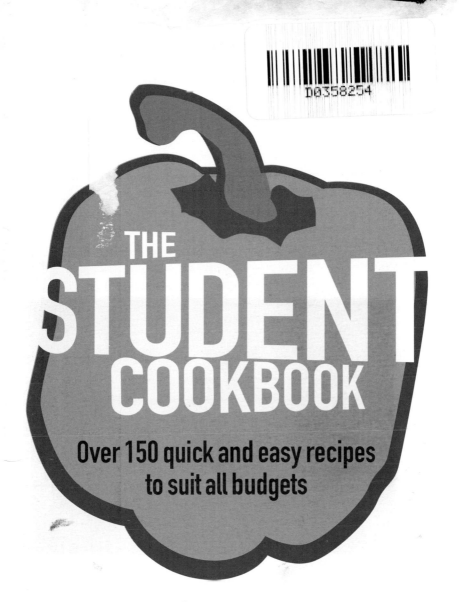

THE STUDENT COOKBOOK

Over 150 quick and easy recipes to suit all budgets

Beverly Le Blanc

ACKNOWLEDGEMENTS

I am indebted to my husband, Philip Back,
who shopped and tested with good spirit, as
well as Sally-Anne Hinchliffe, Norma MacMillan
and Ricki Ostrov, each of whom was greatly
supportive and helpful. I also must thank Norma
MacMillan for permission to use her recipe Lamb
Shanks with Dried Fruit (published in *The Shaker
Kitchen*, Pavilion), and Niru Gupta for her Curried
Mince recipe (published in *Everyday Indian*,
Merehurst, 1995).

I would also like to thank the following friends
who have offered encouragment, ideas and
recipes: my agent Judy Chilcote, Philip Clarke,
Kelly Crossman, Michael Crossman, Phillip
Dudden, Pamela Edward, Else Holst, Lisa Holst,
Henry Johnston, Nancy LeBlanc, Jeani Monce,
Tessa Paul, Susanna Tee, Anne White, William
Windram and Liz Wolf-Cohen.

The nutritional information in this book is for
reference only. The recipes and any suggestions
are to be used at the reader's sole discretion and
risk. Always consult a doctor if you are in doubt
about nutritional or medical conditions.

First published in Great Britain in 2003 by Virgin Books Ltd
This updated edition first published in 2006 by Virgin Books Ltd, Thames Wharf Studios,
Rainville Road, London, W6 9HA

Copyright © Beverly LeBlanc 2003, 2006

ISBN 0 7535 1196 7
      9 7580 75311961

The paper used in this book is a natural, recyclable product made from wood grown in
sustainable forests. The manufacturing process conforms to the regulations of the country
of origin.

Designed by Smith & Gilmour

Printed and bound in Great Britain by Scotprint.

CONTENTS

INTRODUCTION

One of the harshest realities of student life is when you suddenly realise no one is going to cook for you every day anymore. But don't despair. There is no such thing as 'can't cook, won't cook'.

You can get away with Chardonnay and Silk Cuts for a day or two, but after that you are going to need food. And there is nothing wrong with beans on toast once in a while, but it gets boring – and you won't be popular with your flatmates. A regular diet of take-aways will take away all your cash in a flash.

This book won't turn you into a cordon bleu chef, but it will get you through the year. No matter how hung-over you are, how strapped for cash you are, how partied out you are, or how weary you are from cramming for exams, there are plenty of tasty and hasty recipes here. Even if you've never boiled an egg, you'll find plenty you can cook.

The obvious reason to get cooking is to stop the hunger pangs. But there's more to it than that. Food is the fuel that keeps your body and mind going; it's what gives you energy, whether you're studying all day or partying all night. Most people also appreciate that variety is the spice of life, so there is no need to exist on a steady diet of tinned beans and curry.

This book includes essential kitchen survival techniques that are so easy to follow even the newest cook will copy them. Once you can boil or fry an egg, you are well on your way to cooking breakfasts and midnight feasts to soak up the alcohol after a hard night's partying. There is also plenty of variety with pasta and rice recipes, as well as one-pot meals that save on the washing-up, super-speedy snacks that beat the munchies, grazing nosh for small meals and slowly cooked dishes that all but cook themselves while you study. There are even recipes designed to impress – whether cooking for a crowd or a candlelit evening of romance. You'll also find ideas for feasting on a budget, and tips that turn leftovers into a second, or even third, meal with very little effort.

But, of course, a student's life isn't all hard work and study. Take a look at the Cocktail Hour chapter and get the party started. (Just be sure to leave this book by your bed, opened to Hangover Hell (page 26), for gentle tips to ease the pain the morning after.)

As you look through the recipes, easy-to-spot symbols will let you know at a glance which recipes are suitable for vegetarians or vegans, which are quick (on the table in 20 minutes or less) and those that might aid hangover recovery.

Don't think that cooking and eating well means you have to spend a lot of cash on fancy equipment – you can if you want, but these recipes are for the most basic kitchen. On pages 18 and 19 you'll find a list of essentials you shouldn't leave home without.

If you are new to cooking, you are probably new to food shopping as well. So follow the tips for supermarket shopping to stretch your funds, and learn what the essentials are for your cupboard and fridge. Grocery shopping might sound like a chore, but there's nothing quite as comforting as knowing that if you roll in at 3 a.m. you can knock up a bacon buttie or fry an egg. But, when you know the cupboard is really bare, try the ideas for jazzing up a tin of beans or tomatoes if that's all you can afford at the all-night corner shop.

Inviting friends around for a meal can be very pleasurable, but also a nightmare if you aren't organised. Don't put yourself under any undue pressure. Whether a bunch of mates are coming around to watch *Match of the Day* or you want to plan a dinner party, take a look at the recipes starting on page 191.

Eating a balanced and varied diet is also essential to feeling good and looking good. So to keep yourself in top form read the information about healthy eating and see how easy it is to put together a diet that helps you feel good.

So, why not go for it and get cooking? Who knows, it might be the start of a lifelong passion.

EAT WELL TO LIVE WELL

MIX & MATCH

You might think it's easier to live on 'junk food', but just take a minute to consider the term 'junk'. It isn't called junk food for nothing. It has been said many times, but you are what you eat.

Healthy eating isn't a chore or a bore. It is, however, necessary. Your body needs the food you eat to carry out all its functions. So if you don't eat well, you won't function well. And healthy eating doesn't mean a diet of just brown rice, carrot sticks and lettuce leaves. The key to healthy eating is *variety*. Making the effort to eat a varied diet will pay dividends. Not only will your body function efficiently, but you will feel good, look good and have more energy.

There's no problem with the occasional fry-up and chips, as long as that isn't all you eat. Beans on toast has a lot going for it nutritionally – just don't eat nothing else. You need variety in your diet because no single food can provide all the nutrients you need to stay healthy.

Whatever the latest food fads, the basics of healthy eating stay the same – lots of fruit, vegetables and starchy carbohydrates, and a reduction in sugar and fatty foods. Once you get into the habit of eating this way, it will become second nature. It's worth making the effort. Of course there will be days when it's deep-fried fish and chips all round, but you can soon be back on track.

The following pages give you an indication of what to aim for.

Healthy Eating in a Nutshell
▸ Eat lots of the wholegrain starchy foods, such as bread, cereals and rice, and potatoes.
▸ Eat at least five portions of fruit and vegetables every day. These can be fresh, canned, dried or frozen.
▸ Eat moderate amounts of protein, including the vegetarian soya and pulse alternatives, and low-fat dairy products.
▸ Eat very small amounts of foods that are high in fat and contain lots of sugar, such as sweets, savoury snacks and pastries.

Are You Getting Enough?
Study after study has shown that for good health you should eat at least five portions of fruit and vegetables a day. This includes 100 per cent juice (only one glass a day counts). Five portions can sound daunting, but many portion sizes are not large. Take a look at the panel overleaf and you'll see how easy it is to reach the five-a-day target.

HOW MUCH IS A PORTION?

FRUIT:

Apple	1 medium apple
Apple, dried rings	4 rings
Apricot, dried	3 whole
Avocado	1/2 an avocado
Banana chips	1 handful
Banana, fresh	1 medium banana
Blackberries	1 handful (9 or 10)
Cherries, dried	1 heaped tablespoon
Dried fruit, mixed	1 heaped tablespoon
Fig, dried	2 figs
Fruit juice	150 ml/5 fl oz (only 1 glass a day counts)
Fruit salad, canned	3 heaped tablespoons
Fruit salad, fresh	3 heaped tablespoons
Fruit smoothie	150 ml/5 fl oz
Orange	1 orange
Peach, dried	2 halves
Peach, fresh	1 medium peach
Pear, dried	2 halves
Pear, fresh	1 medium pear
Pineapple, canned	1 heaped tablespoon
Pineapple, dried	1 heaped tablespoon
Pineapple, fresh	1 large slice
Plum	2 medium plums
Prune, dried	3 prunes
Raisins	1 tablespoon
Raspberries, fresh	2 handfuls
Strawberries, fresh	7 strawberries

VEGETABLES:

Aubergine	1/3 aubergine
Beans, baked	3 heaped tablespoons (only 1 serving a day counts)
Beans, borlotti	3 heaped tablespoons
Beans, black-eyed	3 heaped tablespoons
Beans, broad	3 heaped tablespoons
Beans, butter	3 heaped tablespoons
Beans, cannelloni	3 heaped tablespoons
Beans, French	4 heaped tablespoons
Beans, kidney	3 heaped tablespoons
Bean sprouts, fresh	2 handfuls
Broccoli	2 spears
Cabbage, shredded	3 heaped tablespoons
Carrots, fresh slices	3 heaped tablespoons
Cauliflower	8 florets
Celery	3 sticks
Chickpeas	3 heaped tablespoons
Courgettes	1/2 large courgette
Cucumber	5 cm/2 inch piece
Leeks	1 leek (white portion)
Lentils	3 tablespoons
Lettuce (mixed leaves)	1 cereal bowl
Mangetout	1 handful
Mushrooms, button	14 mushrooms, or 3–4 tablespoons sliced
Onion	1 medium onion
Parsnip	1 large
Peppers, fresh	1/2 pepper
Spring onions	8 onions
Sweet corn, canned	3 heaped tablespoons
Tomato, fresh	1 medium or 7 cherry

Fruit and vegetables contain a huge number of vitamin and minerals, and chemicals called phytonutrients, that have a range of benefits: they can help protect against killer diseases, such as heart disease and strokes, as well as some cancers. Eating a variety of fruit and vegetables means you are also getting a wide range of nutrients.

Plenty of tempting recipes follow to help you reach the goal. Super-quick and simple recipes like fruit smoothies (page 83)and Banana Wrap To Go (page 81) get you on your way. Make up a large bowl of Dried Fruit Salad (page 76) or Pickled Mixed Veg (page 99) for a dish that counts towards your five. Keep a bowl of apples, bananas and/or oranges in the kitchen for snacks or instant desserts – put one in your bag when you run off to lectures and nibble on that instead of a sugar-laden, high-fat biscuit. Get going and get fruity.

Go for the Carbs
You need carbohydrates in your diet to provide energy all day long. Foods that contain carbohydrates also provide protein and essential vitamins and minerals, especially those from the B group. The good news is they are cheap, filling and easily available. You get a lot of nutritional bang for your pounds from starchy carbohydrates.

There are two main types of carbs: starches and sugars. Starchy carbohydrates, also called complex carbohydrates, are plant-based foods and include bread, cereals, pasta, rice and vegetables, such as parsnips, potatoes and yams. Sugars are found in fruit and vegetables, as well as processed foods, such as biscuits, cakes and sweets.

In a perfect world, about 55 per cent of your daily calories will be made up of starchy carbs. Examples are a big plate of pasta with a small amount of Bolognese Sauce (page 129), or a wholemeal pitta pocket stuffed with a crisp salad.

Go for wholemeal and wholegrain varieties of carbohydrates and you get the added benefit that they contain fibre, which is believed to help reduce the risk of health problems, such as bowel disorders and heart disease.

'CARBS MAKE YOU FAT'
THIS IS ONE OF THE BIGGEST FOOD MYTHS. RARELY IS IT THE CARBOHYDRATES THAT PILE ON THE KILOS – IT'S WHAT YOU PUT ON THEM THAT ADDS THE CALORIES. THINK OF THESE REDUCED-FAT OPTIONS WHEN YOU PREPARE CARBOHYDRATES:
▸ TRY OVEN-BAKED CHIPS (PAGE 44), RATHER THAN DEEP-FRIED ONES.
▸ TOP YOUR JACKET POTATOES WITH RATATOUILLE (PAGE 173), RATHER THAN BUTTER OR SOURED CREAM.
▸ SPREAD YOUR MORNING TOAST WITH MARMITE, RATHER THAN BUTTER OR MARGARINE.

The Plus Points for Proteins

Protein is needed to repair your body's tissues – it is often called the building block of the body. But you don't need to eat a lot every day. In fact, protein foods should only make up about 15 per cent of your food intake.

Protein is made up of amino acids, which are compounds containing carbon, hydrogen, oxygen and nitrogen – these are what support life. There are 20 amino acids commonly found in plant and animal protein. The human body can make twelve of these, but the remaining eight are obtained from the food we eat. These are called essential amino acids. When you eat a variety of foods everyday, your body will combine the nutrients from the different foods to make up the essential amino acids.

Protein comes from both animal and vegetable sources. Although most foods contain at least some proteins, they are especially abundant in animal foods, such as red meats, poultry, fish, dairy products and eggs; some plant foods, such as dried beans and peas, and many nuts are also good sources of protein.

▸ *Vegetarian and Vegan Protein*

What if you are thinking about following a vegetarian or vegan diet? Well, no plant food, other than soya products, contains all the essential amino acids your body needs in the correct proportion. But by eating a variety of foods throughout the day the deficiency in one food will be cancelled out by another. Again, *variety* is the key to healthy eating for non-meat eaters.

Breakfast cereal with cow's milk or soya milk, Three-Cheese Macaroni (page 139), Dhal with Chapatis (page 163), Bean & Pasta Stew (page 164) and Red Beans & Rice (page 162) are vegetarian dishes that contain combined complete proteins.

Sources of Non-meat Protein:

Vegans and vegetarians should eat a variety of these ingredients for a daily dose of protein.

For vegans:

- ▸ Barley
- ▸ Nuts – almonds, brazils, cashews, hazelnuts, peanuts, pine nuts and walnuts
- ▸ Millet
- ▸ Oats
- ▸ Pulses – dried broad beans, peas and lentils
- ▸ Rice – basmati, brown, long-grain, pudding and risotto
- ▸ Seeds – linseed, pumpkin, sunflower and sesame

- Soya products – soya milk, soya flour, tempeh, tofu and most veggie burgers
- Sweet corn

Vegetarians can also add:
- Dairy products – cheese, fromage frais, milk and yogurt; some vegetarians also eat eggs – a great source of protein.

Up from the Farm

Dairy products, including cheese, ice cream, milk and yogurt, are great sources of calcium, protein and vitamins. You need calcium for strong bones, and this is especially important in your late teens and early twenties. There isn't a better excuse for getting your blender out and whizzing up a milk shake or fruit smoothies. Or try the super-quick cheese Quesadilla (page 104).

Sad but true, some dairy products are also high in saturated fats. Healthy-eating guidelines recommend two or three portions of dairy foods a day, so choose lower-fat options, such as semi-skimmed milk and low-fat yogurt.

Cut the Fat

You probably already know that excessive amounts of fat in your diet should be a non-starter. The saturated fats found in most animal-based foods can clog your arteries, increasing your risk of heart disease and strokes.

Although your body needs a small amount of fat for the cells to function properly, for almost everyone, reducing the amount of fat in your diet is essential. Cutting it down, however, is not easy. It seems to be everywhere – it's in processed foods and you use it to cook with. And the other problem is that it tends to be tasty. Just think how much better a slice of toast tastes with butter!

By cooking for yourself, rather than relying on packaged meals, you retain some form of control over the amount of fat in your meals. Most processed and 'fast' foods are, of course, loaded with fat.

The type of fat you eat is important in terms of health. Different foods contain different types of fat:

- *Saturated fat*, found in animal products, is usually solid at room temperature. This includes butter, lard and suet. Diets with lots of saturated fat are linked to heart disease.
- *Polyunsaturated fat*, which is soft or liquid at room temperature, is considered less harmful, but most should still not be consumed in excess. Vegetable oils, such as sunflower and rapeseed, and nut oils, such as groundnut and walnut, as well as sesame oil, are all polyunsaturated.

Polyunsaturated fats can be divided into two types: omega-3 fatty acids and omega-6 fatty acids. Ideally you want to consume more of the omega-3 fatty acids, which come from rapeseed and soya oils and spreads, as these have been shown to be of great benefit to health, including reducing the risk of some cancers and heart disease. Use these in your cooking and for making salad dressings.

► *Trans fats* start out as polyunsaturated, but their chemical components change during processing so they literally transform and become closer to saturated fats. Many margarines contain trans fats, and they are a major ingredient in many processed meals.

► *Monounsaturated fats* are considered the least harmful, but they should still only be eaten in moderation. They are contained in avocados, olives and olive oil and many nuts.

Healthy eating guidelines recommend that fatty foods should not be more than one-third of the day's calorie intake, and no more than 10 per cent should be saturated. You should be aware, however, that there is double the amount of calories per gram in fat as there is in carbohydrate or protein.

Sweet Nothings

Sometimes it's impossible to resist a sugar-coated doughnut, but there is a reason for that. The high sugar content gives you a quick burst of energy, but it won't last. Soon you will be craving another sugar fix. Sugar provides nothing more than empty calories because it doesn't contain any nutrients.

When you want a sugar fix, go for something like a Flapjack (page 122), rather than a chocolate bar. It's sweet and tasty, and the oats it is made with are complex carbohydrates that slowly and steadily raise your blood sugar level. You'll feel satisfied longer.

You can't avoid eating sugar, however, because it occurs naturally in fruit, vegetables and cow's milk, but try to limit the amount of added sugar you eat. This is very difficult to achieve, because sugar is included in so many processed foods. When you look at food labels, you might not see 'sugar' listed as an ingredient, but look for anything ending in 'ose', such as fructose and sucrose – it is sugar by another name.

You can start weaning yourself off sugar by cutting back on how much you add to your morning cuppa.

Vital Vitamins

As you've probably known since you were a schoolchild, vitamins are the essential organic substances that your body needs to function properly. Most vitamins come from the food you eat, although some are manufactured by your body. Your body can store vitamins A, D, E, K and B_{12}, but you need to get a good supply of all others from your diet. (Vegans, however, should consider taking a B_{12} supplement and including soya products that are fortified with B_{12} in their diet, because this nutrient isn't available from any of the other foods on a vegan diet.)

Vitamins are either water-soluble (B complex and C) or fat-soluble (A, D, E and K). Water-soluble vitamins are easily destroyed during food storage and the preparation and cooking processes; fat-soluble vitamins are less likely to be destroyed during the cooking processes.

Mighty Minerals

Minerals are inorganic substances from food that are necessary for your body to carry out many vital functions, from maintaining your nervous system and metabolic processes to your skeleton's strength. You get these from eating a variety of foods.

What You Need – And Where To Get It

The Reference Nutrient Intake (RNI) indicates the average daily amount of vitamins and minerals health experts believe are sufficient to meet the nutritional needs of most people. Some of these vary with age and gender, but the ones in the chart overleaf are for males and females 19–49 years old. (During pregnancy and while breast-feeding there are increased requirements for some, but not all, nutrients. Consult your GP.)

SUPPLEMENTS
IT'S TEMPTING TO THINK THAT IF YOU POP A SUPPLEMENT PILL EVERY MORNING ALL THE BASES ARE COVERED – YOU DON'T HAVE TO GIVE HEALTHY EATING A SECOND THOUGHT AND YOU'LL STILL GET AN ADEQUATE SUPPLY OF ALL THE NUTRIENTS YOU NEED. WRONG! IT IS POSSIBLE TO TAKE TOO MUCH OF A VITAMIN, AND THE RESULT CAN BE TOXIC. IT IS BEST TO CONSULT YOUR GP BEFORE TAKING SUPPLEMENTS.

mg/d = milligrams per day
mcg/d = macrograms per day

VITAMINS	BENEFITS	GOOD SOURCES
VITAMIN A 700 mcg/d for females 600 mcg/d for males	Essential for normal growth and development; good vision, especially night vision; necessary for immune functions and cell maintenance	Butter, cheese, egg yolks, oily fish, liver, whole milk, fortified margarine, tomatoes, leafy dark-green vegetables and orange-coloured fruit
VITAMIN B$_1$ (Thiamin) 0.8 mg/d for females 1 mg/d for males	Helps your body convert carbohydrates into energy to nourish your brain and nervous system	Beef, cheese, eggs, leafy green vegetables, meat, milk, nuts, porridge, pork, pulses, yogurt, wholegrain breads and cereals and fortified breakfast cereals
VITAMIN B$_2$ (Riboflavin) 1.1 mg/d for females 1-3 mg/d for males	Helps cells release energy from fat and protein; keeps your immune system running smoothly; essential for growth and healthy eyes and hair	Cheese, eggs, leafy green vegetables, liver, meat, milk, wholegrain breads and cereals, yeast extract, yogurt and fortified breakfast cereals
VITAMIN B$_3$ (Niacin) 13 mg/d for females 17 mg/d for males	Helps cells release energy from food	Brown rice, chicken, eggs, fish, jacket potatoes, meat, milk, nuts, peanut butter and whole grains
VITAMIN B$_5$ (Pantothenic acid) No RNI	Aids many metabolic reactions, including energy production	Egg yolks, kidneys, liver, nuts, pulses and wheat germ
VITAMIN B$_6$ (Pyridoxine) 1.2 mg for females 1.4 mg for males	Helps the body use protein; keeps immune system healthy; helps form red blood cells	Beef, fish, pork and fortified breakfast cereals
VITAMIN B$_{12}$ (Cyanocobalamin) 1.5 mg for both females and males	Essential for overall growth and the formation of red blood cells; keeps the nervous system healthy	Only found in animal products and fortified food: eggs, meat, milk products, offal and fortified breakfast cereals

Nutrient	What it does	Good food sources
FOLATE/FOLIC ACID 200 mcg/d for both females and males (400 mcg/d for pregnant females during the first trimester; consult your GP)	Aids the production of red blood cells. May protect against heart disease.	Asparagus, beans (fresh and dried), Brussels sprouts, liver, nuts, oranges, peas, leafy dark-green vegetables, wholemeal bread and yeast extract and fortified breakfast cereals (You will see it listed on the label as folic acid, the synthetic form of folate.)
VITAMIN C (Ascorbic acid) 40 mg/d for both females and males	Used in the structure of connective tissue; helps heal wounds and fractures; may help prevent certain types of cancer and heart disease. Increases iron absorption when eaten with iron-rich foods	Fresh fruit, especially citrus, green vegetables, red peppers and potatoes
VITAMIN D (Cholecalciferol) No RNI (except 10 mcg/d for pregnant females; consult your GP)	Promotes the absorption of calcium from food for healthy bones and teeth	Most vitamin D is made by the body when the skin is exposed to sunlight. The few good food sources include egg yolks, oily fish and fortified margarine, powdered milk and breakfast cereals
VITAMIN E No RNI in the UK (EU RNI is 10 mg/d for both females and males)	Protects cell membranes and has a key anti-inflammatory action; may help prevent certain types of cancer and heart disease by its antioxidant actions	Leafy green vegetables, margarine, nuts, peanut butter, salad dressings, vegetable oils, wheat germ and wholegrain cereals; vegetable oils are the best source
VITAMIN K No RNI	Essential for blood clotting and bone formation	Leafy dark-green vegetables, such as Brussels sprouts, Savoy cabbage and spinach

MINERALS	BENEFITS	GOOD SOURCES
CALCIUM 700 mg/d for both females and males	Essential for the development of strong bones and teeth, blood clotting and nerve formation	Bread, dairy products, canned fish, white and brown flours, milk, fortified soya milk and leafy dark-green vegetables
CHLORIDE 2,500 mg/d for both females and males	Needed to maintain the body's fluid balance	The main source is salt
COPPER 1.2 mg/d for both females and males	Helps the body absorb iron from food; assists with bone growth and the formation of connective tissue	Fish, liver and leafy green vegetables
IODINE 140 mcg/d for both females and males	Necessary for proper functioning of the thyroid gland	Milk, seafood, seaweeds
IRON 14.8 mg/d for females, 8.7 mg/d for men	Essential for the formation of red blood cells	Red meat, offal, leafy dark-green vegetables and fortified bread and breakfast cereals
MAGNESIUM 270 mg/d for females 300 mg/d for males	Involved with the production of energy	Nuts, spinach and wholegrain cereals
PHOSPHORUS 550 mg/d for both females and males	Essential for the release of energy for foods and other chemical reactions in the body; also essential for the formation of cells, bone and teeth	Found in most foods. Particularly good sources include cheese, eggs, fish, meat and milk
POTASSIUM 3,500 mg/d for both females and males	Regulates blood pressure and maintains fluid balance; keeps cells functioning properly	All foods, except fats, oils and sugar; bananas and kiwifruit are particularly good sources
SELENIUM 60 mcg/d for females, 75 mcg/d for males	Protects cells against damage from oxidation	Brazil nuts, cereals, cheese, eggs, fish, meat and offal
SODIUM 1,600 mg/d for both females and males	Helps regulate fluid balance; essential for nerve and muscle function; involved in energy use	The main source is table salt
ZINC 7 mg/d for females, 9.5 mg/d for males	Essential for normal growth, as well as reproduction; keeps the immune system healthy; involved in taste perception	Cheese, eggs, meats, peanuts, pulses, sunflower seeds and wholegrain cereal

A BIT OF ROUGH STUFF

Keeping your digestive track functioning efficiently is important. That is why you need fibre in your diet.

Dietary fibre, also called roughage, is naturally occurring, non-digestive substances found in the cell walls of all plants. It does not have nutritional value, but it plays an important role in helping you stay healthy.

There are two types of dietary fibre. Soluble fibre, which you get from eating oats, pulses, fruit and vegetables, can help reduce the risk of heart disease by lowering blood cholesterol levels. It also helps to control blood sugar levels. Insoluble fibre, found in wholegrain cereals, fruit and vegetables, especially leafy green vegetables, adds bulk to food passing through the gut and helps prevent constipation and haemorrhoids. It might also reduce the risk of bowel cancer.

DRINK UP

Ever notice how much the wilting spider plant in the corner of your room perks up when you give it a good drink of water? Well, just as that plant needs water, so do you. Your body is about 70 per cent water, and you can't live without it. You could survive for a couple of weeks without food, but you won't last for more than a couple of days without the miracle liquid – water.

In addition to the liquid you get from foods, you should drink about 8 glasses of water a day, which is 2 litres or $3\frac{1}{2}$ pints. Fruit juices, milk and other liquids that don't include alcohol or caffeine can count towards the goal.

KITTING OUT THE KITCHEN

You don't have to spend a lot of money on flash kitchen equipment, but you are going to need more than just a corkscrew and bottle opener. You probably could make it though the year with just one pan, a bowl and a set of cutlery, but why make life difficult?

Think of kitchen shopping as retail therapy with a difference. It is shopping that will save you time and effort during the hectic term. This doesn't mean you should go out and buy all the fancy, modern electrical gizmos you find. Quite the contrary. When it comes to chopping onions and carrots, for example, a knife and chopping board work just as well as a food processor – and there will be less washing-up when you use a knife.

Look at the following lists and think about the type and amount of cooking you are likely to do before you spend. Storage space will undoubtedly be a consideration as well, so don't just buy lots of large pans, and focus on multifunctional pieces – a wok can be used to fry, simmer and casserole in; a large frying pan with a lid and an ovenproof handle can double as a flameproof casserole that goes in the oven.

Check with your house- or flatmates to find out what they will be bringing before you buy. There is no point in three of you arriving with knives, but no chopping board.

CHEAP SHOPPING
TRY CAR-BOOT OR JUMBLE SALES AND CHARITY SHOPS FOR GOOD-QUALITY, SECOND-HAND KITCHEN EQUIPMENT AT KNOCK-DOWN PRICES. IT IS ALSO WORTH SENDING OUT AN ALL-POINTS-BULLETIN TO RELATIONS BEFORE YOU LEAVE HOME. YOU MIGHT BE SURPRISED BY WHAT PEOPLE HAVE SPARE AT THE BACK OF THEIR CUPBOARDS.

THE BAREST ESSENTIALS

If you want to go minimal that's fine, but this is the least amount of equipment you can get away with unless you plan to spend the whole term at the chippie or take-away.
- *Can opener:* If canned baked beans, pulses and tomatoes feature in your diet, this might be one of the most important pieces of equipment in your kitchen.
- *Chopping board:* These come in polyethylene and wood; try to avoid buying the thin, melamine-coated boards. Wood protects knife blades the best, but polyethylene has the advantage because it can be sterilised after use.
- *Colander:* Essential for draining. Look for a freestanding one that will fit in the sink and has side handles for easy lifting.
- *Corkscrew and bottle opener:* Well, it's obvious, isn't it?
- *Knife:* Knives are the workhorses of the kitchen. A cheap knife with

a flimsy or dull blade can turn the simplest task like chopping an onion into a chore. Buy the best you can afford. There are many knives for specific purposes, but if you only buy one, get a 20–25 cm/8-10-inch chef's knife. Other useful knives include a paring knife with a 10 cm/ 4-inch blade for preparing veggies and fruit, a serrated bread knife and a small serrated knife for slicing tomatoes and peeling oranges. Hold a knife before you buy – it should feel comfortable in your hand.

Store knives in a wooden block or on a magnetic strip secured to the wall. If you just throw knives in a drawer, you can easily cut your fingers, and the blade can become damaged as it knocks around.

Keep your knives sharp – more accidents occur with blunt knives than with sharp ones.

▸ *Wok:* Nothing beats a Chinese wok for fast cooking – and at a pinch it can double as a frying pan or saucepan (buy one with a lid). Chinese supermarkets sell the most inexpensive woks. Buy the largest one you have storage space for. Look for a long handle on one side and a grip handle on the other. Traditional round-bottom woks with a stand only work over a gas flame, but you can buy flat-bottom woks for using over electricity.

WHAT YOU REALLY SHOULDN'T LEAVE HOME WITHOUT

Add these to the list above and you should be able to make every recipe in the book.

▸ *Baking sheet:* You will need this for baking Potato Wedges (page 95), Potato Skins (page 97) and Pitta Crisps (page 100), and if you bake biscuits. If the sheet is too thin, it will warp. Baking sheets are also useful to sit under dishes that might bubble up in the oven, such as Vegetable Lasagne (page 141), to catch any drips and save on the washing-up.

▸ *Blender:* An electrical appliance that can help to cut costs. The money you save by making your own hummus, for example, rather than buying supermarket tubs, more than justifies the expense. A blender is also useful for making large batches of nutritional soups, such as Potato & Leek (page 117).

▸ *Bowls:* Get a selection of sizes. Ovenproof bowls that can be used in both the fridge and the oven are the most useful. Buy bowls in graduated sizes, so they stack inside each other and take up less storage space. Non-metallic bowls, such as glass or earthenware, should be used for tossing salads with dressings that contain vinegar or lemon juice.

▸ *Cake pan(s):* These come in a variety of shapes and sizes. If the idea of home-made Carrot Cake (page 123) and Flapjacks (page 122) appeals, you will need specific pans – the cake is baked in a 23 cm/9-inch round cake pan that is at least 5 cm/2 inches deep; you need a 20 cm/8-inch round sandwich pan for the flapjacks.

▸ *Fish slice:* The thin metal blade on a fish slice means it easily slides under cooking food, so that it can be lifted out of the pan or turned over. Inexpensive and useful for flipping American-style Pancakes (page 70), Eggy Bread (page 69) and Fried Eggs (page 37).

▸ *Flameproof casserole:* An all-in-one cooking pot that really saves on washing-up. These can be used on top of the hob and then transferred directly to the oven. Many are made from enamelled cast iron. Ceramic or earthenware ovenproof casseroles, on the other hand, will crack if used on the hob. Make sure the casserole lid fits tightly so moisture doesn't escape.

Flameproof casseroles can be expensive, so think carefully about what size will be the most useful. They can also be heavy, so it is a good idea to lift before you buy to make sure you can handle it.

▸ *Frying pan:* This is essential kit. A non-stick surface aids omelette- and tortilla-making, but isn't necessary. Instead, put your money towards a good-quality pan with a thick base that conducts the heat evenly. Even simple dishes like Fried Eggs (page 37) are easier to cook in a cast-iron frying pan than a cheap thin one – the eggs don't burn.

If you are cooking for one or two, a 20–25 cm/8–10-inch pan will do, but if you do lots of cooking for a crowd get a 30–35 cm/12–14-inch pan. (Measure across the top, not the base.)

▸ *Garlic press:* You don't need anything fancy – choose a sturdy one that feels comfortable in your hand.

▸ *Glass jars:* Wash and save empty jars in a variety of sizes several months before you leave home for storing dried pulses, pasta and rice, as well as sugar. Jam or peanut butter jars with plastic lids are ideal to use for making Vinaigrette (page 55) in.

▸ *Grater:* There are lots of fancy graters available, but an inexpensive, old-fashioned box grater is perfectly good for grating carrots, cheese and ginger.

▸ *Hand-held electric mixer:* Not essential, but this makes life easier when whisking egg whites for creamy desserts such as Berry Fool (page 211), or making the mixture for Carrot Cake (page 123). You don't need lots of fancy attachments, just blades that work at two or three speeds and are easy to remove. If you don't have an electric mixer you can use a wire whisk, but be prepared to give your arm a good workout.

▸ *Metal spatula:* The characteristic rounded edge of a Tortilla (page 72) is achieved by using a metal spatula to 'tuck in' the edge when it is flipped over.

▸ *Oven gloves:* Buying cheap oven gloves is false economy – you need thickness to prevent burning your skin.

▸ *Ovenproof dishes:* Not all dishes can be put into hot ovens, so make sure you have some that won't break at high temperatures. Inexpensive glass ovenproof dishes will do, but you can find attractively decorated white ceramic ones that also look good on the table – and save on the washing-up. These are available in many shapes and sizes – the only recipe in this book that requires a specific-size dish is Vegetable Lasagne (page 141), which uses a 23 cm/9-inch square ovenproof dish.

▸ *Roasting tin:* If you know the size of your oven, take the measurements with you when you go to buy one of these, otherwise you can end up with a roasting tin that is too large. (If the tin has handles, be sure to include them in the measurement.) Look for a heavy roasting tin, or it will warp at high temperatures.

▸ *Saucepans:* These come in a variety of sizes, so think what you will be using them for before you buy. If pasta features regularly, you need the largest pan you can afford. You will need two pans if you plan to cook lots of risottos – a small one for heating the stock in, and a medium-size pan for stirring the risotto in.

▸ *Tea towels:* The more you have of these, the less anyone has to worry about doing a load of laundry. Stock up.

▸ *Vegetable peeler:* The inexpensive, old-fashioned peeler with a swivel blade works best.

▸ *Wooden spoons:* Get a couple – they're cheap.

. . . and don't forget the washing-up liquid. Somebody has to do it!

OPTIONAL EXTRAS

▸ *Kitchen scales:* Make your life in the kitchen as easy as possible with an inexpensive scale for accurate measuring of everything from breadcrumbs to pasta.

▸ *Measuring jug:* The equivalent of a kitchen scale for liquids. These come in several sizes with graduated measurements etched along the side. Buy one that holds at least 600 ml/1 pint of liquid. If you don't have one, you can get by using a beer mug – a pint mug holds 600 ml/20 fl oz; a half-pint mug holds 300 ml/10 fl oz.

▸ *Measuring spoons:* Measuring spoons are sold in inexpensive sets and used for adding specific quantities of dried ingredients to other Ingredients. These are especially useful when you are new to cooking and following recipes closely. Tapered spoons are best for using with small jars of dried herbs and spices. '

▸ *Pestle and mortar:* Freshly ground spices really enhance cooking, and the easiest way to capture their unbeatable fresh flavour is to use a pestle and mortar. They are also useful for making herb and spice curry pastes, crushing garlic cloves and bashing basil leaves to make pesto sauce.

IT'S TIME TO SHOP

If this is the first time you have ever had to cook for yourself, the chances are this is also the first time you have ever had to shop for groceries. You can do it on an ad hoc basis, running to the shops each time you decide to cook, or you can save yourself a lot of time and money with simple shopping strategies.

To say students have never had it so good is not an overstatement. You can pop into the supermarket – and even the corner shop – and buy a host of affordable ingredients from around the world that only ten years ago were considered exotic luxuries. Even the tightest budget will probably stretch to a bottle of olive oil for salad dressings, and Italian pesto sauce is just as likely to be in your cupboard as a bottle of British Worcestershire sauce.

But think twice when you regularly reach for the ready meals. They will be tempting because they are so easy, but they are the really expensive option. The more you spend on convenience the less you will have to support your social life. It is much less expensive, and often more nutritious, to buy the basic ingredients to cook yourself.

BARGAIN HUNTING

Food shopping is as much about finances as it is about selecting what you put in your trolley. At the start of each term work out how much you and your flatmates will spend on food weekly. Be realistic so you have a chance of sticking to your budget. If you don't, you'll find yourself eating like a king at the beginning of term, but a pauper by the end. (If this does happen, take a look at the When the Cupboard is Bare chapter beginning on page 217 for ideas for feeding on pennies.)

Markets are good hunting grounds for fresh fruit and vegetables, and are usually cheaper than supermarkets. Mind you, the old trick of visiting the supermarket at 3.30 p.m. on a Sunday and getting marked-down foods is worth knowing. Just be sure to take note of the 'use by' dates.

Try these shopping strategies to stretch your pound and keep your cupboard full:

▶ *Don't Shop Hungry:* There is nothing like impulse shopping to blow your food budget! And you are never more vulnerable to the seductive packaging and comforting aromas in a supermarket than when your stomach is empty.

▶ *Look for Own Brands:* Supermarket own brands often represent the best value.

> *Make a List:* Never go shopping without a list. That way you will be able to make sure you pick up all the ingredients you need, without spending lots of money on non-essentials.
> *Shop Around:* Compare prices to establish where to get the best value for money. The local market might provide better bargains than supermarkets. It is also a good idea to keep a record of how much you usually spend for staple ingredients, so you can spot a bargain.

Know Your Dates

You will find 'use by' and 'best before' dates on all packaged food.
> *'Use by' date:* You will find this date on all perishable-food labels. If you find something in your fridge after this date, throw it out. Even if it smells good and looks OK without any mould, bacteria might have developed and the food may not be safe to eat. It is illegal for market traders and shops to sell foods after the 'use by' dates.
> *'Best before' date:* This date is on labels for food that can be stored for longer. When the date has passed, it does not necessarily mean the food has to be thrown out, but that it might be past its best. Dried, frozen and canned foods begin to deteriorate after the 'best before' date.

STOCKING A HEALTHY STORECUPBOARD

The Cans

Get in a supply of canned goods and you'll always be able to knock up a healthy meal in a flash.
> *Baked beans:* A meal on toast.
> *Fish:* Canned anchovies, herring, mackerel, sardines and tuna are good for sandwiches, quick salads, pasta sauces and to combine with freshly cooked rice. They are considerably less expensive than fresh seafood.
> *Pulses:* Canned cannellini, borlotti, butter and kidney beans, chickpeas and lentils are the foundation of many vegetarian meals. They are also a great, inexpensive way to bulk out meat-based casseroles.
> *Sweet corn kernels:* Add to salads, sandwiches, soups and stews. Team with Cheddar cheese for a jacket potato topper. Try Spiced Corn Fritters (page 221) for a quick meal.
> *Tomatoes:* Lots of recipes in this book include a can. Stock up.

STICK WITH SMOOTH
DON'T BUY DENTED OR BULGING CANS, EVEN IF THEY ARE MARKED DOWN AND LOOK LIKE GREAT VALUE. THE SLIGHTEST DAMAGE CAN INDICATE BOTULISM, A VERY SERIOUS TYPE OF FOOD POISONING. DO NOT TASTE ANYTHING IN A DAMAGED CAN – THROW IT AWAY.

The Jars

These are the budget basics:

▸ *Curry powder:* Pick the degree of heat that suits you.

▸ *Herbs & spices:* This list will grow the more you cook and want to expand your repertoire, but start with salt and pepper, dried mixed herbs, dried thyme and bay leaves.

▸ *Honey:* Spread on toast for a quick breakfast.

▸ *Oriental sauces:* Keep jars of hoisin, oyster and Thai fish sauces for quick stir-fries.

▸ *Passata:* Sieved tomatoes, ready to pour into pasta sauces and casseroles.

▸ *Pesto sauce:* Toss with hot pasta or add to mayonnaise-based salads.

▸ *Soy sauce:* For adding a salty/savoury flavour to Oriental-style dishes.

▸ *Sun-dried tomatoes:* Excellent in toasted cheese sandwiches and for adding to pasta sauces.

▸ *Tahini paste:* Sesame seed paste, an essential ingredient for making your own Hummus (page 88).

▸ *Tamarind paste:* A sour flavour to add to Indian dishes.

▸ *Vegetable oils:* Stock up on groundnut and sunflower oil for stir-frying, sunflower and olive oil for everyday cooking and extra-virgin olive oil for Vinaigrette (page 55).

TOO CHEAP TO BE GOOD
PASS ON BUYING 'BLENDED VEGETABLE OIL', EVEN THOUGH IT LOOKS LIKE A BARGAIN BECAUSE IT IS SO CHEAP. IT WILL CONTAIN PALM OIL, WHICH IS HIGH IN SATURATED FAT, AND OTHER HYDROGENATED OILS. LOOK FOR UNBLENDED SUNFLOWER OR GROUNDNUT OILS FOR EVERYDAY COOKING.

▸ *Vinegars:* Red- and white-wine vinegars are inexpensive and ideal for everyday use, but a jar of balsamic vinegar is also useful.

▸ *Worcestershire sauce:* The great British condiment – just the thing to add to any melted cheese sandwich.

If your budget can run to it, these are time-savers:

▸ *Chopped herbs in oil*	▸ *Dried mushrooms*
▸ *Crushed garlic in oil*	▸ *Nut-flavoured oils*
▸ *Curry pastes*	▸ *Ready-made salad dressings*
▸ *Curry sauces*	

The Packets

▸ *Asian noodles:* Supermarkets sell a variety of these, but Oriental food shops might be cheaper. Try Chinese egg and rice noodles and soba noodles with stir-fries.

▸ *Bulgar wheat:* No-cook crushed wheat grains that have a nutty flavour and chewy texture. Pour over boiling water and leave to soak.

▸ *Couscous:* Buy the instant version and all you have to do is pour boiling water over it.

▸ *Dried fruit:* Store a selection for quick energy-rich snacks.

▸ *Pasta:* Unbeatable for quick, cheap meals. Stock a variety of shapes in plain egg and wholemeal. Small pasta shapes are good for adding to soups.

▸ *Rice:* The basis of many filling, inexpensive meals. Stock a variety in airtight containers – basmati, long- and short-grain brown, long-grain white and risotto.

▸ *Stock cubes:* Keep a supply of chicken- and vegetable-flavoured cubes, if you aren't inclined to make your own stock.

KEEP IT COOL – AND CLEAN

Most perishable ingredients – cheese, chicken, eggs, some fruit, mayonnaise, meat, milk, home-made stock, vegetables, yogurt – are stored in the fridge. Follow the storage instructions on packaged goods (see Know Your Dates, page 23), but most loose ingredients should be used within two or three days.

Your fridge can be a breeding ground for bacteria, which can make you very ill. Make sure you regularly clear out any rotting foods. Your nose will tell you instantly if there is anything that should be in the bin instead of the fridge. Also, wipe the base and sides of the fridge at least once a term with an all-purpose kitchen cleaner and cloth.

The older the fridge is, the wiser it is to invest in a fridge thermometer to make sure it keeps foods at a temperature that keeps them safe. Bacteria grow quickly in temperatures above 10°C/50°F and below 65°C/149°F. Ideally, your fridge should be between 0°C/32°F and 5°C/41°F.

Follow these simple tips to keep food poisoning at bay:

▸ Follow all storage information on packaging.

▸ Don't leave the fridge door open longer than necessary. When the door is open, the internal temperature rises.

▸ Completely cool any cooked foods before you put them in the fridge.

▸ To avoid cross-contamination, make sure raw foods are tightly covered and sitting on plates with lips to catch any juices. If the juices from raw food drip onto foods that aren't going to be cooked again, you could get food poisoning.

▸ Store fish, meat and poultry on the bottom shelf, where any juices are less likely to drip on other foods.

SWEET SMELLS
ONCE A TERM PUT AN OPEN PACKET OF BICARBONATE OF SODA ON A SHELF AT THE BACK OF THE FRIDGE, AND IT WILL ABSORB THE UNPLEASANT ODOURS.

HANGOVER HELL

Yes, it is true that medical studies suggest a modest amount of regular alcohol might offer health benefits. Unfortunately, this doesn't apply to the amount of drinking a lot of students indulge in.

Binge drinking all night is not good for you. And the not-so-subtle giveaway is the pounding headache, dizziness, the vomiting and retching that follow too much alcohol.

Too much booze is bad for your body, and the hangover is your body's way of letting you know. Have you ever noticed that as soon as you drink 'too much' you run to the loo all the time? That is the start of your body's payback time.

WHY YOU FEEL SO WRETCHED

When you are hung-over it is because all that going to the loo has left your body depleted in various vitamins and minerals. The pounding headache and vomiting are caused by the loss of potassium and sodium. The alcohol has also depleted the vitamin C in you body; the imbalance of acid and alkaline in your gut is why you feel so queasy, even after the vomiting has stopped.

The weariness that makes you want to roll over and abandon all lectures for the day is not just because you came home with the dawn chorus. It is because your body is working overtime to get better. Also, no matter how much sleep you get, the alcohol still in your system will probably prevent your body from entering REM (Rapid Eye Movement), the stage of sleep that refreshes your body.

Another reason you don't want to move is because the sugars in the alcohol have raised you blood sugar levels. When your blood sugar levels come back down again, the queasy feeling can be due to a fall in glucose. This typically occurs between six and thirty-six hours after an alcoholic binge, especially if you have been drinking on an empty stomach.

BETTER SAFE THAN SORRY

Abstinence is the only 100 per cent effective 'remedy' for a hangover. However, assuming you aren't going down that road, never drink on an empty stomach. Go for bulk and eat starchy foods that provide a slow, long-lasting release of energy. Opt for things like sandwiches made with wholegrain bread and jacket potatoes before you go out. While you are out, beware: traditional bar snacks, such as nuts and crisps, are salty and will only encourage you to drink more. Instead, it would be better to alternate alcoholic and non-alcoholic drinks.

If there is ever a time for a fry-up, it might be before you go out. Alcoholic absorption is much slower after you've eaten something fatty, such as oil or cream.

And girls, remember, your tolerance for alcohol is less than the boys' so don't try to keep up!

DON'T MIX YOUR DRINKS
THINK CAREFULLY BEFORE YOU COMBINE BEER AND WINE IN THE SAME DRINKING SESSION. REMEMBER: 'WINE BEFORE BEER, WILL LEAVE YOU FEELING QUEER. BEER BEFORE WINE, AND YOU'LL FEEL JUST FINE'.

Crystal Clear

Clear drinks, such as gin, vodka and white wine, are less likely to give you a hangover if you drink in moderation. Darker drinks, such as brandy, red wine and whisky, contain congeners, which are by-products of alcohol metabolism. The congeners will leave you feeling worse for wear.

Also, never forget that the cheaper the booze is, the worse your hangover is likely to be!

HANGOVER BUSTERS – WHAT MIGHT HELP YOU RECOVER

▸ *Get some decent sleep.*
▸ *Eat something.* You won't be able to face a feast, but your body needs nourishment and you need to restore your blood sugar levels. A big fry-up might be tempting, but your already precarious stomach doesn't need any grease. Honey Toast (page 67) is a gentle start. The natural sugar in honey is easily absorbed. It raises your blood sugar levels to give you some energy.
▸ *Unzip a banana.* Bananas are like wonder drugs for hangover sufferers. The potassium they contain might help ease the aches and cramps, and their magnesium should help stop the pounding head. Try a sliced banana and peanut butter sandwich to boost the minerals and B-complex vitamins you have lost.
▸ *Down some OJ.* It's good for replacing vitamin C and potassium.
▸ *Scrambled Eggs* (page 38) are high in protein, and might help your overall recovery. They can be soothing for some but induce nausea in others.
▸ *Fresh ginger* can help ease nausea, so try Masala Tea (page 81), or grate some fresh ginger into a mug of black tea and slip slowly.
▸ Many hangover sufferers swear by the *hair-of-the-dog*, or having another alcoholic drink. This might mask unpleasant hangover

symptoms, but it only delays the inevitable. It can make the most horrid symptoms worst. If you insist on going down this road, try a Bloody Mary (page 62), because at least the tomato juice will do you some good – it's a powerhouse of vitamins and should boost your energy.

▸ When you finally crawl out of bed, go for *simple, plain food*: dry toast, Hard-boiled Eggs (page 35), porridge or Crispy Baked Potatoes (page 42).

A WORLD OF CURES

Hangovers are universal. Here is a sample of remedies from around the world. If you think some of these sound awful, pity poor medieval drunks who downed a concoction that included raw eels.

▸ The Irish hair-of-the-dog is Black Velvet: mix equal amounts of Guinness with champagne.

▸ Go Dutch and swallow a soused herring.

▸ In Greece, students 'line' their stomach by swallowing a tablespoon of olive oil before going out, and again before bed. Not a bad idea actually – give it a try.

▸ Some Russians recover from too much vodka by downing heavily salted cucumber juice. Others eat a bowl of black bread soaked in water.

▸ Hung-over Norwegians drink a glass of double cream.

▸ Try black magic. Hung-over Haitians stick 13 black-headed pins in the cork of the bottle they were drinking from.

▸ Look at your health food shop for maté de coca tea. That's an old Inca cure.

▸ Try a plate of Cabbage, Bacon & Tattie Fry (page 65) – ancient Romans swore by cabbage as a hangover cure.

HOW TO USE THIS BOOK

WHAT THE SYMBOLS MEAN

As you flip through the recipes, the easy-to-spot symbols give you a quick clue as to what each recipe is like.

 VEGETARIAN SYMBOL These are recipes suitable for anyone on most vegetarian diets. The recipes do not contain meat or seafood, but do contain eggs and dairy products.

 VEGAN SYMBOL These are recipes suitable for anyone on a vegan diet. You might, however, have to make some of the regular substitutions, such as soya milk for cow's milk. (Or you can use milk from oats, rice or peas.) Be sure to read the labels on packs of pasta and flour tortilla, for example, to make sure they do not contain eggs.

Take a look at the recipes with a vegetarian symbol – many of these will also be suitable if you substitute soya products for the dairy produce.

 QUICK SYMBOL When you want to eat in a hurry, these recipes are for you. All the prep work and cooking time should not take more than 20 minutes in total. That might not sound super-speedy, but remember it is less time than it takes for you to heat the oven and cook most ready-made meals! With these recipes you can be sitting down to eat within 20 minutes of walking into the kitchen.

 HANGOVER BUSTERS These aren't claiming to leave you feeling as right as rain, but they might help you getting back on your feet and feeling better. They will replenish the vitamins and minerals in your body, and start raising your blood sugar levels. When you're feeling really awful, eat small amounts and sip liquids – and remember, the only real hangover buster is moderation while you are drinking.

WELCOME TO THE KITCHEN

No, your mum isn't cooking for you tonight. You're on your own now. You might be reluctant to start cooking, but there comes a time when you just won't be able to face another take-away, or you don't have any money left – all those yummy-looking ready meals at the supermarket will blow your food budget faster than you can say, 'Who's getting the next round?'

If this is literally day one of your cooking experience, don't worry. Once you can boil an egg, you'll be able to feed yourself. The recipes in this chapter are specifically written for novice cooks, and none of the other recipes in the book will be beyond your grasp.

One of the enjoyments of cooking is about experimenting. Try the recipes once as they are written, then feel free to add a bit more of one ingredient and a bit less of another to suit your tastes. These recipes will help you to master the basics so you can flex your muscles in the kitchen. Then you can go on to try the other, slightly more adventurous, dishes in this book.

The big plus for learning to cook, however, is that you can eat good food whenever you want. That's right – whatever you want, whenever you want it. If you want breakfast Bacon, Eggs & Beans before you meet mates at the pub at eight o'clock in the evening, no problem! And if you want Stir-Fried Ginger Pork when you wake up, there isn't any reason why you shouldn't tuck in! Get cooking and indulge yourself!

Other extra-easy recipes for new cooks:
- Bangers & Smashed Potatoes (page 64)
- Cheese Dreams (page 106)
- Chicken & Veg Parcels (page 198)
- Chilli con Carne (page 158)
- Curried Mince (page 157)
- Fruity-Veg Couscous (page 148)
- Garlic Chicken with Roast Veg (page 197)
- Hot Mars Bar Sauce (page 120)
- Jugged Kippers (page 66)
- Lamb Shanks with Dried Fruit (page 171)
- Mary's Beef & Mushroom Casserole (page 175)
- One-pot Creamy Chicken (page 154)
- Oranges in Spiced Wine (page 214)
- Pasta with Almost-Instant Cheese Sauce (page 127)
- Potato & Leek Soup (page 117)
- Ratatouille (page 173)
- Sardines on Toast (page 109)
- Smashed Butter Bean Spread (page 92)
- Stir-fried Ginger Pork (page 183)
- Welsh Rarebit (page 108)

GETTING STARTED

Don't let the thought of cooking overwhelm you. Here are some tips to get yourself organised (so you can cook up a storm) to eat well and save pennies.

▸ *Read the Recipe:* Before you chop the first ingredient or heat the oven, take time to read through the recipe you are planning to cook. Make sure you understand all the steps and have an idea of what is to happen *before* you start. Take a few minutes to ask yourself: Do I have enough time to prepare and cook the recipe before I have to be somewhere else? Do I understand how all the ingredients are prepared? Do I have all the ingredients? If I don't have everything the recipe specifies, do I have something else I can substitute? This is the time to decide to go shopping if you are missing some of the ingredients, not halfway through the recipe.

▸ *Assemble the Equipment:* Make sure you have everything you need to prepare the dish *before* you start preparing the ingredients. Only five recipes in this book require a specific pan or dish (Carrot Cake, Cheese Omelette, Flapjacks, Tortilla and Vegetable Lasagne), but all the others recipes use standard, basic kitchen equipment and most specify a choice of tools for you to choose from.

▸ *Mise en Place:* This fancy-sounding French term translates as 'to put in place', and it means having all your ingredients prepared and ready to combine *before* you start cooking. This is how chefs work, and how the recipes in this book are written. Chop the vegetables, slice the meat, separate the eggs and assemble the herbs, spices and other seasonings as the recipe instructs before you start working at the stove. If you arrange the ingredients in front of you on the work surface, you'll be able to tell at a glance if you are missing anything. Place the prepared ingredients in bowls or put them in small mounds on your chopping board – washed and dried take-away containers are ideal for this.

▸ *Taste:* This hardly sounds like a chore, but it is easy to forget to sample the food you are preparing. Does a dish need more salt or pepper? What about a few more herbs? A little extra spice? You'll never know unless you taste.

Remember, you can always add more of a flavouring, but you can't take it away, so add all the flavouring ingredients in small amounts, constantly tasting after each addition.

Tasting will become second nature as you become an experienced cook – just cook pasta once or twice without adding salt to the water, and you won't forget many more times!

▸ **Wash Up As You Go Along:** If you ever watch professionally trained cooks at work you'll notice the kitchen is almost as tidy when they finish as when they started. There isn't going to be anybody to clean up after you, so make life easy on yourself and don't leave a sinkful of dirty pots and pans. Wipe the work surface as you go, and wash or soak pots and pans before you sit down to eat. This will save you a lot of elbow grease later!

▸ **Experiment:** After you've tried a recipe once or twice and know what its texture and temperature should be like, go ahead and experiment. Feel free to change ingredients and different seasonings.

▸ **Enjoy Yourself:** Remember, you're just cooking a meal, not finding the cure for cancer!

COOKING EGGS

Think of eggs as one of the ultimate and original fast foods. As long as you have a couple of fresh eggs in the fridge you've always got the base for a proper meal that can be on the table in a matter of minutes. Eggs are versatile and combine well with so many different ingredients that there are literally countless variations on the following recipes. You really are only limited by your enthusiasm and imagination.

Boiling Eggs

It's a misnomer to talk about 'boiled' eggs – whether you like yours hard- or soft-boiled, gentle simmering is the best way to cook them. That way they won't rattle around the pan and crack, and the texture won't become rubbery. You can cook as many eggs at one time as will fit in your saucepan in a single layer. When you are hard-boiling eggs, always cook a few extra because they are so useful for quick snacks. See Using Hard-boiled Eggs (page 35).

Hard-boiled Eggs

MAKES **AS MANY EGGS AS WILL FIT IN YOUR PAN**
NO PREP TIME
COOKING TIME: **ABOUT 10 MINUTES**

1. Place the eggs on the bottom of the saucepan. Cover with 2.5 cm/1 inch of water and set the pan over a high heat. Bring the water to a full, rolling boil, then immediately turn the heat to low and leave the eggs to simmer for 10 minutes for large eggs and 9 minutes for medium eggs.

2. Pour off the hot water and run cold water over the eggs in the pan for 1–2 minutes to stop the cooking and cool them. The eggs can now be shelled and eaten immediately. Or store them, unpeeled, in the fridge for up to three days; peeled eggs will keep fresh in a covered bowl of cold water in the fridge for up to two days.

3. To peel a hard-boiled egg, tap it on a firm surface to crack the shell. There is an air pocket at the broad end so it is easiest to start peeling there. Use your fingers to pull off the shell and rub away any of the inner membrane or small pieces of shell from the egg.

Using Hard-boiled Eggs

▸ Use hard-boiled eggs for a super-quick Egg & Ham Sandwich (page 78), or slice and add them to Spinach, Orange & Avocado Salad (page 110), Quesadillas (page 104), or a toasted Cheese Dream (page 106).
▸ *Devilled Eggs:* These make quick, tasty snacks, and will keep, covered with clingfilm, in the fridge for up to two days. Cut each hard-boiled egg in half lengthways. Separate the yolks and whites, and put all the yolks in a small bowl; set aside the whites. Use a fork to smash the yolks and beat in enough mayonnaise, English mustard powder and salt and pepper to taste, to make a thick paste. Spoon the yolk mixture back into the white halves and lightly sprinkle with cayenne pepper.
▸ *Egg Mayonnaise:* Finely chop hard-boiled eggs (both the yolks and the whites) and stir in enough mayonnaise to bind, then season with salt and pepper to taste. You can use this as it is for a sandwich filling, or add any of the following ingredients to taste to make a more substantial salad or sandwich: finely chopped apple and/or celery; English mustard powder; finely chopped fresh chives, parsley and/or coriander; sliced spring onions; sliced sun-dried tomatoes; a handful of chopped walnuts or almonds; or drained, flaked tinned tuna.
▸ *Mimosa Salad:* Very finely chop the hard-boiled yolks and whites separately, then sprinkle them over a green salad tossed with Vinaigrette dressing (page 55) or a bottled dressing just before serving.

Tips for Hard-boiled Eggs

▸ Mark hard-boiled egg shells with an 'H' so they don't get mixed up with uncooked eggs in a communal fridge. Otherwise, you might get a messy surprise when you crack one.

▸ If you're not sure if an egg is cooked or raw, spin it before you crack: a hard-boiled egg spins smoothly and quickly, while an uncooked one wobbles.

▸ Eggs have porous shells, so they can easily absorb strong odours and flavours in the fridge. Keep your eggs covered in the box they come in, or you could have garlic-scented or curry-flavoured eggs.

Soft-boiled Eggs

MAKES **AS MANY EGGS AS WILL FIT IN YOUR PAN**
NO PREP TIME
COOKING TIME: **3–4 MINUTES**

1. Follow the method for Hard-boiled Eggs (page 35), but only leave the eggs to simmer for 3 minutes for a really runny yolk with an unset white, or 4 minutes for a lightly set white.

2. Lift the egg(s) out of the water with a large spoon and put each in an egg cup. Slice off the 'cap' or pointed end of each shell and scoop out the egg with a spoon.

How Fresh Is Your Egg?

Most eggs and egg boxes are stamped with a 'best before' date, but if you buy unstamped eggs – at a farmers' market, for example – or you aren't sure how fresh the ones in your fridge are, here is how to check: gently drop one into a bowl of cold water. A fresh egg will sink to the bottom and lie horizontally, so if the egg floats throw it out, as it is stale.

▸ Store eggs blunt-end up in the fridge.

Lightly Cooked Eggs

Owing to the possible dangers of salmonella food poisoning, it is recommended you do not eat raw or lightly cooked eggs if you are ill or pregnant. Nor should you serve raw or lightly cooked eggs to young children, elderly people, or those with damaged immune systems.

This means no soft-boiled eggs or runny yolks if the eggs are fried, poached or scrambled. The other recipes to avoid in this book are Prairie Oyster (page 62) and Spanish Eggs (page 223).

Fried Eggs

MAKES **AS MANY EGGS AS WILL FIT IN YOUR PAN**
NO PREP TIME
COOKING TIME: **3–4 MINUTES**

WHERE WOULD THE GREAT BRITISH BREAKFAST BE WITHOUT FRIED EGGS? YOU CAN USE
BUTTER, MARGARINE, BACON FAT OR VEGETABLE OIL FOR FRYING EGGS IN, AS LONG AS IT IS
FOAMING OR SIZZLING HOT BEFORE YOU ADD THE EGG(S). IF YOU LEAVE THE EGGS TO COOK
AT THAT HIGH TEMPERATURE, HOWEVER, THEY WILL BECOME RUBBERY, SO TURN THE HEAT
DOWN STRAIGHT AWAY. A NON-STICK FRYING PAN IS IDEAL, BUT IF YOU DON'T HAVE ONE
HEAT THE PAN BEFORE YOU ADD THE FAT AND YOU SHOULDN'T HAVE ANY PROBLEM WITH
THE EGG(S) STICKING. THE WASHING-UP WILL BE EASIER, TOO.

YOU CAN COOK AS MANY EGGS AT A TIME AS WILL FIT IN YOUR FRYING PAN IN A SINGLE
LAYER. IF YOU'RE COOKING FOR A BIG GROUP OF HOUSEMATES, HOWEVER, FRY THE EGGS
IN BATCHES AND SERVE UP AS SOON AS EACH BATCH IS READY: FRIED EGGS THAT ARE KEPT
WARM ARE NOT AT ALL APPETISING. (SEE NOTE ABOUT LIGHTLY COOKED EGGS, PAGE 36.)

1. Heat the frying pan over a medium heat. Add a knob (about 15 g/$^{1}/_{2}$ oz)
of butter or margarine, or 1 tablespoon of sunflower or olive oil, and swirl
it around the pan.

2. As soon as the butter or margarine is foamy, or the oil is sizzling hot,
lower the heat to medium-low and break the egg(s) into the pan.

3. Fry the egg(s) for 3–4 minutes, spooning the fat in the pan over the
yolk(s) until the white(s) are set and just lightly coloured on the edge(s).

4. Use a fish slice to remove the egg from the pan, letting any excess fat
drip back into the frying pan. Serve at once.

VARIATIONS
▶ *Easy-over Eggs:* Fry the egg(s) as above. When the white(s) are set
as you like, use a fish slice to flip the egg(s) over and continue frying
for 30 seconds.

COOK'S TIP
WHEN YOU FRY OR SCRAMBLE EGGS IN BUTTER, THE BUTTER CAN BURN IF IT GETS
TOO HOT. BUTTER MELTED WITH AN EQUAL AMOUNT OF VEGETABLE OIL, SUCH AS
SUNFLOWER, IS A FLAVOURFUL MIXTURE THAT WON'T BURN.

Cracking Up
To crack an egg, tap it at the centre sharply on the edge of a bowl (or
cup). Hold the egg over the bowl and use your thumbs to break the shell
into two pieces along the crack. Carefully pull the halves apart and let
the yolk and white fall into the bowl. Discard the shell and use a spoon to
remove any small pieces that have fallen into the bowl.

Scrambled Eggs

USE 2 EGGS PER SERVING. (SEE NOTE ABOUT LIGHTLY COOKED EGGS ON PAGE 36.) PREP TIME: **LESS THAN 5 MINUTES** COOKING TIME: **LESS THAN 5 MINUTES**

WHEN IT COMES TO HANGOVER-RECOVERY FOOD, TRY SCRAMBLED EGGS. THEY DON'T REQUIRE SKILL OR MUCH EFFORT TO MAKE, AND ARE EASY TO DIGEST WHEN YOUR STOMACH IS FEELING DELICATE. AND, FOR OTHER TIMES, IT IS HARD TO BEAT SCRAMBLED EGGS ON TOAST FOR A QUICK AND EASY MEAL, AND THE VARIATIONS ARE LITERALLY ENDLESS.

1. Heat your frying pan over a medium heat. Break the eggs into a small bowl or cup (see Cracking Up, page 37) and beat with a fork until the yolks and whites are blended – the longer you beat the more air you will incorporate and the lighter the eggs will be. Season to taste with salt and pepper.

2. Melt a knob (about 15 g/½ oz) of butter or margarine, or 1 tablespoon sunflower or olive oil, in the pan. (See Cook's Tip, page 37.) Swirl the fat around the pan.

3. As soon as the butter or margarine is foamy, or the oil is sizzling hot, reduce the heat to medium and pour the eggs into the pan.

4. Use a spoon or fork to stir the eggs constantly until they are thick and creamy. Just before they look as if they are cooked the way you like them, tip them out of the pan. They will continue cooking in the residual heat for 30 seconds or so, and leaving them in the pan will mean your eggs will end up over-cooked, dry and rubbery.

VARIATIONS

▶ *Scrambled Eggs with Bacon:* Heat the frying pan over a medium-high heat. Add rashers of streaky bacon and fry for 8–10 minutes, turning the rashers over once or twice until the bacon is golden-brown and a bit crisp. When the bacon starts sizzling, separate any rashers that are stuck together.

Remove the bacon from the pan and set on folded paper towels to drain. Cover with more paper towels to keep warm. Proceed with the master recipe for scrambling egg, using the bacon fat in the pan, rather than butter, margarine or oil.

▶ *Scrambled Eggs with Mushrooms:* Trim the stalks from about 60 g/ 2 oz button or chestnut mushrooms for each 2 eggs, then thinly slice the mushroom caps. Heat the fat as in the master recipe, add the mushrooms to the pan and fry them, stirring occasionally, for about 10 minutes until they are tender and the liquid they give off has evaporated. Add a little extra butter or oil to the pan, if necessary, then add the eggs and proceed with the master recipe for scrambling eggs.

▸ **Scrambled Eggs with Smoked Salmon and Leeks:** This might sound extravagant, but you can find inexpensive salmon offcuts in supermarkets and at fishmongers: plan on at least 60 g/2 oz per serving. Thinly slice the white part of $^1/_2$ a leek for each 2 eggs. Heat the fat as in the master recipe for scrambling eggs, add the leek and fry, stirring occasionally, for about 5 minutes until it is tender, but not coloured. While the leek is frying, toast one slice of bread per serving and cut the smoked salmon into thin slices. Lightly butter the toast.

When you are ready to scramble the eggs, add a little extra butter or oil to the pan, if necessary, and proceed with the master recipe. Once the eggs are scrambled, tip them on to the toast and top with the smoked salmon.

▸ **Pipérade:** This is a popular Spanish dish that can be eaten at any time of the day. This recipe serves two, but it can easily be doubled or tripled when you have a houseful.

Seed and finely chop 2 tomatoes (page 131). Peel and finely chop 1 onion. Peel and crush 1–2 garlic cloves. Seed, core and thinly slice 1 red, green or yellow pepper. Heat 2 tablespoons of sunflower or olive oil in a large frying pan over a medium-high heat. Add the tomatoes, onion, garlic and salt and pepper to taste, and reduce the heat to medium-low. Fry the vegetables, stirring occasionally, for about 10 minutes until they are tender and pulpy, but not brown. Meanwhile, beat and season 4 eggs as in the master recipe for scrambling eggs, and toast 2–4 slices of bread. Add an extra tablespoon of oil to the pan, then pour in the eggs and scramble with the vegetables as in the master recipe. Spoon the eggs and vegetables on to the hot toast.

▸ Add 1 tablespoon of water or milk when you are beating the eggs, for a fluffier dish.

▸ Add 1 tablespoon of single or double cream while beating the eggs, for a richer-tasting result.

▸ Add freshly chopped herbs to the beaten eggs, such as chives, coriander, dill, parsley or tarragon. Remember that herbs like coriander and tarragon are stronger-tasting than parsley, so adjust the quantities to suit your taste.

▸ Just before you take the eggs out of the pan, stir in grated Cheddar, wensleydale, Parmesan or other hard cheese.

Creamy Mash

MAKES **2–3 SERVINGS**
PREP TIME: **ABOUT 10 MINUTES**
COOKING TIME: **20–30 MINUTES**

WHEN YOU'RE UNDER PRESSURE WITH COURSEWORK, OR HAVE BEEN BURNING THE CANDLE AT BOTH ENDS FOR TOO LONG, A BOWL OF STEAMING MASHED POTATOES IS ONE OF THE ULTIMATE COMFORT FOODS. THIS RECIPE USES A HAND-HELD ELECTRIC MIXER FOR A CREAMY, SMOOTH TEXTURE BUT, IF YOU DON'T MIND A FEW LUMPS, AN INEXPENSIVE POTATO MASHER WORKS JUST FINE. (FOR A QUICKER ROUGH-AND-READY VERSION, SEE THE RECIPE FOR SMASHED POTATOES ON PAGE 64, WHICH USES ONLY A TABLE FORK.)

LEFTOVER MASH WILL KEEP IN THE FRIDGE FOR UP TO THREE DAYS, COVERED WITH CLINGFILM.

2 large floury potatoes (see Potato Primer 1, right, about 500 g/1 lb in total)
45 g/1 ¹/₂ oz butter
4–6 tablespoons milk
Salt and pepper

1. Bring a saucepan of salted water to the boil. Meanwhile, peel the potatoes, then cut them into chunks.

2. Add the potatoes to the boiling water and return the water to the boil.

3. Continue boiling the potatoes for 20–30 minutes until they are soft and a knife slides through them without any resistance. It is important not to over-cook the potatoes, or they will become too soggy, so start testing with the knife after about 18 minutes.

4. Set a colander or sieve in the sink and drain the potatoes. Return the potatoes to the pan, set over a low heat for 1–2 minutes to remove any excess moisture, stirring them frequently.

5. Meanwhile, put the milk in small saucepan over a low heat and warm it just until small bubbles appear around the edge: do not boil.

6. Tip the potatoes into a large bowl and add the butter. Use a hand-held electric mixer on low speed to mash the potatoes. Or, if you don't have an electric mixer, mash firmly and quickly with a masher. As the butter melts, gradually beat in the milk, tablespoon by tablespoon, until the potatoes are smooth, but still with enough body that they don't run off the end of a spoon. Season the potatoes generously with salt and pepper.

VARIATIONS

▸ *Creamy Herb Mash:* Stir 2 tablespoons of very finely chopped fresh basil, chives, parsley and/or watercress into the potatoes before you add the salt and pepper.

▸ *Creamy Garlic Mash:* Peel 1–4 cloves of garlic to taste. Add them to the potatoes after they have cooked for 10 minutes in Step 3 in the master recipe. Drain and mash with the potatoes.

▸ *Creamy Olive Oil Mash:* Replace the milk with extra-virgin olive oil.

COOK'S TIPS

▸ IF YOUR MASHED POTATOES ARE TOO RUNNY, RETURN THEM TO THE PAN OVER A LOW HEAT FOR 1 MINUTE, STIRRING, TO EVAPORATE THE EXCESS MOISTURE.

▸ MASHED POTATOES ARE BEST SERVED STRAIGHT AWAY, BUT IF YOU WANT TO KEEP THEM WARM FOR A HALF AN HOUR OR SO, HEAT THE OVEN TO HIGH AND LIGHTLY BUTTER AN OVENPROOF DISH. PUT THE POTATOES IN THE DISH, SMOOTH THE SURFACE AND BRUSH THE TOP WITH MELTED BUTTER. STIR IN THE BUTTER WHEN YOU ARE READY TO SERVE.

Potato Primer 1

▸ A seemingly endless variety of potatoes are sold, but only certain ones are light and fluffy enough for mashing and baking. Suitable potatoes from a supermarket will be labelled as such, but if you are buying potatoes in a market, look for Cara, King Edward, Maris Piper and Pentland Squire. Do not buy new potatoes or any labelled as 'waxy' or 'suitable for boiling' for baking or mashing, because the texture will be too dense and 'gluey'.

▸ Potatoes need generous seasoning. Cook them in salted water, and season them with plenty of salt and pepper before serving.

▸ If you peel and cut up the potatoes in advance, drop the chunks in a bowl of cold water to prevent the flesh from turning brown. (Be sure to dry them very well, however, if you are making Oven-baked Chips, page 44.)

▸ There are a lot of valuable nutrients just under a potato's skin, which are greatly reduced or lost when it is peeled. Cheesy Potato Skins with Salsa (page 97), Crispy Baked Potatoes (page 42) and Potato Wedges with Blue Cheese Dip (page 95) are among the recipes where the potatoes don't have to be peeled, but can be scrubbed instead.

▸ To scrub potatoes, when you are cooking them with the skins on, use a stiff vegetable brush. Rub firmly under cold, running water to remove any dirt. Use the tip of a small sharp knife to remove any dark indented 'eyes'.

Crispy Baked Potatoes

MAKES **2 SERVINGS**
PREP TIME: **ABOUT 5 MINUTES**
BAKING TIME: **45 MINUTES–1 HOUR**

A BAKED POTATO IS A VERY FILLING GRANT-STRETCHER, AND IS ALSO LIGHT ENOUGH FOR A DELICATE STOMACH TO COPE WITH WHEN YOU'VE PARTIED TOO MUCH AND HAVE TO GET BACK ON YOUR FEET. AS A MEAL ON ITS OWN WITH A SIMPLE TOPPING, SUCH AS GRATED CHEESE, CHOOSE A POTATO THAT WEIGHS AT LEAST 350 G/12 OZ, BUT IF YOU'RE GOING TO HAVE A MORE SUBSTANTIAL TOPPING, SUCH AS CHILLI CON CARNE (PAGE 158), A 225 G/8 OZ POTATO WILL BE SUFFICIENT. (A FEW TOPPINGS ARE SUGGESTED RIGHT, BUT ALMOST ANYTHING THAT TAKES YOUR FANCY – OR JUST ABOUT ANYTHING YOU HAVE IN THE FRIDGE OR CUPBOARD – IS SUITABLE.)

IT'S ALWAYS WORTH BAKING EXTRA POTATOES EVEN IF YOU ONLY WANT ONE AT THE TIME. BAKED POTATOES WILL KEEP IN THE FRIDGE FOR UP TO THREE DAYS, AND CAN BE REHEATED IN A 180°C/350°F/GAS 4 OVEN FOR 10–15 MINUTES: THE SKINS WON'T BE CRISP, BUT THEY WILL STILL MAKE A QUICK, FILLING, CHEAP SNACK. YOU CAN USE EXTRA BAKED POTATOES FOR CHEESE-STUFFED POTATOES (PAGE 147) OR CHEESY POTATO SKINS WITH SALSA (PAGE 97).

2 floury potatoes (see Potato Primer 1, page 41)
Olive or sunflower oil
Salt, ideally coarse sea salt

1. Heat the oven to 230°C/450°F/Gas 8. Thoroughly scrub the potatoes, then dry them with a kitchen towel or paper towels. Poke the potatoes all over with a fork.

2. Using your hands, rub the potatoes all over with a small amount of oil so they are completely coated. Sprinkle all over with salt.

3. Place the potatoes directly on the oven rack and bake for 45 minutes–1 hour, depending on the size. The potatoes are done when the skins are crisp and brown and they feel soft in the centre when poked with a fork: there shouldn't be any resistance.

4. Remove the potatoes from the oven. Make a lengthways cut in the top, using a small sharp knife, then push them open by pressing on both ends. (If they feel too hot, use a folded towel to protect your fingers.) Add the topping of your choice.

TOPPING IDEAS
- Try a dollop of Greek-style or natural yogurt with grated Cheddar or Parmesan cheese.
- Toss drained, canned tuna with mayonnaise and finely sliced sun-dried tomatoes, or drained, canned sweetcorn kernels.
- Mix together soured cream and finely chopped fresh herbs, such as parsley, chives, coriander and/or dill. Or try cottage cheese and herbs for a lower-fat topping.
- Add crumbled, crispy fried bacon to any of the above.
- Aubergine Dip (page 90)
- Blue Cheese Dip (page 94)
- Chilli con Carne (page 158)
- Curried Mince (page 157)
- Guacamole (page 91)
- Hummus (page 88)
- Leftover Mary's Beef & Mushroom Casserole (page 175)
- Ratatouille (page 173)

VARIATION
- For a soft skin instead of a crisp one as in the master recipe, wrap each potato in a piece of foil, shiny side in, before you put it in the oven. The foil stops the natural moisture from escaping, keeping the skin soft.

Time Saver
Insert two long metal kebab skewers through each potato at diagonal angles before you put it in the oven. As the skewers heat, they transfer heat to the centre of the potato, speeding up the cooking time.

Oven-baked Chips

MAKES **2 SERVINGS**
PREP TIME: **ABOUT 10 MINUTES**
COOKING TIME: **20–30 MINUTES**

FEW INEXPENSIVE DISHES CAN BEAT A PLATE OF GOLDEN-BROWN CHIPS. DEEP-FRYING
CHIPS AT HOME, HOWEVER, ISN'T EASY OR SAFE UNLESS YOU HAVE A DEEP-FAT FRYER OR
REALLY GOOD-QUALITY SAUCEPAN AND A THERMOMETER. AND THEN THERE IS THE HEALTH
ASPECT OF FATTY DEEP-FRIED FOOD TO CONSIDER. THESE OVEN-BAKED CHIPS ARE AN
EASY AND HEALTHY ALTERNATIVE. JUST REMEMBER TO PLAN AHEAD, AS THESE AREN'T
QUICK TO BAKE.

2 large floury potatoes (see Potato Primer 1, page 41)
2 teaspoons sunflower oil
2 teaspoons salt
Extra salt and pepper

1. Heat the oven to 220°C/425°F/Gas 7 with a baking sheet inside.

2. Meanwhile, scrub or peel the potatoes. Use a sharp knife to cut each
one lengthways into 0.5 cm/$^1/_4$-inch thick slices, then into 0.5 cm/$^1/_4$-
inch wide sticks; it doesn't matter if some are irregular. As the chips are
cut, put them in a large bowl.

3. Add the oil to the bowl and use your hands to toss and rub the oil all
over the chips. Sprinkle with the salt and toss the chips again.

4. Using oven gloves, carefully remove the baking sheet from the oven.

5. Arrange the chips in a single layer on the baking sheet. Return the
baking sheet to the oven and bake for 20–30 minutes, turning the chips
over several times until they are golden brown and crispy.

6. Sprinkle with extra salt and pepper to taste, and serve at once.

VARIATION
► Add extra flavour to the chips by tossing them in a paper bag while they
are still hot with about 1 teaspoon, or to taste, of any of the following
ingredients: chilli powder, Chinese five-spice powder, English mustard
powder, dried mixed herbs, or grated Parmesan cheese.

Perfect Rice Every Time

Stretch your grant by cooking – rather than buying – rice every time you order an Indian or Chinese take-away. Cooking rice takes little effort and it is a whole lot cheaper when you cook it yourself.

Rice has an unjustified reputation of being difficult to cook, but it really isn't. When you buy rice in a supermarket, just follow the instructions on the packet. But when buying rice in bulk at a health food shop or in a market, use one of the two methods on the following pages, whether you buy long-grain white or brown rice. Try both methods to see which one you like best, then stick with it. Either method will give you tender, separate grains.

Allow 90 g/3 oz of raw white rice per person for a main course, and 60 g/2 oz for a side dish; use 70 g/2$\frac{1}{2}$ oz of raw brown rice for a main course, and 45 g/1$\frac{1}{2}$ oz for a side dish. (If you don't have scales, see Eyeballing It, page 47.)

Leftover cooked rice is very versatile for adding to salads, soups and casseroles, and it freezes well, so get in the habit of cooking double or triple quantities. Cooked rice, however, is a mecca for germs and bacteria so it must be left to cool completely before you put it in the fridge, tightly covered with clingfilm. Then it will keep for one to two days.

Boiled Rice

MAKES **2–3 SERVINGS**
NO PREP TIME
COOKING TIME: **10–12 MINUTES**

180 g/6 oz long-grain white rice
Salt

1. Bring a large saucepan of salted water to the boil over a high heat.

2. Add the rice, stir and return the water to the boil. Continue boiling, uncovered, for 10–12 minutes, stirring occasionally until the rice is fluffy and the grains are separate.

3. To test if the rice is cooked, use a spoon to scoop out a few grains and press them between your fingers; if they are still hard, continue cooking for a few minutes longer.

4. Place a colander or sieve in the sink, then drain the rice in it, shaking to remove any excess water.

VARIATION
▸ *Boiled Brown Rice:* Cook as above, but increase the cooking time to 30–35 minutes.

Basmati Rice
Basmati, a long-grain rice from the foothills of the Himalayas, is traditionally rinsed in several changes of cold water and then left to soak for about 30 minutes before cooking. This is done to remove excess starch that can make the rice stodgy when cooked. Fortunately, most supermarket basmati rice doesn't require any extra preparation and you can cook it like ordinary long-grain rice. Just make sure you read the label before you cook.

If you buy your basmati rice at an Indian market in bulk, however, put it in a strainer and run cold water through it until the water is clear. Then put the rice in a bowl of water, cover and leave to soak for 30 minutes. Drain the rice well, then use the absorption method to cook it on top of the hob. (See Hob Rice, page 47.)

Flavouring Rice
▸ Add extra flavour to rice by cooking it in Chicken or Vegetable Stock (pages 51 and 54), rather than water. If you use a stock cube, however, reduce the amount of salt you add to the water, because stock cubes are salty.
▸ Other flavourings to add to rice while it is cooking include chopped fresh herbs, grated lemon rind and ground spices, such as coriander or cumin.

Hob Rice

MAKES **2–3 SERVINGS**
NO PREP TIME
COOKING TIME: **20 MINUTES, PLUS 5 MINUTES STANDING**

15 g/$^{1}/_{2}$ oz butter or margarine, or 1 tablespoon sunflower oil
180 g/6 oz long-grain white rice
250 ml/8 fl oz water
$^{1}/_{2}$ teaspoon salt

1. Melt the butter or margarine, or heat the oil in a flameproof casserole or large frying pan with a tight-fitting lid over a medium-high heat. Add the rice and stir it around until all the grains are coated.

2. Pour in the water, add the salt and stir. Bring to the boil, without stirring.

3. Turn the heat to its lowest setting, cover the pan tightly and leave the rice to simmer, without lifting the lid, for 20 minutes. Remove the pan from the heat and leave to stand for 5 minutes, still covered.

4. Uncover the pan and stir the rice with a fork to fluff up and separate the grains.

VARIATION
▸ *Brown Hob Rice:* Cook as above, but increase the amount of liquid to 300 ml/10 fl oz, and the cooking time to 30–35 minutes.

Eyeballing It
If you don't have kitchen scales or a measuring jug, you can use an ordinary mug or teacup to measure the rice and water: use two parts water to one part rice for long-grain white rice, or about $2^{1}/_{2}$ parts water to one part brown rice.

The average-size coffee mug holds about 250 g/8 oz long-grain white rice.

Basic Tomato Sauce

MAKES **ABOUT 350 G/12 OZ, ENOUGH FOR
2–3 SERVINGS OF PASTA** PREP TIME: **ABOUT 5 MINUTES**
COOKING TIME: **ABOUT 20 MINUTES**

SUPERMARKETS SELL MANY JARS OF DIFFERENT TOMATO SAUCES THAT SIMPLY NEED
REHEATING. THEY COULDN'T BE QUICKER TO USE, AND IT WILL BE TEMPTING TO STOCK
UP, BUT YOU WILL SOON REALISE IT IS MUCH CHEAPER TO MAKE YOUR OWN.

THIS IS A DEAD SIMPLE RECIPE THAT IS BOUND TO BECOME A REGULAR IN YOUR
REPERTOIRE. ON ITS OWN IT CAN BE TOSSED WITH HOT PASTA OR SPREAD ON PIZZA
BASES, BUT YOU CAN ADAPT IT WITH A VARIETY OF INGREDIENTS YOU MIGHT HAVE
IN THE CUPBOARD. (SEE STORE CUPBOARD PASTA SAUCE, PAGE 223.)

IN SUMMER, WHEN TOMATOES ARE MOST FLAVOURFUL, TRY THE UNCOOKED SAUCE
ON PAGE 131 INSTEAD, FOR TOSSING WITH PASTA.

1 large garlic clove
1 onion
3 tablespoons olive or sunflower oil
1 can (400 g/14 oz) chopped tomatoes
Pinch of sugar
Salt and pepper

1. Peel and crush the garlic. Peel and chop the onion.

2. Heat the oil in a frying pan or saucepan over a medium-high heat.
Add the garlic and onion, and fry, stirring occasionally, for about
5 minutes until the onion is tender, but not brown.

3. Stir in the tomatoes with the juice from the can, the sugar and salt
and pepper to taste, and bring to the boil, stirring occasionally. Lower
the heat and simmer, uncovered, for about 15 minutes until the sauce
reduces and thickens, stirring occasionally to stop the sauce from
sticking to the bottom of the pan. The sauce is now ready for tossing
with freshly cooked pasta or spreading on pizza.

VARIATIONS

► Puree the sauce in a blender or food processor for a smooth version. If you want a really smooth sauce, rub it through a fine sieve with a wooden spoon. Reheat the sauce gently before tossing with pasta.

► For a South-of-France flavour, add a long strip of orange rind while the sauce simmers, remove and discard the rind before serving.

► For an Italian flavour, add fresh basil leaves while the sauce simmers; remove before serving.

► Spice up the sauce by adding 1 seeded and chopped fresh red chilli, or a pinch of dried chilli flakes, with the tomatoes.

► For a more complex flavour, add 1 peeled and finely diced carrot and 1 finely chopped celery stick with the onion.

► *Tomato & Pepper Soup:* To make 4 servings, make the master recipe for Basic Tomato Sauce, but add 2 cored, seeded and chopped red peppers to the onion and garlic, and double the amount of chopped tomatoes. After the sauce has cooked for 15 minutes, stir in 900 ml/1$\frac{1}{2}$ pints of vegetable stock (home-made, page 54, or from a cube) and heat through. Serve chunky as it is, or puree in a blender or food processor and then rub through a fine sieve, if you want a really smooth soup. Reheat before serving.

A Sweet Touch

Adding a pinch of sugar with the tomatoes helps to reduce any acidity.

Making Stock

'Stock' is a liquid used in soups, casseroles, sauces and risottos. You will see it specified in the recipes in this book, as well as other cookery books, because it adds much more flavour than just plain water to dishes. Dissolving a stock cube in hot water is the quick way to make stock, but if you take to cooking you'll find the flavour from a cube isn't as good as your own home-made stock. You're unlikely to keep a stockpot bubbling at the back of the hob like your grandmother might have done, but stock-making is a technique worth learning. Home-made stock helps raise your cooking above the ordinary, even in everyday dishes.

When you go to the trouble of making stock, you might as well make more than you need. It will keep in the fridge, covered, for three days (after this it has to be boiled and left to cool again before refrigerating for another two days). Or the stock can be left to cool and then frozen for up to three months (see Sensational Stocks, page 53).

Chicken Stock

MAKES **ABOUT 1.25 LITRES / 2 PINTS**
PREP TIME: **5–10 MINUTES** COOKING TIME:
ABOUT 1 HOUR, MOST OF WHICH IS UNATTENDED

YOU CAN MAKE THIS WITH THE LEFTOVER CARCASS FROM ROASTED CHICKEN (PAGE 168),
BUT USING INEXPENSIVE CHICKEN WINGS OR THIGHS GETS YOU MORE FLAVOUR – PLUS
PLENTY OF TENDER CHICKEN TO USE IN SANDWICHES, SALADS AND STIR-FRIES.

1 large carrot
1 large onion
1 celery stick
2 whole black peppercorns (optional)
6 chicken wings or thighs on the bone
Several sprigs of fresh parsley (optional)
Pinch of dried thyme (optional)
Salt

1. Scrub or peel and slice the carrot. Peel and coarsely chop the onion.
Chop the celery stick. Use a pestle and mortar or the back of a large
spoon to lightly crush the peppercorns, if using.

2. Put the chicken wings or thighs, vegetables and 1 teaspoon of salt in
a large saucepan or flameproof casserole. Cover with 2 litres/3½ pints
of water and slowly heat until the liquid is trembling, but bubbles don't
break the surface, which will take 10–15 minutes. As the water is heating,
grey scum will rise to the surface. You can't leave the stove at this point,
because you need to spoon off this scum constantly: a large metal spoon
is the easiest to use for this, but an ordinary tablespoon is fine. Do not
let the liquid boil or the stock will become cloudy.

3. When no more scum rises to the surface, add the peppercorns, parsley
and thyme, or whichever flavourings you are using (see Variations on
page 52). Turn the heat to its lowest setting and leave the stock to
simmer until the chicken is cooked through. To test, after 30 minutes
remove one of the chicken pieces, put it on a plate and use the tip of a
knife to pierce it. The juices should be clear; if they are pink, return the
chicken to the stock and continue simmering for 5 minutes longer before
testing again.

4. Remove the chicken pieces from the stock and set them aside. Place
a colander or large sieve over a large heatproof bowl. Strain the stock
into the bowl, pressing down on the vegetables to extract as much of
their flavoursome liquid as possible; discard the vegetables and any
flavourings. (Leave the chicken pieces to cool completely, then cover
with clingfilm and store in the fridge for up to three days.)

5. The stock will now be ready to use. If you are going to use it immediately, skim any fat off the surface with a large metal spoon, or crumple several paper towels and dab the surface to absorb the fat. If you are not using the stock for at least a day, leave it to cool completely, then cover with clingfilm and put in the fridge overnight. During this time any fat on the surface will solidify and can easily be lifted off and discarded.

VARIATIONS

‣ Other flavourings to try include a bay leaf, whole peeled garlic cloves and celery leaves. Or use whole spices, such as star anise, allspice or cloves. Each adds extra and distinctive flavour. Experiment to see what you like the most.

‣ *Chicken-Noodle Soup:* Try this to break a hangover when you can't face a heavy meal, or when you're battling a cold and want some TLC. Cook Asian egg noodles, spaghetti or tagliatelle according to the packet instructions; drain well and set aside. Reheat the stock with the skinned and finely shredded chicken meat, then add the noodles for just long enough to heat through. Add salt and pepper to taste, with lots of chopped fresh parsley, if you have any.

To turn this into more of a meal, add drained, canned sweetcorn kernels, tiny broccoli florets, finely diced celery, scrubbed or peeled finely sliced carrots, sliced mangetout, frozen peas, or sliced mushrooms before you add the noodles. Simmer until the vegetables are heated through and tender when pierced, then add the chicken and noodles, and reheat.

‣ *Oriental Chicken Broth:* Simmer the stock with a sliced 2.5 cm/1-inch piece of fresh root ginger. Use as the base for an Oriental-style soup with Asian noodles and Chinese greens.

Sensational Stocks

► Keep small portions of stock in the ice cube compartment of the fridge and you can be sipping flavoursome home-made soup in almost the time it takes to open a can and heat the contents. Freeze cooled stock in convenient-to-use quantities, so you don't have to thaw more than you need: use a bowl to support a freezerproof bag and add 250–300 ml/8–10 fl oz for single portions.

► You can boil strained stock until it reduces in volume; this will concentrate the flavours. Leave the stock to cool completely, then pour it into an ice-cube tray with dividers and freeze until solid. Remove the stock cubes from the tray and put in a freezerproof bag. You can then use the stock cubes straight from the freezer. Melt them to make stews, casseroles, soups and risottos.

► If you roast a chicken (page 168), save the carcass and bones to make stock. If you have a freezer, you can freeze chicken bones until you have the time and are in the mood to make stock. Crack the frozen bones before you put them in the pot, to release the gelatine – this is what gives home-made stock one of it special qualities.

► 'Take stock and then make stock' is a country saying that makes great sense: the stockpot is a good way to use up slightly-past-their-prime vegetables, which would otherwise be discarded. Do not, however, use any mouldy or rotting vegetables – throw them out!

► Do not add potatoes to a stock, as they will make it cloudy.

► Adding onion skins to a simmering stock will give it a rich, dark colour.

Vegetable Stock

MAKES **ABOUT 1.25 LITRES/2 PINTS**
PREP TIME: **ABOUT 10 MINUTES** COOKING TIME:
1 HOUR, MOST OF WHICH IS UNATTENDED

USE THIS TO ADD EXTRA FLAVOUR TO VEGETARIAN AND VEGAN CASSEROLES,
RISOTTOS AND SOUPS.

10 black peppercorns
5 sprigs fresh parsley
1 garlic clove
2 bay leaves
1 sprig fresh thyme,
   or ½ teaspoon dried

3 large carrots
2 large onions
2 celery sticks
2 large leeks, sliced and rinsed, if necessary
Salt

1. You need a piece of muslin or cotton or a J-cloth about 12.5 cm/
5 inches square, plus some string. Use a pestle and mortar or the back
of a large spoon to lightly crush the peppercorns and the parsley sprig
stalks. Peel the garlic cloves.

2. Put the peppercorns, parsley, bay leaves, thyme and garlic cloves in
the middle of the cloth and tie into a secure bundle with the string.

3. Scrub or peel and chop the carrots. Peel and cut each onion in half.
Chop the celery sticks. Cut each leek in half lengthways, then put the cut
sides down on a chopping board and slice. (If the leek has grit between
the layers, put the slices in a sieve and run cold water over them.)

4. Put the bundle of herbs and spices in a large saucepan or flameproof
casserole with the carrots, onions, celery, leeks and 1 teaspoon salt. Put
the pan over a medium-high heat, add 1.8 litres/3 pints water and slowly
bring to the boil. If any grey scum appears on the surface, use a spoon to
skim it off.

5. As soon as the liquid boils, turn the heat to its lowest setting and leave
the stock to simmer, uncovered, for 45 minutes, removing any scum that
rises to the surface.

6. Set a colander or big sieve over a large heatproof bowl in the sink.
Strain the stock into the bowl, pressing down on the vegetables to
extract as much of their flavoursome liquid as possible; discard the
vegetables and flavouring bundle.

7. The stock is now ready to use, or it can be cooled and refrigerated or
frozen until required (see Chicken Stock, page 51) – cover with clingfilm
and chill for up to 3 days or freeze for up to a month.

Vinaigrette

MAKES **ABOUT 300 ML/10 FL OZ**
PREP TIME: **ABOUT 5 MINUTES**
NO COOKING

VINAIGRETTE IS AN ALL-PURPOSE FRENCH OIL-AND-VINEGAR DRESSING. IT CAN BE TEMPTING TO REACH FOR BOTTLES OF SALAD DRESSING WHEN YOU'RE SHOPPING, BUT GIVE YOUR BUDGET A BREAK AND GET IN THE HABIT OF MAKING YOUR OWN. IT ONLY TAKES MINUTES TO SHAKE UP A BATCH THAT CAN THEN SIT IN THE FRIDGE, READY TO USE, FOR SEVERAL WEEKS. YOU'LL SAVE QUITE A BIT OF MONEY OVER A TERM.

VINAIGRETTES CAN BE AS SHARP OR MILD AS YOU LIKE, AND YOU CAN ALTER THE FLAVOUR BY ADDING MORE OR LESS VINEGAR, SUGAR, MUSTARD, AND SALT AND PEPPER. YOU CAN ALSO REPLACE THE VINEGAR WITH LEMON JUICE, IF YOU PREFER.

IF YOU'VE NEVER MADE SALAD DRESSING BEFORE, START BY MAKING HALF-QUANTITIES AND EXPERIMENT UNTIL YOU FIND THE PROPORTION OF VINEGAR TO OIL THAT SUITS YOU.

250 ml/8 fl oz olive or sunflower oil
6 tablespoons red- or white-wine vinegar
1 teaspoon sugar
1 teaspoon Dijon mustard
Salt and pepper

1. Put all the ingredients in a screw-top jar, screw on the lid and shake vigorously until well blended. Taste and add extra vinegar, sugar, mustard or salt and pepper to taste. Shake again each time before using.

VARIATIONS

▸ *Balsamic Vinaigrette:* Replace 2 tablespoons of the wine vinegar with 2 tablespoons balsamic vinegar.

▸ *Basil Vinaigrette:* Add up to 2 tablespoons of shredded fresh basil leaves for 300 ml/10 fl oz of Vinaigrette, but it is best only to make as much dressing as you will use straight away, as basil looses its freshness quickly and turns an unappetizing black.

▸ *Creamy Vinaigrette:* Add 1–2 tablespoons single or double cream, soured cream or yogurt to the other ingredients before you shake. Use within 3 days.

▸ *Herb Vinaigrette:* Add up to 2 tablespoons chopped fresh parsley, 2 tablespoons fresh snipped chives or 1 teaspoon dried mixed herbs for 300 ml/10 fl oz dressing but, again, it is best to flavour only as much dressing as you will use straight away.

▸ *Mustard Vinaigrette:* Increase the amount of mustard to $1^1/_2$ tablespoons. You can use prepared English, Dijon or wholegrain, each of which gives a different flavour.

▸ *Parmesan Vinaigrette*: Add $1^1/_2$ tablespoons grated cheese to the other ingredients. Do not add salt until after you taste, because the cheese is salty.

▶ Other traditional flavourings to use to taste include: crumbled blue cheese, grated orange or lemon rind, curry powder, dried chilli flakes, crushed coriander seeds and soy sauce. Experiment!

▶ Use honey instead of sugar.

All Dressed Up

▶ When you add dressing to a bowl of lettuce or other salad greens, the idea is to lightly coat each leaf, not drown it. Add a small amount of the dressing, then use salad servers, 2 forks or clean hands to toss the ingredients together. You can always add more dressing, but you can't take it away.

▶ Dressing should be added just before a salad is served. If you do dress a salad in advance the leaves will become limp and unappetizing.

Extra Flavour

▶ Perk up simple grilled chops or chicken breasts and thighs by brushing them with a little Vinaigrette while they are grilling.

Take-away Pizzas at Home

Have you ever added up how much money you spend during a term by just picking up the phone and ringing for a pizza delivery? Make your own pizza and you'll save loads of cash. You can have all the 'extras' you want for a fraction of the price. And you can tailor each pizza to include your favourite topping ingredients, so if you want ham with pineapple chunks, so be it.

Forget any idea you have of it being difficult to make the yeast-dough base. It isn't – you can make up a batch in the time it takes for some TV commercials to run, and then the kneading is a pretty mindless exercise.

In fact, pizza dough is accommodating and will fit in with your schedule. Once the dough is made, you can leave it at room temperature to rise and bake immediately, or you can keep it in a tightly covered bowl in the fridge for up to 24 hours. Just remember to let it come to room temperature before you roll it out. You'll be munching a freshly baked pizza in less time than it would take to have one delivered.

If you still aren't convinced, however, try the ultra-quick Muffin 'Mini Pizzas' (page 105) as a quick, cheap alternative to take-away pizza.

Perfect Pizzas

▸ To knead the dough, shape it into a loose ball. Push the dough at a 45-degree angle from right to left across the front of your body with the heel of your right hand, pushing down firmly. Then use the heel of your left hand and push at a 45-degree angle from left to right. Continue, using alternate hands, until the dough becomes smooth and doesn't stick to your hands. Only add extra flour to prevent the dough from sticking: if you add too much, the pizzas will have a tough texture.

▸ Rub your hands with olive oil to stop the dough sticking to them while you are kneading it.

▸ If you don't have a rolling pin, just use your oiled fingers to pat and press the dough into a circle.

▸ To determine if the dough has risen enough in Step 7, stick your finger into it. If the indentation remains, the dough is ready to use.

Tomato Pizzas with Herbs

MAKES **TWO 30 CM/12-INCH PIZZAS**
PREP TIME: **ABOUT 5 MINUTES, PLUS KNEADING
AND RISING** BAKING TIME: **15 MINUTES**

THIS IS A SIMPLE VEGETARIAN PIZZA, BUT A LONG LIST OF OTHER TOPPING IDEAS FOLLOWS.

FOR THE DOUGH:
400 g/14 oz plain white flour
1 sachet easy-blend dried yeast
1 teaspoon sugar
1 teaspoon salt
1 tablespoon olive oil, plus extra for greasing
About 250 ml/8 fl oz warm water

FOR THE TOPPINGS:
6–8 tablespoons tomato sauce, home-made (page 48) or bottled
125 g/4 oz mozzarella cheese, drained and thinly sliced
1 teaspoon dried mixed herbs

1. Put the flour, yeast, salt and sugar in a large mixing bowl and stir together. Use the spoon to make a well in the centre. Pour the olive oil and 200 ml/7 fl oz of the water into the well.

2. Gradually stir the flour into the liquids until a soft, sticky dough forms. Slowly add the remaining water if the dough feels dry.

3. Lightly flour the work surface and tip the dough out onto it. Sprinkle the dough very lightly with a little extra flour and knead (see Perfect Pizzas, page 57) for up to 10 minutes until it becomes smooth and doesn't stick to your hands any more.

4. Wash and dry the bowl, then lightly rub the inside with olive oil. Shape the dough into a ball and put it in the bowl. Roll the dough around so it is coated with oil: this prevents a dry skin from forming as it rises.

5. Cover the bowl tightly with clingfilm and set aside to rise until the dough doubles in volume. The exact time will depend on the temperature of the room, but it should take 30 minutes–1 hour. (Alternatively, put the covered bowl in the fridge for up to 24 hours; see the introduction.)

6. Meanwhile, heat the oven to 220°C/425°F/Gas 7 with 2 baking sheets inside.

7. When the dough has risen, lightly flour the work surface again. Turn out the dough onto the surface and press down on it to extract the air. Lightly knead again for 1 minute.

8. Cut the dough into 2 equal pieces and shape each into a ball. Use a lightly floured rolling pin and roll 1 ball into a 30 cm/12-inch round.

9. Remove a baking sheet from the oven and sprinkle it with flour. Put the pizza base on the baking sheet. Spread with half the tomato sauce, until it is no closer than 0.5 cm/$\frac{1}{4}$ inch from the edge. Scatter with half the cheese and sprinkle with half the herbs.

10. Remove the other baking sheet from the oven. Put the first pizza in the oven to bake for 15 minutes, or until the edge is golden brown and the cheese has melted.

11. While the first pizza is baking, roll out the remaining dough and top with the remaining ingredients. When you take the first pizza out of the oven, put the second one in to bake.

VARIATIONS
▸ *Pizza Americana:* Roll out the dough and cover the pizza bases with tomato sauce as in the master recipe. Omit the herbs and instead add sliced pepperoni with the mozzarella. Bake as above.
▸ *Pizza Bianca:* This is a simple Italian classic. Omit the tomato sauce. Instead, roll out the dough as in the master recipe and brush the base with olive oil. Scatter with the drained and sliced mozzarella cheese and season with sea salt and pepper. Bake as in the master recipe.
▸ *Pizza Romana:* Roll out the dough and cover the pizza bases with tomato sauce as in the master recipe. Omit the herbs and top the pizzas with sliced Parma ham, sliced red onion and sliced mozzarella cheese. Season with pepper. Bake as in the master recipe.
▸ *California-style Pizza:* Replace the mozzarella with sliced goat's cheese. Roll out the dough and cover the pizza bases with the tomato sauce as in the master recipe. Add sliced sun-dried tomatoes and sliced stoned black olives. Bake as above, and scatter fresh basil leaves over the top before cutting.
▸ *Mushroom Pizza:* Sauté 250 g/8 oz thinly sliced brown or chestnut mushrooms with 1 or 2 peeled and crushed garlic cloves in 2 tablespoons olive oil for about 10 minutes until the mushrooms are brown and the excess liquid they give off evaporates. Toss with finely chopped fresh parsley and salt and pepper to taste. Roll out the dough and cover the pizza bases with the tomato sauce as in the master recipe. Add the mushrooms and bake as above.

ALL-DAY BREAK-FASTS

There are no acceptable excuses for skipping breakfast.

You've probably already been told a million times that breakfast is the most important meal of the day. Well, it's true. Neither hangovers nor oversleeping, nor just not being hungry, are good enough reasons not to eat something when you get up – whatever the time of day.

Nutritional research constantly shows that eating breakfast helps to improve your mental and physical performance and contributes important nutrients to your diet.

'Breakfast' literally means to break the fast. When you get up, your body will probably have been fasting for at least eight hours, and it needs food to convert into the physical and mental energy you require. Running out the door without eating something first is like setting off on a car journey with an empty petrol tank.

And if you think you can save calories and lose weight by skipping breakfast, think again. Many studies have concluded that breakfast skippers end up consuming more calories during the rest of the day than those who feed their face first thing. When you make time for breakfast, you will be less likely to crave a mid-morning snack. And we all know that those quick snacks contain more calories than nutrients.

Breakfasts kick-starts your metabolism. When you skip breakfast, however, your metabolic rate drops so your body burns fewer calories throughout the day.

Eating breakfast every day can be a good first step towards consuming the five portions of fruit and vegetables a day you need as part of a healthy, balanced diet.

But if the idea of conventional breakfast dishes, such as bacon and eggs or a bowl of cereal, don't appeal, that's no problem. The selection of drinks and sandwich recipes in this chapter can help you think outside the 'breakfast box' and get you going, whether you're eating on the run or have time for a leisurely start. And, if you don't get up before lunchtime, you'll still find plenty of recipes that hit the spot.

Other recipes to start the day:
- Boiled Eggs (page 35)
- Leftover Vegetable Lasagne (page 141)
- Sardines on Toast (page 109)
- Scrambled Eggs (page 38)

Bloody Mary

 MAKES **1 DRINK**
PREP TIME: **LESS THAN 5 MINUTES**

GENERATIONS OF STUDENTS HAVE RELIED ON THIS HAIR-OF-THE-DOG TO VANISH THE
AGONY OF THE NIGHT BEFORE, BUT BEWARE – THE SLUG OF VODKA ONLY POSTPONES THE
INEVITABLE. THE TOMATO JUICE CAN HELP YOU GET ON YOUR FEET AGAIN, SO IT MIGHT BE
A GOOD IDEA TO CONSIDER THE VIRGIN MARY ALTERNATIVE, BELOW.

60 ml / 2 fl oz vodka
1 teaspoon lemon juice
1/2 teaspoon Worcestershire sauce
125–180 ml / 4–6 fl oz tomato juice
Celery salt (optional)
Salt and pepper

1. Put the vodka, lemon juice and Worcestershire sauce in a glass and
stir together. Top up with tomato juice, then add celery salt and salt and
pepper to taste. Stir again. Add ice cubes.

VARIATIONS
▶ *Bloody Bull:* Replace half the tomato juice in the Bloody Mary recipe
with beef stock and add several dashes of hot-pepper sauce.
▶ *Red Snapper:* Replace the vodka in the Bloody Mary recipe with gin.
▶ *Virgin Mary:* This will probably do more good if you are nursing a
hangover than a Bloody Mary, and it makes a refreshing drink for other
times. Make as above, but omit the vodka.

Prairie Oyster

 MAKES **1 DRINK**
PREP TIME: **LESS THAN 5 MINUTES**

NOT FOR THE FAINT HEARTED. THIS IS AN AMERICAN COWBOY CURE FOR HANGOVERS,
USED SINCE THE MID-NINETEENTH CENTURY.

1 egg
2 teaspoons Worcestershire sauce
1 teaspoon vinegar
2 dashes hot-pepper sauce
Salt and pepper

1. Break the egg into a tumbler. Add the Worcestershire sauce, vinegar,
hot pepper sauce and salt and pepper to taste. Down it in one if you're
macho enough.

Eggs, Bacon & Beans

MAKES **2 SERVINGS**
PREP TIME: **LESS THAN 5 MINUTES**
COOKING TIME: **8–10 MINUTES**

THIS AND THE FOLLOWING RECIPE MAKE HEARTY STARTS TO THE DAY THAT WILL POSTPONE
LUNCH HUNGER PANGS FOR SEVERAL HOURS. THESE CAN ALSO BE TEMPTING WHEN YOU
COME HOME AFTER A LATE NIGHT AND HAVEN'T EATEN ANYTHING.

1 can (400 g/14 oz) baked beans
6 rashers streaky bacon
4 eggs
Brown sauce, to serve (optional)

1. Empty the can of beans into a small saucepan over a medium heat
and heat through, stirring occasionally.

2. Put the bacon on a chopping board and cut off the rinds, if necessary.
Put the bacon in a large frying pan over a medium-high heat without any
extra fat and fry for 8–10 minutes, turning the rashers over once or twice
until the bacon is golden brown and a bit crisp. When the bacon starts
sizzling, separate any rashers that are stuck together.

3. Remove the bacon from the pan and set on folded paper towels to
drain. Cover with more paper towels to keep warm, and set aside.

4. Break the eggs into the bacon fat in the pan. Fry the eggs for 3–4
minutes, spooning the bacon fat over the yolks until the whites are just
set and lightly coloured around the edge. Use a fish slice to remove the
eggs from the pan and serve at once with the bacon and beans. Add a
dash of brown sauce for an authentic 'caff' flavour.

VARIATIONS
▸ *Eggs, Bacon & Chips:* This is for when you're not in a hurry. Make
Oven-baked Chips (page 44), then fry the bacon and eggs as in the
master recipe above.
▸ Don't throw out any leftover beans. Instead, take a look at Jazzing
Up a Can of Kidney Beans (page 222).

Bangers & Smashed Potatoes

MAKES **2 SERVINGS**
PREP TIME: **ABOUT 5 MINUTES**
COOKING TIME: **20–30 MINUTES**

1 large floury potato (see
   Potato Primer 1, page 41)
Sunflower oil

2 pork sausages
Butter (optional)
Salt and pepper

1. Bring a small saucepan of salted water to the boil. Meanwhile, peel or scrub the potato, then cut it into chunks.

2. Add the potato to the boiling water and return the water to the boil.

3. Continue boiling the potato for 20–30 minutes until it is soft and a knife slides through it without any resistance. It is important not to over-cook the potato chunks, or they will become too soggy, so start testing with the knife after about 18 minutes.

4. Meanwhile, coat the base of your frying pan with a small amount of oil and put it over a medium heat. Prick the sausages in a couple of places with a fork. Add the sausages to the pan and fry, shaking the pan occasionally, for 6–10 minutes until the skins are brown all over and the juices are clear when you pierce them with the tip of a knife. The exact cooking time will depend on the thickness of the sausages.

5. Place a colander or sieve in the sink and drain the potato chunks, shaking to remove any excess moisture. Put the potatoes in a bowl and use a fork to smash. Beat in a knob of butter, if you like, and season with salt and pepper. Serve with the sausages and tuck in!

VARIATIONS

▶ *Olive Oil Smash:* Well, maybe not for breakfast, but smashed potatoes made with olive oil, rather than butter, are good with grilled chops and chicken breasts, as well as sausages. As you smash the potatoes in Step 5 in the master recipe, drizzle in 1–2 tablespoons olive oil. Season to taste with salt and pepper.

▶ *Pan Gravy:* Serve the potatoes with an easy-to-make pan gravy, rather than butter, if you like. Pour off all but 2 tablespoons of the fat in the pan. Sprinkle with about $^1/_2$ tablespoon plain white or wholemeal flour and stir for 1–2 minutes. Stir in 200 ml/7fl stock, water or wine and bring to the boil, stirring and scraping the bottom of the pan. Leave to bubble until the gravy thickens. Season with salt and pepper to taste, if necessary, and then spoon over the potatoes.

Cabbage, Bacon & Tattie Fry

MAKES **2–3 SERVINGS**
PREP TIME: **ABOUT 5 MINUTES**
COOKING TIME: **ABOUT 20 MINUTES**

THINK OF THIS AS BUBBLE AND SQUEAK MADE FROM SCRATCH, RATHER THAN USING THE
LEFTOVERS FROM A TRADITIONAL ROAST LUNCH. THIS IS GOOD AFTER A LONG HARD NIGHT,
WHEN YOU DON'T HAVE TO BE ANYWHERE IN A HURRY.

LEFTOVERS WILL KEEP IN THE FRIDGE FOR UP TO THREE DAYS, READY TO BE REHEATED
FOR A VERY QUICK MEAL.

4 rashers streaky bacon
1 can (560 g/$18^1/_2$ oz) new potatoes
1 wedge Savoy cabbage, about 300 g/10 oz
Salt and pepper

1. Put the bacon on a chopping board and cut off the rinds, if necessary.
Place the bacon in a large frying pan over a medium-high heat without
any extra fat and fry for 8–10 minutes, turning the rashers over once or
twice until the bacon is golden brown and a bit crisp. When the bacon
starts sizzling, separate any rashers that are stuck together.

2. Meanwhile, place a sieve over the sink and drain the can of potatoes,
then pat them dry with paper towels. Coarsely chop each potato. Cut the
tough core out of the cabbage, then thinly slice the leaves.

3. Remove the bacon from the pan and set on folded paper towels to
drain. Cover with more paper towels to keep warm.

4. Add the potatoes to the bacon fat in the frying pan and fry, stirring
occasionally, for 2 minutes. Add the cabbage and continue frying for
about 5 minutes longer until it is tender and the potatoes are heated
through. If the cabbage starts to catch on the bottom of the pan, stir
in a couple tablespoons of water.

5. Cut the bacon into bite-size pieces and stir into the pan. Warm the
bacon through, if necessary, then season with salt and pepper to taste.

VARIATIONS

▸ For a vegetarian version, omit the bacon and fry the potatoes and
cabbage in 4 tablespoons of sunflower or olive oil.
▸ Omit the canned potatoes and use leftover chopped Crispy Baked
Potatoes (page 42) or Potato Wedges (page 95). If you have leftover
Creamy Mash (page 40), or potato flesh when you make Cheesy Potato
Skins (page 97), stir it into the pan to reheat after the cabbage has
cooked for 3 minutes.

Jugged Kippers

MAKES **2 SERVINGS**
PREP TIME: **8–10 MINUTES**
NO COOKING

KIPPERS FOR BREAKFAST MIGHT SEEM LIKE A REALLY OLD-FASHIONED, FUDDY-DUDDY IDEA, BUT THEY ARE SPOT-ON FOR A SUPER-QUICK MEAL THAT DOESN'T REQUIRE EFFORT – AND THEY ARE LOADED WITH THE OMEGA-3 OILS THAT ARE LINKED WITH GOOD HEALTH. KIPPERS ARE OFTEN GRILLED, BUT THAT CAN STINK OUT THE ENTIRE FLAT OR HOUSE UNLESS YOUR KITCHEN IS EQUIPPED WITH A TOP-RATE EXTRACTOR. SO, INSTEAD, TRY THIS NO-COOK METHOD – NO ONE ELSE WILL BE ABLE TO SMELL WHAT YOU'VE EATEN, AND YOU'LL SEE THIS ISN'T SUCH AN OUT-OF-DATE IDEA. WHOLEMEAL OR WHITE TOAST IS THE PERFECT ACCOMPANIMENT.

2 smoked kippers fillets
Butter
Pepper

1. Bring a kettle or saucepan of water to the boil. You need a tall heatproof jug, such as the lining for a cafeteria, a large measuring jug or an earthenware water jug. Put the kippers in the container, with the tails sticking up.

2. Pour the boiling water over the fish and leave them to stand for 8–10 minutes until the flesh flakes easily.

3. Remove the kippers from the water and pat off any excess with paper towels. Eat the kippers while they are still hot with a little butter spread over them and sprinkled with pepper.

Raisin-Cinnamon Porridge

MAKES **2 SERVINGS**
PREP TIME: **2 MINUTES**
COOKING TIME: **ABOUT 5 MINUTES**

300 ml/10 fl oz milk
250 g/8 oz rolled porridge oats
60 g/2 oz raisins or sultanas
Pinch of salt
Ground cinnamon, to taste
Brown sugar, to serve

1. Put the milk, oats, raisins or sultanas, and salt in a saucepan over a high heat and bring to the boil, stirring. Lower the heat and simmer, stirring, for 4–5 minutes until the porridge is thick and creamy.

2. Stir in cinnamon to taste and spoon into bowls. Sprinkle with brown sugar and serve hot.

Honey Toast

MAKES **1 SERVING**
PREP TIME: **HARDLY ANY**
COOKING TIME: **3–4 MINUTES**

THE FIRST STEP ON THE ROAD TO HANGOVER RECOVERY DOESN'T GET ANY EASIER OR QUICKER THAN THIS. AND WHEN YOU'RE PUSHED FOR TIME, RUSHING OFF TO LECTURES, THINK TOAST: IT'S QUICK, IT'S EASY AND THE BREAD CONTAINS A HOST OF THE VITAMINS AND MINERALS YOU NEED EVERY DAY TO REMAIN HEALTHY.

2 slices white or wholemeal bread
Butter or margarine
Honey

1. Heat the grill to high, if you don't have a toaster. Toast the bread in a toaster, or under the grill for 1^1/$_2$–2 minutes on each side until golden brown.

2. Lightly spread with butter or margarine, then top with honey.

Toast Toppings:
- ► Cinnamon and sugar
- ► Grated cheese
- ► Greek-style yogurt
- ► Honey and banana
- ► Jam or jelly
- ► Marmalade
- ► Marmite
- ► Peanut or other nut butter

Mushrooms on Toast

MAKES **2 SERVINGS**
PREP TIME: **LESS THAN 5 MINUTES**
COOKING TIME: **ABOUT 10 MINUTES**

125 g/4 oz chestnut or button mushrooms, wiped
15 g/½ oz butter or margarine
Small pinch of dried thyme (optional)
2 slices white or wholemeal bread
2 tablespoons single or double cream
Salt and pepper

1. Heat the grill to high, if you don't have a toaster. Trim the mushroom stalks, if necessary. If the mushrooms are large, thickly slice the caps, but you can leave small ones whole.

2. Melt the butter in a frying pan over a medium heat. Add the mushrooms, thyme, if you are using, and salt and pepper to taste, and fry the mushrooms, stirring occasionally, for 8–10 minutes until they are soft, but not all the liquid they give off has evaporated.

3. Meanwhile, toast the bread in the toaster or under the grill for 1½–2 minutes on each side until golden brown.

4. Stir the cream into the pan juices and let it bubble for a few seconds. Add extra salt and pepper, if necessary, then spoon the mushrooms and pan juices over the toast.

VARIATION
▶ *Devilled Mushrooms on Toast:* Prepare the mushrooms as in the master recipe above. Melt the butter and add the mushrooms. Omit the thyme, but stir 2 teaspoons mushroom ketchup, 2 teaspoons of Worcestershire sauce, 1 teaspoon English mustard powder and a pinch of cayenne pepper into the pan. Fry the mushrooms for 8–10 minutes, stirring occasionally until they are soft, but not all the liquid they give off has evaporated. If you want, stir in the cream.

Eggy Bread

MAKES **1 SERVING**
PREP TIME: **LESS THAN 5 MINUTES**
COOKING TIME: **ABOUT 5 MINUTES**

THIS IS AN EXCELLENT WAY TO USE BREAD THAT IS STARTING TO DRY OUT, RATHER THAN THROWING IT AWAY. AMERICANS CALL THIS 'FRENCH TOAST' AFTER THE FRENCH NAME, *PAIN PERDU*, OR LOST BREAD, MEANING BREAD THAT IS ABOUT TO BE THROWN AWAY.

1 large egg
1 tablespoon milk
A knob of butter, or 1 tablespoon sunflower oil
2 slices of bread
Salt and pepper
Honey or jam, to serve

1. Crack the egg into a shallow dish, such as a soup plate or quiche dish. Add the milk and beat together with salt and pepper to taste.

2. Melt the butter in a large frying pan over a medium heat. Quickly dip the bread slices into the egg mixture to coat both sides, then let any excess egg drip back into the dish.

3. Add the bread slices to the hot butter or oil and fry for 1–2 minutes on each side until set and golden brown. Serve with honey or jam spread over the top.

VARIATIONS
▸ *Herbed Eggy Bread:* Try this when breakfast is late in the day, and a savoury dish can be more appetising than a sweet one. Add ½ tablespoon of chopped fresh herbs, such as parsley and/or chives, or a pinch of dried mixed herbs, to the egg and milk mixture. Serve with grilled chestnut or portobello mushrooms and grilled bacon.
▸ *Orange Eggy Bread:* Add the finely grated rind of 1 orange and a pinch of ground cinnamon to the egg and milk mixture. Serve with golden syrup, honey or marmalade for spreading over the top.
▸ Sift icing sugar over the top of the bread slices.
▸ Maple syrup is another delicious topping.

Breakfast Drop Scones

MAKES: **ABOUT 16**
PREP TIME: **ABOUT 5 MINUTES**
COOKING TIME: **ABOUT 15 MINUTES**

THIS RECIPE IS SO EASY THAT, ONCE YOU MAKE IT, YOU WON'T BE TEMPTED TO BUY DROP SCONES AGAIN

150g/ 5 oz plain white flour
2 tablespoons sugar
2 teaspoons baking powder
$^1/_2$ teaspoon of salt
250 ml/ 8 fl oz milk
1 large free-range egg
1 tablespoon sunflower or rapeseed oil, plus extra for cooking
Butter and maple syrup to serve

1. Heat the oven on a low setting so you can keep the drop scones warm until all are cooked.

2. Put the flour, sugar, baking powder and salt in a large bowl and stir together. Use the spoon to make an indentation in the centre of the dry ingredients

3. Measure the milk into a measuring jug, then crack in the egg, add the oil and beat together. Slowly pour these liquid ingredients into the dry ingredients and beat together until a smooth batter forms. If a few lumps remain, don't worry as they will disappear during the cooking.

4. Heat the largest frying pan you have, ideally non-stick, over a medium-high heat. Use a pastry brush or crumpled piece of kitchen paper to lightly grease the base of the pan. Drop the batter in large spoonfuls on to the surface, spacing them well apart. The pancakes should spread to 7.5 cm/ 3 inches across. Add as many drop scones as will fit in your pan without them touching.

5. Reduce the heat to medium and leave the drop scones to cook for about 1 minute, or until small bubbles appear all over the surface. Use a fish slice or a metal spatula to flip the drop scones over and leave them to cook for another minute or so until they are set and golden brown on the bottom.

6. Transfer the drop scones to a plate and keep warm in the low oven. Continue as before until all the batter is used. Serve the drop scones with a little butter for smearing over the surface and maple syrup.

VARIATIONS

▸ *Banana Drop Scones:* Use half plain white and half plain wholemeal flours. Add 1 thinly sliced banana and 1 teaspoon of ground cinnamon or 1 teaspoon of vanilla to the batter in Step 3 of the master recipe. You can also stir in 1 grated apple. Cook the drop scones as the master recipe

▸ *Blueberry Drop Scones:* Stir about 150 g/ 5 oz blueberries into the batter in Step 3 of the master recipe. Cook these over a slightly lower heat, as the high sugar content of the blueberries can cause them to burn.

COOK'S TIP
ONLY FLIP THE DROP SCONES ONCE OR THEY WILL BE TOUGH

Save Time

There is no point in making a whole batch of batter for just one serving of three or four scones and then throwing away the excess. Store the leftover batter in a clean screw-top jar in the fridge for up to 3 days, and give it a good stir before using.

Berry Ripple

MAKES **2 SERVINGS**
PREP TIME: **LESS THAN 5 MINS**
NO COOKING

IF YOU KEEP A BAG OF FROZEN MIXED BERRIES IN THE ICE-CUBE COMPARTMENT OF YOUR FRIDGE, TAKE A HANDFUL OUT TO THAW BEFORE YOU GO TO BED. IF YOU'RE REALLY GROGGY IN THE MORNING, JUST TOSS THEM WITH A BOWL OF YOGURT. BUT, IF YOU'RE NOT IN A FOG, OR TOO SHORT OF TIME, TRY THIS CREAMY START TO THE DAY.

100 g/3 ½ oz mixed berries, thawed if frozen
honey (optional)
300 g/10 oz Greek-style yogurt, or vanilla-flavoured yogurt
nuts or sunflower seeds (optional)

1. Put the berries in a blender and blitz to a puree. Taste and add a little honey, if you like.

2. Spoon the yogurt into a bowl. Add the berry puree and gently fold together until you have a ripple effect. Sprinkle with a few nuts or sunflower seeds.

Smash away

If you're making this just for yourself, it hardly seems worth the effort of cleaning the blender. Instead, just use your fork and smash the berries into a chunky sauce.

Tortilla

MAKES **2 SERVINGS**
PREP TIME: **ABOUT 5 MINUTES, PLUS 10 MINUTES STANDING**
COOKING TIME: **ABOUT 30 MINUTES**

HERE IS A DELICIOUS MEAL-IN-A-PAN MADE WITH THE MOST BASIC OF INGREDIENTS –
EGGS, ONION AND POTATOES. IT'S WORTH MASTERING THIS TRADITIONAL SPANISH DISH
BECAUSE IT IS SO INEXPENSIVE, AND ALSO BECAUSE IT IS SO VERSATILE. YOU CAN EAT IT
HOT OR AT ROOM TEMPERATURE, AND IT'S GOOD FOR BREAKFAST OR ANY MEAL OF THE DAY.
YOU WON'T BE ABLE TO BEAT THIS WHEN YOU WANT A BREAK FROM CRAMMING ON A SUNNY
SPRING DAY, AND HEAD OUT FOR A PICNIC.

THINK OF THIS AS A MAKE-AHEAD BREAKFAST. IT TAKES TOO LONG TO PREPARE WHEN YOU
ARE IN A HURRY, BUT WHEN YOU HAVE ONE IN THE FRIDGE YOU CAN JUST GRAB A SLICE AND
GO. (FOR LUNCH OR SUPPER, EAT THIS WARM OR AT ROOM TEMPERATURE WITH A SALAD OR
CHUNKS OF FRENCH BREAD.)

A NON-STICK FRYING PAN MAKES THE TORTILLA EASIER TO FLIP OVER, BUT AN ORDINARY
FRYING PAN WORKS AS LONG AS YOU HEAT IT WELL BEFORE YOU ADD THE OIL.

200 g/7 oz waxy potatoes (see Potato Primer 2, right)
1/2 onion
Up to 4 tablespoons olive oil
4 large eggs
Salt and pepper

1. Scrub or peel the potatoes, then cut them into thin slices. Peel and thinly
slice the onion.

2. Heat a 20 cm/8-inch frying pan, preferably non-stick, over a high heat.
Add 2 tablespoons of the oil and heat until you can feel the heat rising, then
swirl the oil around the pan. Lower the heat, add the potatoes and onion and
fry for 15–20 minutes, stirring occasionally, until the potatoes are tender
when you pierce them with a fork.

3. Meanwhile, beat the eggs together in a large bowl and season generously
with salt and pepper; set aside.

4. Set a large sieve over a heatproof bowl and drain the potatoes and onion,
reserving any oil that drips into the bowl. Very gently stir the vegetables into
the the bowl with the eggs and set aside for 10 minutes.

5. Use a wooden spoon or spatula to remove any crusty bits stuck to the
base of the frying pan. Reheat the pan over a medium-high heat with 4
tablespoons of oil, using any reserved oil. Swirl the hot oil around to coat the
whole base and side of the pan. Add the potato and egg mixture and smooth
the surface, pressing the vegetables into an even layer.

6. Cook for 7–8 minutes, shaking the pan occasionally, until the base is set.
Use a metal spatula or round-bladed knife to loosen the side of the tortilla.

Place a large plate over the top of the pan and, wearing oven gloves, carefully invert the pan and plate together so the tortilla drops onto the plate.

7. Add 1 tablespoon oil to the pan, heat and swirl it around. Carefully slide the tortilla back into the pan, cooked side up. Run the spatula or knife around the tortilla to 'tuck in' the edge.

8. Continue cooking for 3 minutes, or until the eggs are set and the base is golden-brown. Remove the pan from the heat and slide the tortilla onto a plate. Leave to stand for at least 5 minutes before cutting.

VARIATION
▸ To make a tortilla for 4 servings, use a 25 cm/10-inch frying pan, preferably non-stick. Follow the master recipe left and above, but use 125 ml/4 fl oz of olive oil, 750 g/1$\frac{1}{2}$ lb potatoes, 1 large onion and 6 large eggs.

COOK'S TIP
IF YOU ARE HESITANT ABOUT TURNING OVER THE TORTILLA IN STEP 6, YOU CAN FINISH COOKING IT UNDER A HOT GRILL UNTIL THE EGGS ON TOP ARE NO LONGER RUNNY. BE SURE THE HANDLE OF YOUR FRYING PAN IS FLAMEPROOF BEFORE YOU TRY THIS.

Potato Primer 2
For a dish like tortilla you need a potato that holds its shape when cooked. These will be labelled as suitable for boiling and salads at a supermarket. If you're shopping at a market, however, look for Maris Peer, Pentland Dell, Romano or Shetland potatoes. Or, ask the merchant. He or she will be able to advise you.

Cheese Omelette

MAKES **1 SERVING**
PREP TIME: **LESS THAN 5 MINUTES**
COOKING TIME: **LESS THAN 5 MINUTES**

MAKE THE EFFORT TO PERFECT OMELETTE-MAKING AND YOU CAN ALWAYS HAVE A FRESHLY COOKED MEAL AT ANY TIME OF THE DAY, EVEN IF THERE IS LITTLE MORE THAN JUST TWO EGGS IN THE FRIDGE. IT CAN TAKE A COUPLE ATTEMPTS BEFORE YOU GET THE TECHNIQUE RIGHT, BUT THAT'S NOT A PROBLEM BECAUSE THE WORST THAT CAN HAPPEN IS YOU END UP WITH SCRAMBLED EGGS.

ALL OTHER EGG RECIPES ARE COOKED OVER A LOW OR MEDIUM HEAT, BUT OMELETTES NEED A HIGH HEAT TO SET THE BOTTOM LAYER QUICKLY.

LOW-SIDED OMELETTE PANS MAKE THE JOB SUPER-EASY, BUT THEY AREN'T NECESSARY, AND IT IS ONLY WORTH INVESTING IN ONE IF YOU MAKE LOTS OF OMELETTES. A NON-STICK PAN IS IDEAL, BUT, AGAIN, AN ORDINARY ONE WILL DO. (SEE NOTE ON LIGHTLY COOKED EGGS, PAGE 36.)

60 g/2 oz cheese, such as Cheddar, Cheshire or Wensleydale
2 large eggs
2 tablespoons milk
A knob of butter
Salt and pepper

1. Finely grate the cheese. Break the eggs into a bowl. Add the milk, and salt and pepper to taste, to the eggs and quickly beat until just blended: do not over-beat or the omelette's texture will be rubbery.

2. Heat a 20 cm/8-inch frying pan over a medium-high heat until very hot – flick a few drops of water into the pan and if they 'hop' about, the pan is hot enough.

3. When the pan is hot, add the butter and use a fork to rub it over the base and around the side as it melts.

4. When the butter has stopped sizzling, immediately pour in the eggs. Shake the pan forwards and backwards over the heat while you use a fork to stir the eggs around the pan in a circular motion, holding the fork almost parallel to the base. Do not scrape the base of the pan while you do this.

5. As the omelette begins to set, use the fork to push the cooked egg from the edge towards the centre, so that the remaining raw egg fills the space and comes in contact with the heat on the base of the pan. Continue doing this until the omelette looks set on the bottom, but is still slightly runny on top, which won't take longer than 3 minutes.

6. Sprinkle all but 1 tablespoon of the cheese over the centre of the omelette. Tilt the pan slightly away from the handle, so that the omelette slides towards the edge. Use the fork to fold the top half over the filling.

7. Slide the omelette onto a plate and sprinkle the remaining cheese over the top. Serve at once – omelettes become unappetising when they are left to stand.

VARIATIONS
▸ *Herb Omelette:* Add 1 tablespoon of finely chopped fresh herbs, such as parsley and/or chives, when you beat the eggs.
▸ *Mushroom Omelette:* Before you start the omelette, wipe and slice 60 g/2 oz of button or chestnut mushrooms. Melt about 15 g/¹/₂ oz of butter in the frying pan over a medium-high heat. Add the mushrooms, ¹/₂ finely chopped onion and salt and pepper to taste, and fry, stirring occasionally, until the mushrooms are soft and the liquid they give off evaporates. Make the omelette as in the master recipe and add the mushrooms instead of the cheese.
▸ *Ratatouille Omelette:* Replace the cheese in the master recipe with leftover Ratatouille (page 173).
▸ When the fridge is really bare you can make omelettes with water, rather than milk. The butter can also be replaced with sunflower oil, but the flavour won't be as rich.

Big Isn't Always Better
The size of your frying pan will determine the size of omelette you can make. If the pan is too large for the number of eggs you use, the mixture will spread out too thinly and your omelette will be dry; if the pan is too small, the omelette will be over-cooked on the bottom and too runny on top.

The master recipe uses a 20 cm/8-inch frying pan to make a single-serving omelette with 2 eggs. For a larger omelette to share, use a 25 cm/10-inch pan with 4 large eggs, 90 g/3 oz grated cheese, 2 tablespoons milk or water and 15 g/¹/₂ oz of butter. (Measure across the top of the pan, not the base.)

Dried Fruit Salad

MAKES **4–6 SERVINGS**
PREP TIME: **ABOUT 2 MINUTES, PLUS COOLING**
COOKING TIME: **5 MINUTES**

KEEP A BOWL OF THIS IN THE FRIDGE AND YOU CAN DIP INTO IT FOR A VITAMIN-RICH BREAKFAST OR SNACK AT ANYTIME OF THE DAY. THIS WILL KEEP, TIGHTLY COVERED WITH CLINGFILM, IN THE FRIDGE FOR UP TO FOUR DAYS.

2 green cardamom pods
1 cinnamon stick
500 ml/16 fl oz orange juice
1 star anise (optional)
125 g/4 oz dried apricots
125 g/4 oz dried peaches
125 g/4 oz dried apples
4 tablespoons dried cranberries
4 tablespoons sultanas or raisins
Greek-style or natural yogurt, to serve (optional)

1. Use a pestle and mortar or the back of a large metal spoon to lightly crush the cardamom pods. Break the cinnamon stick in half.

2. Pour the orange juice in to a saucepan and place over a high heat. Add the cardamom pods, cinnamon stick and star anise, if using, and slowly bring to the boil. Turn the heat to its lowest setting and leave the mixture to simmer for 5 minutes.

3. Meanwhile, put the dried fruits in a large heatproof bowl. Pour the hot juice and spices over the fruit and leave the mixture to stand until completely cool, stirring occasionally. Cover the bowl tightly with clingfilm and chill overnight. Serve in a bowl with a good dollop of yogurt, if you like.

VARIATIONS
▸ Treat the list of dried fruit above as just a suggestion. Supermarkets and health food shops sell a variety, so use whatever you have to hand.
▸ To transform this into a dessert that is good served hot or cold over vanilla ice cream, replace the orange juice with dry red wine.

Make-Your-Own Muesli

MAKES **ABOUT 12 SERVINGS**
PREP TIME: **LESS THAN 10 MINUTES**
NO COOKING

THINK OF THIS TRADITIONAL SWISS BREAKFAST CEREAL WITH MIXED GRAIN FLAKES AND DRIED FRUIT AS A TWO-FOR-ONE START TO THE DAY – IT SAVES YOU TIME AND MONEY. FEW BREAKFASTS ARE QUICKER THAN A BOWL OF MUESLI WITH A SPLASH OF CHILLED MILK, AND YOU'LL STRETCH YOUR CASH IF YOU GO TO A HEALTH FOOD SHOP AND BUY THE INGREDIENTS TO MIX YOURSELF. SUPERMARKET BOXES OF MUESLI ARE CONVENIENT, BUT MUCH MORE EXPENSIVE. AND, ONCE YOU'VE MADE YOUR OWN, YOU'LL NEVER WANT TO GO BACK TO SHOP-BOUGHT AGAIN. ADD MORE OR LESS OF EACH INGREDIENT UNTIL YOU GET A COMBINATION YOU REALLY LIKE.

MUESLI ALSO TASTES GOOD WITH A FRESH BANANA OR STRAWBERRIES SLICED OVER IT. STORE THIS IN AN AIRTIGHT CONTAINER AND YOU'LL HAVE AN INSTANT BREAKFAST OR SNACK FOR ANY TIME OF THE DAY.

$1/2$ mug ready-to-eat dried apricots
100 g/$3^1/_2$ oz hazelnuts
100 g/$3^1/_2$ oz unblanched almonds
4 mugs jumbo porridge oat flakes
2 mugs barley flakes
1 mug dried apple flakes

1 mug raisins or sultanas
$1/2$ mug wheat germ
4 tablespoons sesame seeds
1 tablespoon ground cinnamon
Soft light brown sugar

1. Cut the dried apricots into small pieces. Coarsely chop the hazelnuts and almonds.

2. Put the apricots, hazelnuts and almonds in a large bowl with the oat flakes, barley flakes, apple flakes, raisins or sultanas, wheat germ, sesame seeds and cinnamon. Add sugar to taste and toss together. Transfer to an airtight container.

VARIATIONS
Other popular ingredients include:
- ► Bran
- ► Desiccated coconut
- ► Dried apple rings
- ► Dried bananas
- ► Dried figs
- ► Dried pears
- ► Wheat flakes

COOK'S TIPS
► TO PREVENT DRIED FRUIT FROM STICKING TO THE KNIFE WHEN YOU CHOP IT, SPRINKLE THE FRUIT WITH A LITTLE OF THE BROWN SUGAR FIRST.
► IF ANY OF THE DRIED FRUIT HAS HARDENED, PUT IT IN A HEATPROOF BOWL AND POUR OVER ENOUGH BOILING WATER TO COVER. LEAVE IT TO STAND FOR 15 MINUTES AND IT WILL PLUMP UP AGAIN. PAT DRY WITH PAPER TOWELS BEFORE USING.

Fried Egg & Ham Sandwich

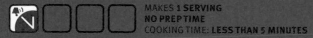

MAKES **1 SERVING**
NO PREP TIME
COOKING TIME: **LESS THAN 5 MINUTES**

WHY STOP AT THE SANDWICH SHOP WHEN YOU'RE ON YOUR WAY TO LECTURES? BOUGHT SANDWICHES REALLY ARE THE EXPENSIVE BREAKFAST OPTION. THIS RECIPE, ALONG WITH THE FOLLOWING ONE, GIVES YOU A FISTFUL OF BREAKFAST TO EAT ON THE GO.

Butter or margarine, or sunflower or olive oil
1 egg
2 slices white or wholemeal bread
1 slice cooked ham

1. Heat your frying pan over a medium-high heat. Add a knob (about 15 g/ ½ oz) of butter or margarine, or 1 tablespoon sunflower or olive oil, and swirl it around the pan.

2. As soon as the butter or margarine is foamy, or the oil is sizzling hot, reduce the heat to medium-low and break the egg into the pan. Fry the egg for 3–4 minutes, spooning the fat from the pan over the yolks until the white is just set and lightly coloured on the edge.

3. Use a fish slice to flip the egg over and continue frying 1 minute longer, or until the yolk is firmly set.

4. Butter the bread on one side of each slice, if you like. Put the ham on one buttered side, add the fried egg and top with the other slice of bread, buttered side down.

VARIATIONS
‣ *Bacon & Egg Buttie:* Fry 2 or 3 rashers of streaky bacon (page 63) and add to the sandwich instead of the ham.
‣ Spread the bread with ketchup, brown sauce or mustard.
‣ For a reduced-fat version, keep a supply of Hard-boiled Eggs (page 35) in the fridge and use a sliced egg, rather than a fried egg.

Sausage & Marmalade Sandwich

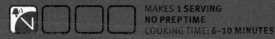

MAKES 1 SERVING
NO PREP TIME
COOKING TIME: 6–10 MINUTES

2 sausages
Vegetable oil, such as sunflower
2 slices white or wholemeal bread
Butter
Marmalade

1. Coat the base of your frying pan with a small amount of oil and place over a medium heat. Prick the sausages in a couple of places with a fork. Add the sausages and fry, shaking the pan occasionally, for 6–10 minutes until the skins are brown all over and the juices run clear when you pierce one with a knife. The exact cooking time will depend on the thickness of sausages.

2. Meanwhile, butter both slices of bread on one side, if you like.

3. Remove the sausages from the pan and slice each in half lengthways. Put the 4 sausage halves on the buttered side of one slice of bread. Spread the other slice of bread with marmalade and put on top of the sausages, marmalade side down.

Time Savers
▸ Slice each sausage in half lengthways before you add them to the pan and fry cut-side down.
▸ Cook extra sausages to use as a quick filling for Quesadillas (page 104) with grated cheese.

Vegetable Strata

MAKES: **4–6 SERVINGS**
PREP TIME: **ABOUT 20 MINUTES, PLUS OVERNIGHT 'RESTING'** COOKING TIME: **ABOUT 1 HOUR**

IF YOU'VE GOT FRIENDS COMING TO VISIT FOR THE WEEKEND, OR JUST LIKE THE IDEA OF RELAXED, LATE BREAKFASTS AND SUNDAY BRUNCHES, THIS TRADITIONAL ITALIAN RECIPE IS THE ONE TO USE. ALL THE REAL WORK IS DONE THE NIGHT BEFORE, SO THE ONLY THING LEFT TO DO IN THE MORNING IS TO PUT IT IN THE OVEN.

4 spring onions
1 red or green pepper
1 small courgette
225 g/8 oz Cheddar cheese
about 175 g/6 oz white or
    wholemeal bread
3 medium eggs

Butter or vegetable oil for the baking
    pan or ovenproof dish
450 ml/16 fl oz milk
1 teaspoon dry mustard
$^{1}/_{2}$ teaspoon salt
$1^{1}/_{2}$ teaspoons dried basil
Pepper

1. Trim and finely slice the spring onion. Cut the pepper in half, remove the core and seeds and finely chop the flesh. Dice the courgette. Put the vegetables in a bowl and toss them together. Set aside.

2. Coarsely grate the cheese using the large holes of a grater. Use a sharp knife to cut the bread into 1 cm/$^{1}/_{2}$ inch cubes. Grease the inside of a 20 cm/8 inch baking pan or ovenproof dish with the butter or oil.

3. Sprinkle the bread cubes over the base of the pan or dish. Scatter with half the cheese. Arrange the mixed vegetables over the bread, then scatter with the remaining cheese.

4. Put the eggs, milk, basil, mustard and salt in the bowl the vegetables were in and beat them together. Pour the egg mixture over the vegetables, then cover the dish with cling film. Put in the fridge and leave overnight.

5. In the morning, preheat the oven to 180°C/350°F/Gas 4 and bring a kettle of water to the boil. Sprinkle the top of the strata with the basil and pepper.

6. Put the baking pan or ovenproof dish in a larger roasting pan and pour in enough boiling water to come halfway up the sides. Place the roasting pan in the oven and bake for 1 hour, or until the top is golden. Remove the strata from the oven and leave to stand for 2–3 minutes before cutting into squares to serve.

Banana Wrap To Go

MAKES **1 SERVING**
PREP TIME: **LESS THAN 5 MINUTES**
NO COOKING

1 soft flour tortilla
Honey
1 large banana
Natural yogurt
Ground cinnamon (optional)

1. Spread one side of the tortilla with honey.

2. Unpeel the banana and cut it into slices. Arrange the slices on half the tortilla, then add dollops of yogurt and sprinkle with cinnamon, if using. Fold the tortilla over to cover the banana, then roll up.

VARIATION

► Replace the honey with a chocolate-hazelnut spread.

Masala Tea

MAKES **2 SERVINGS** PREP TIME: **LESS THAN 5 MINUTES, PLUS A FEW MINUTES STEEPING**
SIMMERING TIME: **ABOUT 10 MINUTES**

INVIGORATE YOURSELF IN THE MORNING WITH GINGER-SPICED HERBAL TEA. MANY HERBALISTS BELIEVE GINGER AIDS BLOOD FLOW TO THE BRAIN, INCREASING MENTAL SHARPNESS, AND IT HELPS SETTLE YOUR STOMACH WHEN YOU DON'T FEEL WELL.

4 black peppercorns
3 green cardamom pods
2 cinnamon sticks
1 cm/^{1}/$_2$-inch piece fresh root ginger

500 ml/16 fl oz water
2 tea bags, flavour of your choice
Honey (optional), to taste

1. Use a pestle and mortar or the back of a large spoon to crush the peppercorns and cardamom pods lightly. Break the cinnamon sticks in half.

2. Put the ginger, peppercorns, cardamom and cinnamon in a saucepan with the water. Bring to the boil, then lower the heat and simmer for 10 minutes.

3. Return the water to the boil. Add the tea bags, turn off the heat, cover the pan and leave to steep for 1–2 minutes. Strain into mugs and add honey to taste, to sweeten if you are not a vegan.

Kick-Start Shake

MAKES **1 SERVING**
PREP TIME: **ABOUT 2 MINUTES**
NO COOKING

GET YOUR BLENDER GOING FIRST THING IN THE MORNING AND WHIZ UP THIS BREAKFAST-IN-A-GLASS IN SECONDS. THIS TASTES GREAT AND PACKS A NUTRITIONAL PUNCH.

150 ml/5 fl oz milk
100 g/3$^{1}/_{2}$ oz Greek-style or natural yogurt
2 tablespoons orange juice
1 small banana
$^{1}/_{2}$ tablespoon wheat germ
$^{1}/_{2}$ teaspoon honey, or to taste

1. Put the milk, yogurt, orange juice, broken-up banana, and wheat germ in a blender and whiz until smooth. Add honey to taste and whiz again. It's ready to drink.

VARIATIONS

▸ *Banana Shake:* Put 125 ml/4fl oz milk, 150 g/5 oz vanilla-flavoured yogurt, 1 broken-up banana, $^{1}/_{2}$ tablespoon wheat germ and a dash of freshly grated nutmeg in a blender and whiz until smooth. Add honey or sugar to taste and whiz again.

▸ *Fruit-of-the-Forest Shake:* Put 100 g/3$^{1}/_{2}$ oz frozen fruit-of-the-forest berries in a blender with 150 g/5 oz Greek-style or natural yogurt, 2 tablespoons milk and 2 tablespoons orange juice. Whiz until slushy, adding extra milk or orange juice if you want a more liquid drink.

▸ *Honey-Milk Drink:* Put 200 ml/7fl oz milk, 3 tablespoons Greek-style or natural yogurt, 1 tablespoon honey, $^{1}/_{2}$ tablespoon wheat germ and a squeeze of lemon juice in a blender and whiz until smooth.

▸ *Mango-Banana Shake:* Put $^{1}/_{2}$ ripe mango, $^{1}/_{2}$ banana, 75 ml/2$^{1}/_{2}$ fl oz milk, 4 tablespoons orange juice and 2 tablespoons Greek-style or natural yogurt in a blender and whiz. Add honey to taste and whiz again.

▸ *Mixed Berry Shake:* Replace the banana in the master recipe with 90 g/3 oz strawberries, raspberries or a combination.

▸ *Orchard Shake:* Put 125 ml/4 fl oz milk, $^{1}/_{2}$ grated apple or pear, $^{1}/_{2}$ banana and $^{1}/_{2}$ tablespoon wheat germ in a blender and whiz until smooth. Add honey to taste and whiz again.

▸ *Peanut Butter Shake:* Put 180 g/6 oz Greek-style or natural yogurt, $^{1}/_{2}$ banana, 2 tablespoons smooth peanut butter and 2 tablespoons orange juice in a blender and whiz until smooth. Add honey to taste and whiz again.

Yogurt-Apricot Smoothie

MAKES **1 SERVING**
PREP TIME: **LESS THAN 5 MINUTES**
NO COOKING

ANOTHER NUTRITIONAL POWERHOUSE TO WHIZ UP IN A FLASH.

150 g/5 fl oz Greek-style or natural yogurt
125 ml/4 fl oz orange juice
60 g/2 oz ready-to-eat dried apricots
1 teaspoon honey or sugar, or to taste

1. Put the yogurt, orange juice, apricots and honey or sugar in the blender and whiz. Add extra honey if you want a sweeter drink.

VARIATIONS
▸ *Yogurt-Berry Smoothie:* Replace the dried apricots with fresh, hulled strawberries.
▸ If you are organised enough to plan ahead, pour the orange juice over the apricots and leave to stand overnight.

Lassi

MAKES **1 SERVING**
PREP TIME: **LESS THAN 5 MINUTES**
NO COOKING

THIS TRADITIONAL INDIAN YOGURT DRINK IS GENTLE AND SOOTHING IN THE MORNING, ESPECIALLY AFTER A ROUGH NIGHT BEFORE. IT ALSO MAKES A GOOD ALCOHOL-FREE ALTERNATIVE TO LAGER WITH CURRIED MINCE (PAGE 157).

250 g/8 oz natural yogurt
4 tablespoons water
Pinch of salt
Pinch of sugar
Pinch of ground cumin
Ice cubes

1. Put the yogurt, water, salt and sugar in a tall glass and blend with a fork. Add extra salt, sugar or cumin to taste. Add ice cubes and sprinkle with ground cumin.

Stress-busting Smoothie

MAKES **1 SERVING**
PREP TIME: **LESS THAN 5 MINUTES**
NO COOKING

WHEN THE PRESSURE OF EXAMS IS BUILDING UP, TRY A GLASS OF THIS. IT WILL HAVE A
MORE CALMING EFFECT THAN TEA OR COFFEE. DATES ARE ALSO SAID TO HELP IMPROVE
MEMORY AND CONCENTRATION.

100 g/3^1/$_2$ oz stoned dates
1 tablespoon ground almonds
1 teaspoon ground ginger
300 g/10 oz Greek-style or natural yogurt or silken tofu
honey (optional)

1. Use a small knife to chop the dates. Put the dates, ground almonds
and yogurt in a blender and whiz. This should be sweet enough, but add
a little honey, if you want.

Purple Haze

MAKES **1 SERVING**
PREP TIME: **LESS THAN 5 MINUTES**
NO COOKING

IT'S WORTH KEEPING A BAG OF FROZEN BLUEBERRIES IN THE FREEZER COMPARTMENT OF
YOUR FRIDGE. THEY CONTAIN A POWERHOUSE OF ANTIOXIDANTS AND VITAMIN C – BOTH OF
WHICH ARE GOOD FOR YOU AND CAN HELP REPAIR SOME OF THE DAMAGE DONE BY
UNHEALTHY LIFESTYLE CHOICES.

125 g/4 oz frozen blueberries
300 g/10 oz vanilla-flavoured yogurt, or silken tofu
^{1}/$_2$ banana (optional)
lemon juice
honey

1. Put the blueberries, yogurt or tofu, and banana, if using, in a blender
and whiz. Add lemon juice and/or honey to taste.

Cinnamon Smoothie

MAKES **1 SERVING**
PREP TIME: **LESS THAN 5 MINUTES**
NO COOKING

1 banana
150 ml/5 fl oz milk
150 g/5 oz Greek-style or natural yogurt
1 teaspoon orange-flower or plain honey
ground cinnamon

1. Put the banana, milk, yogurt and honey in a blender and whiz. Add a good pinch of ground cinnamon and whiz again. Drink as it is, or pour it over ice cubes.

Hot Ginger Soother

MAKES **1 SERVING**
PREP TIME: **LESS THAN 5 MINUTES**
COOKING TIME: **ABOUT 15 MINUTES**

SIP THIS AT THE FIRST SIGN OF A SORE THROAT. GINGER HAS MANY MEDICINAL QUALITIES, AND ONE OF THEM IS FIGHTING INFECTIONS. THIS DRINK WILL ALSO HELP WITH HANGOVER RECOVERY, SETTLING STOMACHS AND EASING HEADACHES.

2.5 cm/1 in piece fresh ginger
450 ml/15 fl oz water
fresh lemon juice
honey

1. Leave the ginger unpeeled, but cut it into a couple of slices, then smash the slices with anything heavy you can fine – use a tin of beans, the handle of a big knife or the side of a cleaver.

2. Put the ginger in a saucepan with the water and bring to the boil. Reduce the heat to low, put a lid on the pan and simmer for about 20 minutes. Remove the ginger slices, pour into a mug and add lemon juice and honey to taste.

VARIATIONS
► Hot Toddy: Add a teabag and leave it to seep for a few minutes, then strain into a mug. Add a good slug of whiskey, along with the lemon juice and honey. When you've got a bad cold that leaves you bunged up with a sore throat, sip this before you go to bed – chances are you'll be feeling better in the morning.
► Vegans can omit the honey and sweeten with sugar instead.

GRAZING NOSH

Remember when your mum insisted you ate three meals a day and frowned on snacks between meals? Well, all that is changing. The good news is that snacking throughout the day can be beneficial for you.

Health experts now think 'grazing', or eating small meals every three or four hours, might be the answer to healthy eating. Stretching the traditional three daily meals to six smaller ones can help you get the mix of nutrients you need to stay healthy and keep your energy levels steady. Just remember that, when you are eating more frequently, you must scale down your portions. Eat the quantities you are served as appetizers when you eat out.

This doesn't, of course, mean you can get away with chips and curries all day, every day. Avoid fat-laden, high-sugar processed foods and fried foods. Go for variety. Put fresh fruit and veggies at the top of your list of snack foods, and be sure to include plenty of rice, grains and pulses in your diet over the course of a day. (If, however, you prefer the idea of three conventional meals a day, that is also fine, and you'll find plenty of recipe ideas in other chapters for putting together varied and healthy meals.)

The quick-and-easy recipes in this chapter banish the munchies and satisfy snack attacks without costing a lot of cash – or requiring much effort on your part. Try the dips, home-made crisps with their lower fat content than the ones you buy, toasted sandwiches, soups and salads when you don't want to spend a lot of time fussing in the kitchen. You'll also find recipes here for feeding a crowd without breaking the bank.

Take note of the recipes in this chapter and your take-away fund can be spent on going out instead.

More grazing nosh:
- Banana Wrap To Go (page 81)
- Crispy Baked Potatoes (page 42)
- Dried Fruit Salad (page 76)
- Fish Finger Sandwich (page 220)
- Make-Your-Own Muesli (page 77)
- Mushrooms on Toast (page 68)
- Oven-baked Chips (page 44)
- Pad Thai (page 187)
- Take-away Pizzas at Home (page 57)
- Tortilla (page 72)

Hummus

MAKES **ABOUT 500 G/1 LB**
PREP TIME: **ABOUT 10 MINUTES**
NO COOKING

THIS MIDDLE EASTERN CHICKPEA DIP KEEPS FOR UP TO TWO WEEKS IN THE FRIDGE, SO THERE ISN'T ANY POINT IN MAKING A SMALL AMOUNT. PUT THE LEFTOVERS IN A BOWL WITH A THIN LAYER OF OLIVE OIL ON THE SURFACE, THEN COVER TIGHTLY WITH CLINGFILM AND CHILL UNTIL YOU WANT A DIP. COMPARE THE PRICE OF MAKING THIS RECIPE WITH THAT OF A SMALL TUB FROM THE SUPERMARKET AND YOU'LL SEE WHY IT MAKES SENSE TO MAKE YOUR OWN.

COUNTER THE RELATIVELY HIGH-FAT CONTENT OF THIS BY SERVING IT WITH A SELECTION OF FRESHLY CUT VEGETABLES – SCRUBBED OR PEELED CARROT STRIPS, CELERY STRIPS, BROCCOLI OR CAULIFLOWER FLORETS AND RED PEPPER STRIPS. HUMMUS IS ALSO GOOD WITH PIECES OF PITTA BREAD, OR PITTA CRISPS (PAGE 100), OR SPREAD A LITTLE ON SANDWICHES IN PLACE OF MAYO.

2 garlic cloves
2 cans (400 g/14 oz) chickpeas
2 tablespoons olive oil, plus a little extra to serve
5 tablespoons tahini sauce (page 24)
About 2 tablespoons lemon juice, or to taste
Salt and pepper
Cayenne pepper (optional)
Chopped fresh coriander or parsley (optional)

1. Peel and crush the garlic cloves.

2. Place a strainer in the sink and tip in the chickpeas. Rinse them with cold water and shake dry.

3. Put the chickpeas in a blender with the garlic and oil and whiz until they are chopped. Add the tahini sauce and 2 tablespoons of lemon juice and whiz again until blended, but not completely smooth.

4. Taste and add extra lemon juice, if you like, and salt and pepper to taste. Spoon the hummus into a bowl and drizzle with a little extra olive oil. Sprinkle with cayenne pepper and chopped herbs, if you like.

COOK'S TIP
IF YOU DON'T HAVE A BLENDER OR FOOD PROCESSOR, MASH THE CHICKPEAS WITH A POTATO MASHER OR FORK.

Tzatziki

MAKES **ABOUT 300 G / 10 OZ**
PREP TIME: **ABOUT 10 MINUTES**
COOKING TIME: **ABOUT 1 MINUTE**

A GREEK DIP TO MUNCH WITH A SELECTION OF FRESH VEGETABLE PIECES, PITTA CRISPS (PAGE 100) OR CRISPS.

1 large cucumber
1–2 garlic cloves, to taste
Several sprigs of fresh dill
300 g / 10 oz Greek-style yogurt
1 tablespoon olive oil
2 tablespoons sesame seeds
Salt and pepper
Cayenne pepper, to serve (optional)

1. Line a bowl with a clean tea towel. Coarsely grate the cucumber into the towel. Gather the 4 corners of the cloth into a bundle and squeeze with your hand to extract as much moisture as possible. Pour the liquid out of the bowl, then put the cucumber in the bowl and set aside.

2. Peel and finely chop the garlic. Finely chop the dill.

3. Stir the yogurt into the cucumber. Add the garlic, dill and olive oil and stir until blended. Season with salt and pepper to taste. (See Plan Ahead, below.)

4. Put the sesame seeds into a small, dry frying pan over a medium heat and toast, stirring constantly, until they are golden and give off their aroma. Immediately tip the sesame seeds into the yogurt. Dust with a little cayenne pepper, if you like, and serve at once.

Plan Ahead
For a party, make this through to Step 3. It will keep for up to a day in the fridge, but don't add the toasted sesame seed or chopped coriander until just before you are ready to serve. Take the dip out of the fridge about 10 minutes in advance and stir well.

VARIATION
► Fresh dill gives this an authentic flavour, but if you don't have any, use parsley.

Aubergine Dip

MAKES **ABOUT 400 G / 14 OZ**
PREP TIME: **ABOUT 15 MINUTES**
COOKING TIME: **ABOUT 20 MINUTES**

WHEN YOU'RE FEELING REALLY IMPOVERISHED, GIVE YOURSELF AN INDULGENCE.
THIS SIMPLE DIP IS ALSO KNOWN AS 'POOR MAN'S CAVIAR', SUPPOSEDLY BECAUSE
THE FLAVOUR IS CONSIDERED GOOD ENOUGH FOR A MILLIONAIRE'S TABLE.

THIS GOES PARTICULARLY WELL WITH PITTA CRISPS (PAGE 100) OR PLAIN PITTA BREAD,
AND ANY LEFTOVERS CAN DOUBLE AS A PASTA SAUCE.

1 large aubergine
1 can (400 g / 14 oz)
   crushed tomatoes
1 spring onion
1 large garlic clove
4 tablespoons olive oil

1–2 tablespoons lemon juice, to taste
Pinch of ground cumin
Salt and pepper
Chopped fresh parsley,
   to garnish (optional)

1. Heat the oven to 230°C/450°F/Gas 8. Poke the aubergine all over
with a fork and place it on a baking sheet. Roast the aubergine for about
20 minutes until it feels very soft when you squeeze it. Remove the
aubergine from the oven and set it aside until it is cool enough to handle.

2. Meanwhile, put a strainer over a bowl and tip the can of tomatoes with
the juices into it, then set aside to drain until required. Finely chop the
white and green parts of the spring onion. Peel and crush the garlic clove.

3. When the aubergine is cool enough to handle, cut it in half and use
a spoon to scoop out the flesh, and discard the skins.

4. Put the aubergine flesh in a blender with the garlic and olive oil and
whiz until smooth. Add 1 tablespoon of the lemon juice and the cumin and
whiz again. Taste and add extra lemon juice and salt and pepper to taste.

5. Put the aubergine mixture in a bowl and stir in the spring onions and
drained tomatoes. If the mixture seems too thick, thin it with a little of
the reserved tomato juices from the can. Sprinkle with chopped parsley,
if you have any.

VARIATION
▶ To 'stretch' the dip, add several spoonfuls of Greek-style or natural
yogurt or tahini sauce (page 24) in Step 4.

COOK'S TIP
DON'T THROW AWAY THE STRAINED TOMATO JUICE. IT WILL KEEP IN THE FRIDGE, TIGHTLY
COVERED WITH CLINGFILM, FOR UP TO TWO DAYS. ADD IT TO PASTA SAUCE, OR DRINK IT
FOR BREAKFAST – TOMATO JUICE MIGHT HELP YOU RECOVER FROM A HANGOVER.

Guacamole

MAKES **ABOUT 300 G/10 OZ**
PREP TIME: **10–15 MINUTES**
NO COOKING

SUPERMARKETS REDUCE THE PRICE OF AVOCADOS WHEN THEY BECOME VERY RIPE AND SOFT, AND THOSE ARE EXACTLY THE ONES YOU NEED FOR THE ROUGH-AND-READY MEXICAN DIP. TAKE ADVANTAGE OF THE BARGAINS!

THIS DIP CALLS OUT FOR A BAG OF CORN CHIPS TO DUNK INTO IT. A HEALTHIER, LOWER-FAT OPTION, HOWEVER, IS A SELECTION OF FRESH VEGETABLES CUT INTO BITE-SIZE PIECES.

1 large tomato	Small bunch of fresh coriander or parsley,
1 large garlic clove	rinsed and dried
1 fresh green chilli	2–3 tablespoons lemon juice, to taste
2 large, ripe avocados	

1. Cut the tomato in half and use a small spoon to scoop out and discard the seeds. Cut the tomato flesh into small dice. Peel and very finely chop the garlic.

2. Hold the chilli by the stem end and cut in half lengthways. Use the tip of a knife to scoop out the seeds, then finely slice the flesh. (See Hot Stuff, page 189.)

3. Remove the coriander or parsley leaves from the stalks and finely chop them; discard the stalks.

4. Seed the avocado (see below). Scoop the avocado flesh into a bowl with 2 tablespoons of the lemon juice. Mash it up with a fork, then stir in the tomato, garlic and chilli.

5. Add extra lemon juice and salt and pepper to taste. Sprinkle with the chopped coriander or parsley.

COOK'S TIP
AVOCADO FLESH BECOMES BROWN WHEN IT IS CUT AND EXPOSED TO OXYGEN. THIS IS WHY IT IS IMPORTANT TO MASH THE AVOCADO WITH LEMON JUICE IN STEP 4. IF YOU ARE NOT SERVING THIS STRAIGHT AWAY, COVER IT TIGHTLY WITH CLINGFILM BEFORE YOU PUT IT IN THE FRIDGE.

Seeding an Avocado

Use a small sharp knife and cut lengthways through the skin and flesh to the seed. Use both hands to twist each half of the avocado in opposite directions to separate them: one half will come away free, and the other half will contain the seed.

Hold the half with the seed firmly in the cup of one hand. With your other hand, tap the blade of the knife into the seed. Slightly twist the knife to loosen the seed, then lift it up and the seed should come with it.

Smashed Butter Bean Spread

MAKES **ABOUT 400 G/14 OZ**
PREP TIME: **ABOUT 10 MINUTES**
NO COOKING

THIS IS A QUICK AND EASY WAY TO MAKE A DIP WHEN YOU DON'T HAVE A BLENDER
OR FOOD PROCESSOR – OR JUST WANT TO SAVE ON THE WASHING-UP! SERVE WITH
PITTA CRISPS (PAGE 100), OR SPREAD ON BREAD AND ADD A COUPLE LEAVES OF
ICEBERG LETTUCE AND TOMATO SLICES TO MAKE A FILLING SANDWICH.

1 can (400 g/14 oz) butter beans
1 lemon
About 4 tablespoons Greek-style yogurt
1 teaspoon ground turmeric
Pinch of ground coriander
Cayenne pepper
Salt and pepper
Chopped fresh parsley, to serve (optional)

1. Place a sieve in the sink and tip the can of butter beans into it.
Rinse the beans under cold water, then shake off the excess water.
Transfer the beans to a bowl.

2. Grate the rind of the lemon into the beans. Use a fork to start breaking
up the beans.

3. Put 4 tablespoons of the yogurt in a bowl with the turmeric and
coriander. Stir this into the beans. If the mixture is too thick, add more
yogurt. Add cayenne pepper and salt and pepper to taste. Sprinkle
with parsley, if you have any.

VARIATIONS
▸ For a sharper flavour, add more lemon juice.
▸ Red kidney beans and white cannellini beans also work well in this.
▸ Omit the turmeric and coriander, and instead use 2 tablespoons of
bottled pesto sauce.
▸ Or omit the turmeric and coriander, and instead use 1 tablespoon
of mild to strong curry paste, to taste.

Smoked Fish Spread

MAKES **2 SERVINGS**
PREP TIME: **ABOUT 5 MINUTES**
NO COOKING

SMOKED MACKEREL, TROUT, SALMON OFFCUTS AND EVEN DRAINED CANNED SARDINES
ARE FINE TO USE FOR THIS SIMPLE PÂTÉ THAT MAKES A QUICK SNACK. YOU CAN ALSO
SERVE THIS AS A FIRST COURSE FOR A DINNER PARTY.

THIS WILL KEEP IN THE FRIDGE FOR UP TO 48 HOURS, BUT BE SURE TO COVER THE
BOWL TIGHTLY WITH CLINGFILM – OR EVERYTHING ELSE WILL TASTE OF SMOKED FISH.

250 g/8 oz smoked mackerel, or other smoked fish
125 g/4 oz Greek-style yogurt
Finely grated rind and juice of 1 lemon
1 tablespoon chopped fresh parsley, or $^1/_2$ teaspoon dried thyme
Pinch of cayenne (optional)
4 slices wholemeal bread
Salt and pepper

1. Heat the grill to high if you don't have a toaster. Flake the fish into a
bowl, removing all the skin and small bones. Add the yogurt and lemon
rind to the bowl and use a fork to mash the ingredients together.

2. Slowly add the lemon juice, teaspoon by teaspoon, to taste. Stir
in the herbs and season to taste with salt and pepper and a pinch of
cayenne, if you like.

3. Meanwhile, toast the bread in the toaster, or under the grill for
$1^1/_2$–2 minutes on each side until golden brown. Spread the fish mixture
on the hot toast and cut the toast into triangles.

VARIATIONS
▸ For a smooth spread, put all the ingredients in a blender or food
processor and whiz until blended.
▸ For a chunkier version, add grated radishes and finely chopped celery.
▸ For a stronger-tasting version, stir in 1–2 teaspoons creamed
horseradish.
▸ Drained and flaked canned tuna also works well in this recipe.

Pitta Pockets with Crunchy Salad

MAKES **ABOUT 400 G / 14 OZ**
PREP TIME: **ABOUT 5–10 MINUTES**
NO COOKING

STUFF A PITTA BREAD FOR A TASTY SNACK AT ANY TIME OF THE DAY.

1 carrot
$\frac{1}{2}$ courgette
1 spring onion
1 tomato
Handful spinach leaves
4 tablespoons Hummus, either home-made (page 88) or bottled
1 white or wholemeal pitta bread

1. Scrub or peel and coarsely grate the carrot. Coarsely grate the courgette. Finely slice the white and green parts of the spring onion. Cut the tomato in half and scoop out the seeds, then finely dice the flesh.

2. Rinse the spinach in cold water and pat dry. Cut out the central stems if the leaves are large. Roll the spinach leaves up like a cigar, then cut them crossways into thin slices.

3. Put the carrot, courgette, spring onion, tomato and hummus in a bowl and stir together. Stir in the spinach.

4. Cut the pitta bread in half from top to bottom at the centre point to make 2 pockets. Spoon the salad into the pockets.

VARIATIONS
▸ *Ham & Cheese Pitta Pockets:* Spread a little pickle on the inside of the pitta bread, then stuff with sliced cheese, sliced cooked ham and shredded Iceberg lettuce leaves.
▸ *Chicken Salad Pitta Pockets:* Mix skinless cooked chicken with chopped celery, halved seedless green grapes and mayonnaise. Stir in some shredded lettuce leaves and stuff the salad mixture into the pitta bread.
▸ Other fillings for the pitta pockets include leftover Chilli con Carne (page 158), Guacamole (page 91), Smashed Butter Bean Spread (page 92) and Ratatouille (page 173).

Potato Wedges with Blue Cheese Dip

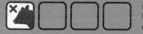

MAKES 4–6 **SERVINGS; 24 WEDGES**
PREP TIME: **ABOUT 15 MINUTES**
COOKING TIME: **30–35 MINUTES**

DO NOT PEEL THE POTATOES FOR THIS RECIPE. IF YOU BUY THEM IN BAGS AT THE
SUPERMARKET THEY WILL ONLY NEED A QUICK WIPE, BUT IF YOU HAVE BOUGHT THEM
FROM A MARKET YOU MIGHT HAVE TO GIVE THEM A GOOD SCRUB UNDER COLD WATER
TO GET RID OF ALL THE DIRT. IN EITHER CASE, MAKE SURE THEY ARE DRY BEFORE YOU
PUT THEM IN THE OVEN.

4 large baking potatoes (see Potato Primer 1, page 41)
1 garlic clove
2 tablespoons olive oil
1¹/₂ teaspoons salt
Pepper

FOR THE BLUE CHEESE DIP:
125 g/4 oz blue cheese, such as Stilton or Dutch blue cheese
300 ml/10 fl oz soured cream or crème fraîche
Snipped fresh chives (optional)

1. Heat the oven to 200°C/400°F/Gas 6 with a baking sheet inside.

2. Wipe or scrub the potatoes, as necessary (see introduction), and dry
them with paper towels or a tea towel. Put a potato on a chopping board
and cut it in half. Place a potato half, cut side down, on the chopping
board and cut into 3 long wedges. Set the wedges aside in a large bowl.
Continue with the remaining potatoes to make 24 wedges in total.

3. Peel and very finely chop the garlic clove, then add it to the bowl
with the potato wedges.

4. Add the oil to the bowl and use your hands to toss and rub the oil
and garlic all over the potato wedges. Sprinkle in the salt and toss the
potato wedges again, then season with pepper to taste.

5. Using oven gloves, carefully remove the baking sheet from the oven.

6. Arrange the potato wedges on the baking sheet in a single layer.
Return the baking sheet to the oven and bake for 30–35 minutes, turning
the potatoes over once, until they are golden brown and crispy.

7. Meanwhile, make the Blue Cheese Dip. Crumble the cheese into a bowl and use a fork to mash it up. Add the soured cream or crème fraîche and continue mashing until blended. Add salt and pepper to taste. Stir in the chives, if you are using. Cover with clingfilm and chill until required. (This can be made up to 2 days in advance and kept in the fridge, covered with clingfilm.)

8. Remove the potato wedges from the oven and leave until cool enough to handle. Serve warm or at room temperature with the chilled dip.

VARIATIONS
▸ Other dips that go well with these potato wedges are Hummus (page 88) and Tzatziki (page 89). Or serve the wedges with a bowl of plain tomato ketchup.
▸ Thin the dip with a little Greek-style or natural yogurt and use it as a salad dressing.
▸ The dip is also good spooned over a hot Crispy Baked Potato (page 42).

Cheesy Potato Skins with Salsa

MAKES **4–6 SERVINGS; 24 POTATO SKINS** PREP TIME: **ABOUT 5 MINUTES, PLUS BAKING THE POTATOES AND LEAVING THEM TO COOL** COOKING TIME: **15–20 MINUTES**

THIS ISN'T A SPUR-OF-THE-MOMENT SNACK, UNLESS YOU'VE HAD THE FORESIGHT TO PLAN AHEAD AND HAVE EXTRA CRISPY BAKED POTATES (PAGE 42) IN THE FRIDGE. BUT, IF YOU GET IN THE HABIT OF PUTTING EXTRA POTATOES IN THE OVEN WHENEVER YOU BAKE ANY, IT WON'T TAKE LONG FOR THIS OH-SO-SIMPLE, FILLING SNACK TO TRANSPORT YOU TO COUCH POTATO PARADISE.

THIS IS ALSO GOOD, CHEAP PARTY NOSH.

4 large baking potatoes (see Potato Primer 1, page 41)
Olive or sunflower oil
Salt, ideally coarse sea salt, but ordinary will do
45 g/1^1/$_2$ oz Cheddar cheese

FOR THE SPICY SALSA:
1 large tomato
1 small onion
^{1}/$_2$ fresh green chilli, or to taste
2 teaspoons white-wine vinegar
1 spring onion

1. To bake the potatoes, heat the oven to 230°C/450°F/Gas 8. Rub the potatoes with the olive oil and salt as on page 42, then bake for 45 minutes – 1 hour until crisp and brown, and so they feel soft in the centre when poked with a fork: there shouldn't be any resistance.

2. Remove the potatoes from the oven and set aside until they are cool enough to handle. Lower the oven temperature to 190°C/375°F/Gas 5.

3. Meanwhile, coarsely grate the cheese and set aside.

4. When you can handle the potatoes, cut each potato in half and scoop out the centres, leaving a 0.5 cm/^{1}/$_4$-inch shell on each. (Don't throw away the potato flesh; see page 65.)

5. Cut each potato half into 3 long strips. Put the potato skins, flesh-side up, on a baking sheet. Equally sprinkle the cheese over the potato skins.

6. Put the baking sheet in the oven and bake for 15–20 minutes until the cheese melts.

7. Meanwhile, make the Spicy Salsa. Cut the tomato in half and use a small spoon to scoop out the seeds. Finely dice the tomato flesh and put it in a bowl. Peel and finely chop the onion, then add it to the tomato.

8. If you want a blow-the-top-off-your-mouth hot, spicy salsa, very thinly slice the chilli without removing the seeds (see Hot Stuff, page 189) before adding it to the bowl, otherwise seed and slice the chilli. Stir in the vinegar, then cover and set aside or chill until required. Finely chop the white part of the spring onion and set aside.

9. To serve, sprinkle the spring onion slices over the salsa. Leave the potato skins until they are cool enough to handle, then serve them hot or at room temperature with the salsa as a dip.

VARIATION

▸ Sprinkle the potato skins with crumbled, crisp bacon before you add the cheese.

▸ If you can't be bothered to make the salsa, serve the potato skins plain or with a bowl of tomato ketchup as a dip.

COOK'S TIP
THE POTATOES ARE EASIEST TO SCOOP OUT WHEN THEY ARE HOT. IF YOU'VE BAKED THEM IN ADVANCE, REHEAT THEM AT 180°C/350°F/GAS 4 FOR 10–15 MINUTES. IF YOU WANT TO USE BAKED POTATOES WITHOUT REHEATING THEM FIRST, USE A SMALL SHARP KNIFE TO CUT THE FLESH AWAY FROM THE SKINS.

Red-Hot Salsa
For a real blast of heat in the salsa, use the small, thin red chillies, called bird's-eye chillies. Anyone who tries this will sit up and take notice!

Pickled Mixed Veg

MAKES **6–8 SERVINGS**
PREP TIME: **10–12 MINUTES, PLUS CHILLING**
NO COOKING

NIBBLE THESE INSTEAD OF REACHING FOR A HIGH-FAT BAG OF CRISPS THE NEXT TIME YOU
SETTLE DOWN FOR A SESSION IN FRONT OF THE TV. THE VEGGIES HAVE A SWEET-SHARP
FLAVOUR, AND WILL REMAIN CRISP IN THE FRIDGE FOR UP TO FIVE DAYS.

8 tablespoons sugar, or to taste
250 ml/8 fl oz white distilled vinegar, or white-wine vinegar
250 ml/8 fl oz water
A selection of about 1 kg/2 lb fresh vegetables, such as broccoli,
   carrots, cauliflower, courgettes and red, yellow or orange peppers

1. Put the sugar in a large bowl and add the vinegar and water, stirring
until the sugar dissolves. Add more sugar or vinegar to taste, then set
aside while you prepare the vegetables.

2. Prepare the vegetables as required: cut broccoli and cauliflower into
bite-size florets; scrub or peel carrots and then slice; rinse courgettes
and then slice; core, seed and cut peppers into thin strips.

3. Add the vegetables to the bowl and stir them around. If they aren't
covered with liquid, stir in more vinegar and water. Tightly cover the
bowl with clingfilm and chill for at least 1 hour.

VARIATION
► For a spicy kick, add a large pinch of dried chilli flakes to the liquid
and leave to infuse for at least 30 minutes. Remove and discard the
chilli flakes before you add the vegetables – unless you want a really
hot and spicy flavour, in which case leave them in the liquid.

Pitta Crisps

MAKES **4–6 SERVINGS; 32 PIECES**
PREP TIME: **ABOUT 5 MINUTES**
COOKING TIME: **ABOUT 20 MINUTES**

TRY THESE FOR A REDUCED-FAT ALTERNATIVE TO MUNCHING YOUR WAY THROUGH A BAG
OF ORDINARY POTATO CRISPS. (TAKE A LOOK AT THE TORTILLA CHIPS VARIATION, BELOW,
IF YOU ARE OUT OF PITTA BREADS.)

4 white or wholemeal pitta breads
Olive oil

1. Heat the oven to 180°C/350°F/Gas 4. Carefully cut each pitta bread
through the pocket into 2 pieces. (A serrated bread knife if ideal, but
an ordinary knife will do.)

2. Cut each pitta bread half into 4 wedges, to make 32 pieces in total.

3. Place the pitta bread pieces on a baking sheet with the rough inside
facing upwards. Very lightly brush the top of each pitta wedge with olive oil.

4. Place the baking sheet in the oven and bake for 20 minutes, or until
the pitta chips are golden brown and crisp. Leave to cool completely.
Serve with the dip of your choice, or store in an airtight container for
up to three days.

VARIATIONS
► *Tortilla Chips:* Heat the oven to 180°C/350°F/Gas 4. Lightly brush 4
soft flour tortillas with olive or sunflower oil and season each with salt
and pepper to taste. Stack the tortillas on top of each other and use a
sharp knife to cut the stack into 12 wedges, to make a total of 48 pieces.

Arrange the tortilla wedges in a single layer on 1 or 2 baking sheets.
Bake for about 5 minutes until they are crisp and golden. Leave to cool
completely. Serve with the dip of your choice, or store in an airtight
container for up to three days.
► Spice up the Pitta Crisps or Tortilla Chips with a sprinkling of cayenne
pepper, instead of the black pepper in the master recipe.

COOK'S TIP
IF YOU DON'T HAVE A PASTRY BRUSH FOR ADDING THE OLIVE OIL IN STEP 3, DIP
A CRUMPLED PAPER TOWEL INTO A SMALL BOWL OF OIL AND THEN USE TO LIGHTLY
BRUSH THE OIL OVER THE PITTA WEDGES.

Caerphilly Sausage Rolls

MAKES **4–6 SERVINGS; 24 ROLLS**
PREP TIME: **ABOUT 20 MINUTES, PLUS CHILLING**
COOKING TIME: **ABOUT 20 MINUTES**

HERE'S A VEGETARIAN VERSION OF A GREAT BRITISH PARTY FAVOURITE. REMEMBER TO REMOVE THE PASTRY FROM THE FREEZER IN ENOUGH TIME FOR IT TO THAW.

¹/₂ bunch fresh parsley
3 slices day-old wholemeal or white bread
180 g/6 oz Caerphilly or Wensleydale cheese
1 onion
2 eggs, plus 1 extra yolk
A little plain white flour
350 g/12 oz frozen puff pastry, thawed
1 tablespoon Dijon, prepared English or wholegrain mustard
Salt and pepper

1. Rinse the parsley and shake off the excess water; then set aside to dry while you prepare the other ingredients.

2. Make the bread into crumbs (page 102). Put the breadcrumbs in a large bowl. Finely grate the cheese into the bowl.

3. Peel and very finely chop the onion, then add it to the bowl. Very finely chop the parsley leaves and stems, then add them to the bowl. Beat the egg with the extra yolk.

4. Add all but 2 tablespoons of the egg mixture to the bowl with salt and pepper to taste. Wet your hands and use them to mix and squeeze all the ingredients together. Divide the mixture into 2 portions and shape each into a 'rope', about 45 cm/18 inches long and 2.5 cm/1 inch thick.

5. Lightly dust the work surface and a rolling pin with flour. Roll out the dough into a 45 x 25 cm/18 x 10-inch rectangle. Cut the dough in half lengthways.

6. Brush the dough with the mustard, leaving about 0.5 cm/¹/₄ inch free on each long edge.

7. Place one cheese 'rope' in the centre of on each piece of pastry. Use your finger to lightly brush water along the long pastry edges that aren't covered with mustard.

8. Fold each pastry strip over the filling and press the long edges together.

9. Use a sharp knife to trim the short open ends. Cut each roll into 12 equal-size pieces, each about 4 cm/1¹/₂ inches wide.

10. Place the sausage rolls on a plate, cover with clingfilm and chill for at least 30 minutes, or up to 1 day. (If you are not baking straight away, cover the reserved egg mixture tightly with clingfilm.)

11. Heat the oven to 220°C/425°F/Gas 7.

12. Place the sausage rolls on a baking sheet and brush with the reserved beaten egg. Bake for 15–20 minutes until the pastry is risen and golden. Remove the sausage rolls from the oven and leave to cool to room temperature. These will keep in an airtight tin for up to 2 days.

Making Breadcrumbs
Day-old bread is best to make crumbs from. If you have a food processor, just tear the bread into small cubes and process until crumbs form. Otherwise, rub the bread up and down the coarse or medium side of a grater.

Store leftover breadcrumbs in an airtight container in the fridge for up to a week.

Nachos

MAKES **2–3 SERVINGS**
PREP TIME: **LESS THAN 5 MINUTES**
COOKING TIME: **ABOUT 10 MINUTES**

THESE TEX-MEX SNACKS ARE A MUST WHEN YOU ARE DRINKING TEQUILA SLAMMERS (PAGE 234) OR CHILLED LAGER! AND THEY'RE GOOD ANY OTHER TIME WHEN YOU WANT A WARM, QUICK SNACK. JUST REMEMBER THAT THESE ARE BEST SERVED HOT, STRAIGHT FROM THE OVEN. DON'T LEAVE THEM SITTING AROUND – THEY ARE VERY UNAPPETISING ONCE THEY COOL.

180 g/6 oz Cheddar cheese
250 g/8 oz corn chips

1. Heat the oven to 200°C/400°F/Gas 6. Coarsely grate the cheese.

2. Spread out the corn chips in a single layer in an ovenproof dish, quiche dish or roasting tin.

3. Sprinkle the cheese over the chips. Bake for 10 minutes, or until the cheese melts. Use a fork to scoop up portions of cheesy chips.

VARIATIONS

▶ For an 'I'm-more-macho-than-you' version, sprinkle the corn chips with sliced red or green chillies before you add the cheese. (See Hot Stuff, page 189.)
▶ When you take the nachos out of the oven, top them with soured cream and sliced stoned black olives or sliced pickled green chillies. (Look for the pickled chillies in supermarkets where Mexican ingredients are sold.)

COOK'S TIPS
▶ COOK THE NACHOS IN BATCHES IF YOUR BAKING DISH OR TIN ISN'T LARGE ENOUGH TO HOLD THE CORN CHIPS IN A SINGLE LAYER.
▶ CUT THE WASHING-UP TIME BY LINING THE COOKING CONTAINER WITH A PIECE OF KITCHEN FOIL, SHINY SIDE DOWN. THE MELTED CHEESE WILL DRIP ON TO THE FOIL, SO NO ELBOW GREASE IS REQUIRED!

Quesadillas

MAKE 2 SERVINGS
PREP TIME: **LESS THAN 5 MINUTES**
COOKING TIME: **ABOUT 5 MINUTES**

ANOTHER QUICK TEX-MEX-STYLE SNACK THAT HITS THE SPOT WHEN YOU'RE DRINKING TEQUILA OR LAGER. QUESADILLAS (PRONOUNCED KEH-SAH-DE-YAHS) ARE FLOUR TORTILLAS FOLDED OVER A SAVOURY FILLING AND THEN DRY-FRIED UNTIL WARMED THROUGH. (TAKE A LOOK BELOW FOR OTHER TEMPTING FILLING IDEAS.)
 YOU WON'T FIND A QUICKER 'TOASTED' CHEESE SANDWICH THAN THIS.

**125 g/4 oz Cheddar cheese
2 soft flour tortillas**

1. Finely grate the Cheddar cheese.

2. Heat a dry frying pan that is large enough to hold a flour tortilla over a medium-high heat until you feel the heat rising from the surface.

3. Lay one tortilla in the pan. Sprinkle half the cheese over one half of the tortilla. Fold the plain half of the tortilla over the cheese to make a Cornish pasty shape and lightly press both halves together.

4. Dry-fry the quesadilla for 30 seconds–1 minute until you can see that the cheese has started to melt.

5. Flip the quesadilla over and continue heating it for about 1 minute longer to crisp the bottom. Tip the quesadilla out of the pan and cut it into wedges. Repeat with the remaining tortilla and cheese.

VARIATIONS
► For spicy heat, top the cheese with sliced green chillies (seeded or unseeded, as you like). Or add a little Spicy Salsa (page 97).
► Add finely sliced leftover chicken, pork or beef to the filling for a more substantial sandwich.
► Refried beans (sold in cans in the Mexican food section of supermarkets) are another traditional filling.
► Try a combination of all these filling – let your imagination loose.

COOK'S TIP
IF YOUR FRYING PAN IS TOO SMALL TO HOLD THE TORTILLA FLAT, HEAT THE OVEN TO 230°C/450°F/GAS 8 WITH A BAKING SHEET INSIDE. PLACE THE TORTILLA ON THE HOT BAKING SHEET, SPRINKLE WITH THE FILLING OF YOUR CHOICE AND FOLD IT OVER INTO A CORNISH PASTY SHAPE. BAKE FOR 3–5 MINUTES UNTIL THE TORTILLA IS TOASTED AND THE CHEESE HAS MELTED. CUT THE TORTILLA INTO WEDGES TO SERVE.

Muffin 'Mini Pizzas'

MAKES **2 SERVINGS; 4 MUFFIN HALVES**
PREP TIME: **ABOUT 10 MINUTES**
COOKING TIME: **UP TO 10 MINUTES**

OK, MAYBE NOT A TRUE PIZZA, BUT QUICKER THAN MAKING A TAKE-AWAY PIZZA AT HOME (PAGE 57) OR RINGING FOR A DELIVERY WHEN A SNACK-ATTACK STRIKES.

1 courgette
1 orange, red or yellow pepper
1 tablespoon olive oil
1 teaspoon dried mixed herbs
2 muffins, split in half
125 ml/4 fl oz tomato sauce, either home-made (page 48) or bottled
125 g/4 oz mozzarella cheese, drained
Salt and pepper

1. Heat the grill to the highest setting. Line the grill pan with foil.

2. Cut the ends off the courgette and discard, then thinly slice the courgette. Core, seed and slice the pepper.

3. Put the courgette and pepper slices in the grill pan, drizzle with the olive oil and sprinkle with the dried herbs. Use your hands to toss everything together so the vegetables slices are coated with oil and herbs.

4. Spread the vegetables into a layer in the grill pan and add the muffins, uncut sides up, on the side of the pan. Grill for about 5 minutes until the vegetables begin to soften and the muffins are toasted on the bottoms.

5. Remove the muffin halves from the grill pan and continue grilling the vegetables until they are tender, about 2 minutes longer. (Do not turn off the grill.) Spread the uncut sides of the muffins with the tomato sauce, equally dividing the sauce between them. Top the muffin halves with the grilled vegetables.

6. Cut the mozzarella into 4 slices, then chop each slice of cheese. Sprinkle the mozzarella over each mini pizza.

7. Return the mini pizzas to the grill pan for 3–5 minutes until the cheese melts and the muffins are crisp around the edges.

Cheese Dreams

MAKES **2 SERVINGS**
PREP TIME: **LESS THAN 5 MINUTES**
COOKING TIME: **LESS THAN 5 MINUTES**

AN INSTANT PICK-ME-UP THAT IS ESPECIALLY GOOD AFTER A LONG SESSION IN THE PUB.

1–2 tomatoes, depending on their size
2 slices white or wholemeal bread
Butter or margarine
4 slices cheese, such as Cheddar

1. Heat the grill to high. Thinly slice the tomatoes so you have enough slices to completely cover each slice of bread.

2. Grill the bread for 1$\frac{1}{2}$–2 minutes on one side until golden brown.

3. Turn the toast over and lightly butter the untoasted sides. Arrange the tomato slices over top of each slice of toast, then add the cheese slices. Return to the grill and toast until the cheese melts.

VARIATIONS
▸ *Fried Cheese Dream:* To make 1 sandwich, lightly butter 2 slices of white or wholemeal bread. Sandwich the tomato and cheese slices between the buttered sides of the bread. Lightly butter a plain side, and put the sandwich, buttered side down, in a frying pan over a medium heat. Fry for 3–5 minutes until the bread becomes golden and the cheese starts to melt. Lightly butter the top of the sandwich, then flip it over and continue frying until the second side is golden and the cheese has melted.
▸ *Fried Ham & Cheese Dream:* Make as above, but insert a slice of cooked ham with the cheese and tomato slices.
▸ Spread the untoasted side of the bread with Marmite, brown sauce, pickle or mustard, rather than butter, before you add the tomato slices.
▸ Use a different cheese, such as Cheshire, Parmesan or wensleydale.
▸ Scatter sliced spring onions over the tomatoes before you add the cheese.

Mozzarella Melts

MAKES **2 SERVINGS**
PREP TIME: **ABOUT 5 MINUTES**
COOKING TIME: **LESS THAN 5 MINUTES**

A LADETTE VERSION OF THE PREVIOUS RECIPE. THIS IS A FILLING SNACK,
OR YOU CAN SERVE IT AS FIRST COURSE FOR A DINNER PARTY.

2 slices ciabatta bread
1–2 tomatoes, depending on their size
Olive oil
60 g / 2 oz mozzarella cheese, drained
Salt and pepper

1. Heat the grill to high. Use a serrated bread knife to slice each piece
of ciabatta bread horizontally in half, to make 4 pieces in total.

2. Thinly slice the tomatoes so you have enough slices to cover the
pieces of ciabatta bread. Slice the mozzarella as thinly as you can;
it doesn't matter if the slices are irregular.

3. Toast the bread, cut sides up, for 1½–2 minutes until it just starts
to turn golden brown.

4. Drizzle the toasted sides with a small amount of olive oil. Add the
tomato slices so the top of each bread slice is covered. Season with
salt and pepper.

5. Top the tomatoes with the mozzarella slices. Return the slices of
ciabatta bread to the grill and continue toasting until the cheese melts.

VARIATIONS
► Add flaked, drained canned tuna to each slice of bread before you
top with the cheese.
► If you don't have any fresh tomatoes, use home-made (page 48) or
bottled tomato sauce. Or drain a can of chopped tomatoes through a
sieve and use the tomatoes. (Drink the juice, or add it to pasta sauce.)

Welsh Rarebit

MAKES **2 SERVINGS**
PREP TIME: **LESS THAN 5 MINUTES**
COOKING TIME: **ABOUT 5 MINUTES**

125 g/4 oz Cheddar cheese
A knob of butter
1$\frac{1}{2}$ teaspoons mustard powder
2 tablespoons lager or brown ale
2 slices white bread
Worcestershire sauce

1. Heat the grill to high. Finely grate the cheese into a saucepan.

2. Add the butter, mustard powder and lager or ale to the pan over a low heat. Stir until the cheese and butter melt and a creamy sauce forms.

3. Meanwhile, toast the bread for 1$\frac{1}{2}$–2 minutes until golden brown on one side.

4. Turn the slices of toast over and spread the cheese mixture over the untoasted sides. Add a few drops of Worcestershire sauce to each slice.

5. Return the slices of toast to the grill and continue toasting until the cheese becomes golden brown and bubbles. Cut into quarters to serve.

VARIATIONS
‣ *Golden Buck:* Add a poached egg to the top of each Welsh rarebit.
‣ Top the untoasted bread with tomato slices, Hard-boiled Eggs (page 35) or crumbled cooked sausages before you add the cheese sauce.
‣ Or add sliced, cooked chorizo sausage before you add the cheese sauce. Don't forget to remove the sausage casing, if necessary.
‣ Stir the finely chopped green and white parts of a spring onion into the cheese mixture.
‣ Vary the cheese you use. Cheshire and Parmesan also work well.

Sardines on Toast

MAKES **2 SERVINGS**
PREP TIME: **LESS THAN 5 MINUTES**
COOKING TIME: **LESS THAN 5 MINUTES**

ONCE YOU'VE GOT THE CAN OPEN, THIS IS CUPBOARD TO MOUTH IN LESS THAN LESS THAN FIVE MINUTES.

2 slices white or wholemeal bread
1 can (125 g/4 oz) sardines in tomato sauce

1. Heat the grill to high, if you don't have a toaster. Toast the bread in the toaster, or under the grill for 1½–2 minutes on each side until golden brown.

2. Tip the contents of the can of sardines into a bowl and smash with a fork. Spread on the toast.

VARIATIONS
▸ If this isn't quick enough, make a bap sandwich with the sardines, straight from the tin.
▸ Add a dab of mustard to plain sardines on toast.
▸ Flake the sardines into a bowl, removing any skin and tiny bones, and stir in 2–3 tablespoons of mayo and the finely chopped green and white parts of a spring onion.

Spinach, Orange & Avocado Salad

MAKES **2 SERVINGS**
PREP TIME: **10–15 MINUTES**
NO COOKING

WHEN YOU WANT THE VIRTUOUS FEELING FROM EATING A HEALTHY SALAD, THIS IS FOR YOU. THIS IS A POWERHOUSE OF ESSENTIAL VITAMINS AND MINERALS.

1 orange
1 avocado
250 g/8 oz baby spinach leaves
4 tablespoons vinaigrette dressing, home-made (page 55) or bottled
2 tablespoons toasted pumpkin seeds

1. Use a small serrated knife to cut the ends off the orange. Then slowly slice off the orange peel and white pith to expose the orange segments, working over a bowl to catch any juices. Set the orange segments and any juice aside. (Take your time, because if you leave any white pith on the orange segments they will taste very bitter.)

2. Place a colander or sieve in the sink. Add the spinach leave and rinse with cold water, then pat them completely dry with paper towels or a tea towel. Put the spinach leaves in a large bowl.

3. Seed the avocado (page 91), then peel the avocado flesh and cut it into slices.

4. Add the avocado slices and orange segments to the spinach leaves. Add the dressing, then use salad servers, 2 forks or clean hands to toss the ingredients together. (Remember, you can always add more dressing, but you can't take it away.) Sprinkle with the pumpkin seeds. Serve at once so the avocado doesn't turn brown.

VARIATIONS
► For a non-vegetarian version, add crisp fried bacon pieces or cold cooked ham slices.
► Drain canned chickpeas also go well tossed with the other ingredients.
► Perk up the flavour by adding peppery-flavoured rocket or watercress leaves.

Casbah Salad

MAKES **2–4 SERVINGS** PREP TIME: **ABOUT 10 MINUTES, PLUS 20 MINUTES FOR THE BULGAR WHEAT TO SOAK AND UP TO 4 HOURS CHILLING. NO COOKING**

THIS MIDDLE EASTERN SALAD, MADE WITH CRACKED WHEAT, IS WIN-WIN. NOT ONLY IS IT HEALTHY AND GOOD FOR YOU, WHEN YOU MAKE IT YOURSELF, RATHER THAN BUYING IT IN A SMALL TUB AT THE SUPERMARKET, YOU GET A WHOLE LOT MORE FOR A WHOLE LOT LESS. AND THE VARIATIONS (SEE RIGHT) ARE ENDLESS, SO YOU'LL NEVER GET BORED WITH IT.

SERVE THIS WITH PITTA CRISPS (PAGE 100), BUT WHITE OR WHOLEMEAL PITTA BREAD IS MORE TRADITIONAL. OR, FOR AN END-OF-TERM LUNCH, SERVE THIS AS PART OF A BUFFET WITH PROVENÇALE-STYLE LEG OF LAMB (PAGE 200) AND RATATOUILLE (PAGE 173) OR RICE-STUFFED PEPPERS (PAGE 144).

60 g/2 oz bulgar wheat
Large bunch fresh flat-leaf parsley
Large bunch fresh mint
2 tomatoes
1 red onion

1 lemon
Large pinch ground cumin
Olive oil
Salt and pepper

1. Bring a kettle or saucepan of water to the boil. Put the bulgar in a large bowl and stir in ½ teaspoon salt. Pour over enough boiling water to cover, then set aside to soak for 20 minutes, or until the liquid is absorbed and the grains are tender and puffed up.

2. Meanwhile, rinse the parsley and mint under cold water, then shake dry. Set aside to dry completely while you prepare the other ingredients.

3. Cut the tomatoes in half and use a small spoon to scoop out and discard the seeds. Cut the tomato flesh into fine dice. Peel and finely chop the red onion.

4. Very finely chop the parsley leaves and stalks. Remove the mint leave from the stalks and chop them finely.

5. Use your hands to squeeze all the moisture from the bulgar wheat, then put it into a large bowl. Add the tomatoes, onion and herbs, and toss together with a large spoon or clean hands.

6. Finely grate the lemon rind into the bowl. Cut the lemon in half and squeeze the juice over the other ingredients in the bowl. Sprinkle with 2 tablespoons olive oil and add the cumin and salt and pepper to taste. Toss together again and add extra lemon juice and/or olive oil to taste.

7. Serve at once, or cover and chill for up to 4 hours. Remove from the fridge and leave to come to room temperature before eating. Toss again and adjust the seasoning, if necessary, before serving.

VARIATIONS

▸ *Chicken Casbah Salad:* Add skinless, boneless cooked chicken to the salad just before serving.

▸ Bulgar wheat is a really cheap ingredient when you are feeding a crowd. Double or triple the quantities in the master recipe and add any of the following for a party salad: chopped cucumber, very finely chopped garlic, blanched green beans, stoned black olives, toasted pine nuts, sliced spring onions and sliced sun-dried tomatoes.

Sizzling Fish Finger Salad

MAKES **2 SERVINGS**
PREP TIME: **ABOUT 5 MINUTES**
COOKING TIME: **ABOUT 12 MINUTES**

4 fish fingers
60 g/2 oz Cheddar cheese
2 large handfuls of mixed salad leaves
2 tablespoons lemon-flavoured vinaigrette dressing, either
   home-made (page 55) or bottled, or a salad dressing of your choice
Chopped fresh parsley, to serve (optional)

1. Heat the grill to high. Place the fish fingers on a baking sheet and grill for 10–12 minutes, turning them over once, or according to the instructions on the fish finger packet.

2. Meanwhile, grate the cheese into a large bowl. Add the lettuce leaves and use your hands or 2 forks to toss the cheese and leaves together. Add the Vinaigrette or salad dressing and toss with 2 forks until the leaves are coated.

3. Divide the salad between two plates. When the fish fingers are cooked, immediately cut them into bite-size pieces and place on top of the salad. Sprinkle with chopped parsley, if you have any.

Sesame-Lemon Chicken Wings

MAKES **2–3 SERVINGS; 12 WINGS**
PREP TIME: **ABOUT 5 MINUTES**
COOKING TIME: **35–40 MINUTES**

A FINGER-LICKING, LIP-SMACKING SNACK. PILE THESE HIGH AND TUCK IN.

THESE ARE CHEAP AND MAKE IRRESISTIBLE PARTY NOSH. AND FORGET ABOUT KNIVES AND FORKS. CHICKEN WINGS ARE MEANT FOR EATING WITH YOUR FINGERS – THAT MEANS LESS WASHING-UP FOR YOU.

NOT ALL SUPERMARKETS STOCK CHICKEN WINGS, SO YOU MIGHT HAVE TO GO TO A BUTCHER TO BUY THEM.

12 chicken wings
1 lemon
2 tablespoons olive oil
1$^1/_2$ teaspoons demerara sugar
Pinch of cayenne powder, or to taste
1 tablespoon sesame seeds
Salt and pepper

1. Heat the oven to 190°C/350°F/Gas 5. Line a roasting tin with foil, shiny side up, and place a rack in the tin. Lightly grease the rack. Use a pair of tweezers or your fingers to pull out any fine feathers in the chicken wings. Use a knife or kitchen shears to cut off the thin end of each wing, and discard. (The tips are so thin they burn easily and there isn't enough meat on them to bother with.)

2. Finely grate the rind from the lemon into a large bowl, then squeeze the juice from both halves into the bowl. Use a small spoon or your fingers to fish out any seeds.

3. Stir in the olive oil, sugar, cayenne and salt and pepper to taste. Add the chicken wings to the bowl and toss them around so they are well coated.

4. Place the chicken wings on the rack and roast for 35–40 minutes until the skin turns crisp and golden-brown and the sesame seeds begin to toast.

5. Line a large plate with a double thickness of paper towels. Place the chicken wings on the plate to drain and leave until completely cool. Serve with lots of paper napkins!

VARIATION
▸ *Chinese-style Chicken Wings:* Heat the oven to 190°C/375°F/Gas 5 and line the roasting tin as in the master recipe left. Prepare the chicken wings as shown. To make the glaze, mix together 6 tablespoons tomato ketchup, 4 tablespoons soft light-brown sugar, 2 tablespoons soy sauce, 1 tablespoon rice vinegar or dry sherry and 1 tablespoon sesame, groundnut or sunflower oil. Stir in 2 peeled and very finely chopped garlic cloves. Roast the chicken wings as in the master recipe.

Marinate for Extra Flavour
If you plan ahead, leave the chicken wings to marinate in the spicy lemon mixture, or the Chinese-style glaze, for at least 2 hours, but ideally overnight, in the fridge. Just remember to remove the bowl from the fridge 15 minutes before putting the chicken wings in the oven.

Nice & Juicy
For maximum juice from the lemon, roll it around on the work surface, pressing down firmly with your hand before you squeeze out the juice. You will also get more juice from a lemon when it is at room temperature, rather than straight from the fridge.

Sticky Ribs

MAKES **2–3 SERVINGS** PREP TIME: **ABOUT 15 MINUTES,
PLUS AT LEAST 4 HOURS MARINATING THE RIBS**
COOKING TIME: **ABOUT 20 MINUTES**

ANOTHER SNACK TO EAT WITH YOUR FINGERS – CHEAP ENOUGH THAT YOU CAN MAKE A BIG
PILE OF THEM TO FILL UP A CROWD. YOU WON'T BE ABLE TO BEAT THESE AS AN ICE-BREAKER
AT BEGINNING-OF-TERM PARTIES – AFTER ALL, WHO CAN BE INHIBITED WHEN THEY'RE
MUNCHING ON PORK RIBS WITH STICKY FINGERS, AND WITH SAUCE-SMEARED LIPS?
CHILLED LAGER IS THE NATURAL DRINK TO SERVE WITH THESE.

2.5 cm/1-inch piece fresh root ginger
1 large garlic clove
150 ml/5 fl oz orange juice
6 tablespoons red-wine vinegar
1 tablespoon Worcestershire sauce
2 teaspoons soy sauce
3 tablespoons soft light-brown sugar
2 tablespoons lemon juice
900 g/2 lb pork spareribs
Sunflower or groundnut oil for brushing the grill rack

1. Peel and finely grate the ginger. Peel and very finely chop the garlic.

2. Put the garlic and ginger in a large bowl and stir in the orange juice,
vinegar, Worcestershire sauce, soy sauce, sugar and lemon juice. Add
the ribs and stir them around with your clean hands so they are coated
with the marinade. Cover the bowl with clingfilm and chill for at least
4 hours.

3. Remove the ribs from the fridge 15 minutes before you want to cook
so they come to room temperature. Heat the grill to its highest setting.
Line the grill pan with kitchen foil, shiny side up. Lightly brush the grill
rack with oil.

4. Arrange the ribs on the grill rack in a single layer. Grill for about
15 minutes, turning the ribs over occasionally and brushing with the
reserved marinade.

5. Leave the ribs until they are cool enough to handle, then serve with
lots of paper napkins.

Curried Lentil Soup

MAKES **4 SERVINGS**
PREP TIME: **10–15 MINUTES**
COOKING TIME: **ABOUT 25 MINUTES**

TEAM THIS WITH SHOP-BOUGHT CHAPATIS OR CHUNKS OF FRENCH BREAD FOR AN INEXPENSIVE FILLER-UPPER. (THE ADDITION OF BREAD ALSO MAKES THIS INTO A COMPLETE PROTEIN FOR VEGETARIANS.)

LEFTOVERS WILL KEEP, COVERED WITH CLINGFILM, IN THE FRIDGE FOR UP TO THREE DAYS, OR CAN BE FROZEN FOR UP TO A MONTH.

200 g/7 oz red or yellow lentils
1 large garlic clove
1 onion
1 carrot
1 celery stick
2 tablespoons olive oil
1 tablespoon mild to hot curry paste, to taste

1 litre/1¹/₂ cups vegetable stock, either home-made (page 54) or from a cube
¹/₂ tablespoon red-wine vinegar
Salt and pepper
Finely chopped fresh coriander, to serve (optional)
Greek-style or natural yogurt (optional), to serve

1. Place a sieve in the sink, add the lentils and rinse well with cold water; then set them aside until required.

2. Peel and finely chop the garlic. Peel and finely chop the onion. Scrub or peel and finely chop the carrot. Finely chop the celery.

3. Heat the oil in a large saucepan or flameproof casserole over a medium heat. Add the garlic, onion, carrot and celery, and fry, stirring occasionally, for about 2 minutes. Stir in the curry paste and continue frying for about 3 minutes until the vegetables are tender, but not brown.

4. Stir in the stock and bring to the boil. Lower the heat, cover the pan and simmer, stirring occasionally, for 20 minutes, or until the lentils are very tender and starting to fall apart.

5. You now have to decide if you want a smooth or chunky soup. You can puree all the soup in a blender, puree only three-quarters for a smooth soup with a little texture, mash the lentils with a potato masher for a semi-smooth soup or serve it as it is.

6. Reheat the soup, if necessary. Add salt and pepper to taste. Sprinkle with chopped coriander, if you have any, and add a dollop of yogurt to each bowl if you are not a vegan.

Potato & Leek Soup

MAKES **4 SERVINGS**
PREP TIME: **10–12 MINUTES**
COOKING TIME: **ABOUT 25 MINUTES**

THERE ARE SEVERAL REASONS WHY THIS IS A SOUP TO MASTER WHEN YOU'RE NEW TO COOKING. FIRST, IT IS INEXPENSIVE AND EASY AND, SECOND, IT'S AN ALL-PURPOSE MEAL IN A MUG: ENJOY IT PIPING HOT IN THE WINTER, OR WELL CHILLED IN THE SUMMER. ANY LEFTOVERS CAN BE KEPT IN THE FRIDGE, COVERED, FOR UP TO THREE DAYS, OR FROZEN FOR UP TO ONE MONTH.

2 large leeks
2 floury potatoes (see Potato Primer 1, page 41)
2 tablespoons olive oil, or 30 g/1 oz butter
1 litre/2^1/$_2$ pints vegetable stock,
    home-made (page 54) or from a cube
4 tablespoons single cream
Salt and pepper
Snipped chives, to serve (optional)

1. Cut each leek in half lengthways, then place, cut sides down, on a chopping board and slice thinly. (If the leeks have grit between the layers, put the slices in a sieve and run cold water over them.)

2. Peel the potatoes and cut them into small cubes.

3. Heat the oil or melt the butter in a large saucepan or flameproof casserole over a medium heat. Add the leeks and potatoes and season with salt and pepper. Stir the vegetables around for 3–5 minutes, or until the leeks are soft, but not brown.

4. Pour in the stock, turn up the heat and bring to the boil. Lower the heat and leave the soup to simmer, stirring occasionally, for 20 minutes, or until the potatoes are very soft and starting to fall apart.

5. Add salt and pepper to taste – don't forget, potatoes need generous seasoning. You can either serve the soup as it is with a coarse texture, or transfer it to a blender or food processor and puree until smooth.

6. Stir in the cream and adjust the seasoning, if necessary. Serve hot or chilled, sprinkled with chives, if you have any.

VARIATIONS

- To make a vegan version, omit the single cream.
- Crème fraîche makes a delicious alternative to single cream.

Minestrone

MAKES **4 SERVINGS**
PREP TIME: **10–15 MINUTES**
COOKING TIME: **ABOUT 20 MINUTES**

THIS HEARTY ITALIAN VEGETABLE SOUP NEEDS NOTHING MORE THAN A CHUNK OF GOOD BREAD TO MAKE A CHEAP, FILLING MEAL. LEFTOVERS WILL KEEP IN THE FRIDGE, COVERED WITH CLINGFILM, FOR UP TO A DAY, BUT IF YOU LEAVE THEM LONGER THAN THAT THE PASTA MIGHT BECOME MUSHY.

3 carrots
2 celery sticks
1 large garlic clove
1 onion
125 g/4 oz back bacon
1 can (400 g/14 oz) cannelloni beans
2 tablespoons olive oil
2 cans (400 g/14 oz) chopped tomatoes
1 litre/1½ pints vegetable stock, either home-made (page 54)
    or from a cube
150 g/5 oz frozen peas
150 g/5 oz short-cut pasta, such as macaroni
Salt and pepper
4 tablespoons bottled pesto sauce
Grated fresh Parmesan cheese, to serve

1. Scrub or peel the carrots, then cut them into small dice. Trim and cut the celery stalks into small dice. Peel and finely chop the garlic. Peel and finely chop the onion.

2. Put the bacon on a chopping board and cut off the rinds, if necessary, then coarsely chop. Place a strainer in the sink, tip in the can of beans and rinse them under cold water. Set the beans aside until required.

3. Heat the olive oil in a large saucepan or flameproof casserole over a medium heat. Add the carrots, celery, garlic, onion and bacon and fry for about 5 minutes, or until the vegetables are soft, but not brown.

4. Stir in the tomatoes with the juice from the can, the stock and salt and pepper to taste, and bring to the boil. Lower the heat, partially cover the pan and simmer, stirring occasionally, for 15 minutes.

5. Add the beans, peas and pasta. Return the soup to the boil, then lower the heat again, partially re-cover the pan and simmer for 10 minutes longer, or until the pasta is tender to the bite and the flavours are blended.

6. Season with salt and pepper to taste and stir in the pesto sauce. Serve with plenty of grated cheese for sprinkling over the tops.

VARIATIONS

▸ Italian cooks rarely make this the same way twice. Use whatever fresh vegetables you have, and don't feel constrained by the ingredients list. Shredded cabbage, chopped red and green peppers, diced turnips and fresh tomatoes in season are other often-used vegetables. Drained and rinsed canned chickpeas and kidney beans also feature in many versions of this soup.

▸ For a vegetarian or vegan version, omit the bacon.

▸ If you don't have any small pasta shapes, break spaghetti into the soup in Step 5.

Hot Mars Bar Sauce

MAKES **2–4 SERVINGS**
PREP TIME: **LESS THAN 5 MINUTES**
COOKING TIME: **LESS THAN 5 MINUTES**

POUR THIS RICH, THICK SAUCE OVER ICE CREAM FOR AN IRRESISTIBLE HOT-FUDGE SUNDAE. YOU DON'T HAVE TO BE AN EXPERIENCED COOK TO MAKE THIS – BUT EVERYONE WILL AWARD YOU MICHELIN STARS.

150 ml/5 fl oz double cream
1 Mars bar (85 g)

1. Heat the cream in a small saucepan over a medium-high heat until small bubbles appear around the edge.

2. Break the Mars bar into small pieces. Add the pieces to the saucepan and stir until the Mars bar melts: it doesn't matter if some small pieces remain. Spoon the hot sauce over ice-cold ice cream.

VARIATION

▸ *Hot Coffee-Mars Bar Sauce:* Replace the double cream with ¹/₂ mug of leftover coffee. Pour the coffee into a small saucepan and heat until small bubbles appear around the edge. Add the broken up Mars bar and continue as in the master recipe.

Fruidités with Yogurt-Vanilla Dip

MAKES **2–4 SERVINGS**
PREP TIME: **5–15 MINUTES, DEPENDING ON YOUR**
SELECTION OF FRUIT NO COOKING

THINK OF THIS AS A CROSS BETWEEN A SWEET SNACK AND A DESSERT – PERFECT FOR A
GIRLIE NIGHT IN FRONT OF A TEAR-JERKER VIDEO WITH A COUPLE OF BOTTLES OF BUBBLY.
OR TRY THIS AS A HEALTHY ALTERNATIVE TO REACHING INTO THE BISCUIT TIN. SNACK AWAY
WHILE YOU ARE MAKING A CONTRIBUTION TO YOUR 'FIVE-A-DAY' FRUIT AND VEGETABLES.

A selection of fresh fruit, such as cherries, melon slices, oranges,
   star fruit, strawberries and pineapple wedges

FOR THE YOGURT-VANILLA DIP:
300 g/10 oz Greek-style yogurt
1 teaspoon vanilla extract
Icing sugar, to taste

1. Begin by making the Yogurt-Vanilla Dip. Put the yogurt in a bowl. Stir
in the vanilla. Sift 2 tablespoons icing sugar over the yogurt and stir it in.
Taste and sift in extra sugar until you reach the level of sweetness you
like. Cover with clingfilm and chill until required.

2. Prepare the fruit as necessary. Rinse and dry cherries. Cut melon
into thin wedges and remove the peel and seeds. Peel oranges and then
separate into segments, using a small serrated knife to scrape off any
white pith. Trim any dark lips from star fruit, then cut into thin slices.
Quickly rinse strawberries, then pat dry with paper towels. Use a small
sharp knife to remove any tough central core from the pineapple, then
cut off the thick peel and cut the flesh into bite-size pieces.

3. If you aren't eating the fruit at once, cover tightly with clingfilm and
chill until required. Arrange the fruit on a plate with the bowl of dip in
the centre.

Flapjacks

MAKES **8 PIECES**
NO PREP TIME
COOKING TIME: **ABOUT 25 MINUTES**

180 g/6 oz butter
60 g/2 oz golden granulated sugar
2 tablespoons honey or golden syrup
200 g/7 oz rolled oats

1. Heat the oven to 180°C/350°F/Gas 4. Grease a 20 cm/8-inch round sandwich tin or a 17.5/7-inch square roasting tin with a little butter.

2. Put the butter, sugar and honey or golden syrup in a saucepan over a medium heat and stir with a wooden spoon until the butter and honey melt and the sugar dissolves.

3. Remove the pan from the heat and stir in the rolled oats, stirring until they are well coated. Spoon the mixture into the prepared tin and smooth the surface.

4. Bake the flapjacks for 25 minutes, or until golden brown. Remove the tin from the oven and use a sharp knife to mark into 8 equal-size wedges. Leave the flapjacks to cool completely in the tin.

5. When the flapjacks are cool, use a knife to cut them into wedges, as marked. Store in an airtight container for up to a week.

VARIATIONS
▸ *Ginger Flapjacks:* Add ¹/₂ a teaspoon of ground ginger with the oats in Step 3 of the master recipe above.
▸ *Spiced Flapjacks:* Add ¹/₂ a teaspoon of ground mixed spice with the oats in Step 3 of the master recipe above.

COOK'S TIP
MEASURING HONEY CAN BE MESSY. BUT IF YOU WIPE A SMALL AMOUNT OF BUTTER OR SUNFLOWER OIL OVER YOUR MEASURING SPOON BEFORE YOU MEASURE THE HONEY, IT WILL FLOW OFF THE SPOON SMOOTHLY.

Carrot Cake

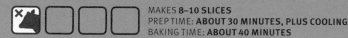

MAKES **8–10 SLICES**
PREP TIME: **ABOUT 30 MINUTES, PLUS COOLING**
BAKING TIME: **ABOUT 40 MINUTES**

WHEN YOU COME HOME AFTER A DAY OF LECTURES, IT IS DIFFICULT TO BEAT THIS WITH A CUP OF TEA AS A PICK-ME-UP. YOU'LL HAVE A DIFFICULT TIME RESISTING A SECOND SLICE.

300 g/10 oz carrots, about 2
150 g/5 oz walnut halves
4 large eggs
300 ml/10 fl oz sunflower oil, plus a little extra for greasing the tin
300 g/10 oz self-raising flour
300 g/10 oz demerara sugar
2 teaspoons ground cinnamon

FOR THE CREAM CHEESE ICING:
180 g/6 oz butter, at room temperature
500 g/1 lb icing sugar
150–200 g/5–7 oz cream cheese
2 teaspoons vanilla extract

1. Heat the oven to 180°C/350°F/Gas 4. Lightly grease the side and bottom of a 23 cm/9-inch round cake tin that is 5 cm/2 inches deep. Line the base with a circle of greaseproof paper, and lightly grease the paper.

2. Scrub or peel the carrots, then coarsely grate them. Coarsely chop the walnut halves into small pieces. Sprinkle the walnut pieces with a tablespoon or so of the flour and lightly toss together, then set aside.

3. Crack the eggs into a large bowl and beat them with an electric hand-held mixer or a whisk. Beat in the oil.

4. Add the remaining flour, sugar and cinnamon to the bowl and lightly stir together with a large spoon. Add the carrots and walnuts and continue stirring until all the ingredients are blended.

5. Spoon the mixture into the cake pan and level the surface. Bake for 40 minutes, or until the top is set, the side starts to come away from the pan and a toothpick stuck in the centre comes out clean.

6. Remove the cake from the oven and run a round-bladed knife between the cake and the tin. Leave the cake to stand for 10 minutes, ideally on a wire rack or a grill pan rack. (Make sure the grill pan isn't covered with bacon grease.)

7. After 10 minutes, invert the cake onto the wire rack and lift off the pan. Remove and discard the lining paper, then leave the cake to cool completely.

8. Meanwhile, make the icing. Cut the butter into small pieces and put it in a mixing bowl. Use an electric hand-held mixer or wooden spoon and beat the butter until it is soft and creamy. Sift in the icing sugar and continue beating until the mixture is blended and smooth.

9. Add 150 g/5 oz of cream cheese and continue beating until the icing becomes firm. If it is too stiff, add more cream cheese.

10. Use a serrated knife, such as a bread knife, to slice the cake horizontally into 2 layers. Put one layer, cut side up, on a plate and cover with half the frosting. Top with the second layer, cut side down, and spread the remaining frosting over the top.

COOK'S TIPS
▸ TOSSING THE WALNUT PIECES WITH FLOUR HELPS PREVENT THEM FROM SINKING TO THE BOTTOM OF THE CAKE WHILE IT BAKES.
▸ IF YOU DON'T HAVE A LONG SERRATED KNIFE TO SLICE THE CAKE IN STEP 10, LEAVE IT WHOLE AND ONLY MAKE HALF THE AMOUNT OF ICING. SPREAD THE FROSTING ON TOP OF THE SINGLE-LAYER CAKE.

Sifted, not Shaken
Always sift icing sugar before you add it to a creamy or liquid mixture. Lumps will form if you stir it straight from the box into the mixture.

If lumps do form, however, use a wooden spoon to press the mixture through a fine sieve, which should remove them.

PACKING IN THE CARBS

Carbs count. A big plate of carbohydrates gives you the energy to go all day and into the night. They will keep you fuelled to run from lectures to tutorials, and keep you going when you are out clubbing.

Carbohydrate is one of the key nutrients your body needs to function properly. Without carbohydrates you won't have any energy. Healthy eating guidelines recommend that carbohydrates make up more than half of each meal. Overall, carbohydrates are excellent low-fat sources of energy.

The good news is that carbohydrates are inexpensive. Stock up on bread, pasta, canned or dried pulses, rice, seeds and plenty of fresh vegetables and fruit, and you'll be well on your way to eating your body's needs without spending lots of cash.

The recipes in this chapter are all really easy, and many can be on the table in less than 20 minutes from the time you walk into the kitchen. Some of the Italian pasta recipes suggest specific shapes simply because of conventions but, in reality, any shape will do. Don't avoid making Spag Bol, for example, because you only have pasta tubes in the cupboard. Keep a selection of dried Italian pasta shapes and rice in your cupboard and you'll never be at a loss of what to make in a hurry.

Other recipes that give you plenty of carbs:
- Cabbage, Bacon & Tattie Fry (page 65)
- Casbah Salad (page 111)
- Chicken with Rice & Peppers (page 153)
- Creamy Mash (page 40)
- Curried Lentil Soup (page 116)
- Hummus (page 88)
- Oven-baked Chips (page 44)
- Pasta with Garlic & Chillies (page 219)
- Perfect Rice (page 45)
- Potato Wedges with Blue Cheese Dip (page 95)
- Red beans & Rice (page 162)
- Sausages with Lentils (page 161)
- Smashed Butter Bean Spread (page 92)
- Spiced Rice (page 208)
- Tortilla (page 72)

Pasta with Almost-Instant Cheese Sauce

MAKES **2 SERVINGS**
PREP TIME: **ABOUT 5 MINUTES**
COOKING TIME: **10–12 MINUTES**

YOU'LL BE CHALLENGED TO FIND A QUICKER HOT MEAL!

200 g/7 oz dried pasta, such as bows, corkscrews or twists
90 g/3 oz Parmesan or Cheddar cheese
2 tablespoons olive oil
Salt and pepper

1. Bring a large saucepan of salted water to the boil over a high heat. Stir in the pasta, return the water to the boil and continue boiling for 10–12 minutes, or according to the packet instructions, until the pasta is tender to the bite.

2. Meanwhile, grate the cheese into a large bowl. Add the olive oil and beat until a thick paste forms.

3. Set a colander or sieve in the sink. Drain the pasta, reserving 2–3 tablespoons of the cooking water. Immediately add the hot pasta to the large bowl and stir until the cheese melts and coats the pasta. If the sauce seems too thick, stir in a little of the reserved cooking water. Season with salt and pepper to taste.

VARIATIONS

► Add frozen peas to the pan with the pasta for the last 5 minutes of cooking time. Or add drained canned sweet corn kernels or chickpeas for the final 2 minutes cooking.
► Stir in drained and sliced sun-dried tomatoes in oil after the cheese melts. If you fancy this option, use the oil from the jar, rather than the plain olive oil.
► Add finely shredded fresh basil or chopped parsley after the cheese melts in Step 3.
► Splash a small amount of balsamic vinegar over each serving.

Is It Done?

Neither under-cooked nor over-cooked pasta is appetising. Pasta is ready to eat when it is *al dente*, or tender to the bite. The only accurate way to check if pasta is cooked is to fish out a piece and bite it: no whiteness should remain in the centre and it should feel tender, but still slightly firm. The residual heat will finish the cooking, and the pasta won't become mushy. Undercooked pasta is very difficult to digest.

Perfect Pasta

▸ Always boil pasta in the largest pan you have. Ideally you want a pot large enough to hold 2 litres/3 ⅓ pints of water to cook 200 g/ 7 oz pasta.

▸ Cook pasta in salted water, otherwise it will be bland regardless of how tasty the sauce is.

▸ The cooking water should be at a full, rolling boil when you add the pasta.

▸ Stir the pasta as you add it to the boiling water to prevent pieces sticking together. Stir several times while the pasta is cooking as well.

▸ Most dried pasta cooks in 10–12 minutes, and fresh pasta cooks in 2–3 minutes. Read the packet labels, though, because some inexpensive dried pasta cooks faster and can become mushy.

▸ Do not rinse pasta after you drain it. The starch will help any sauce stick to the pasta.

Pasta Bolognese

☐ ☐ ☐ ☐ MAKES **2 SERVINGS**
PREP TIME: **ABOUT 10 MINUTES**
COOKING TIME: **ABOUT 40 MINUTES**

SPAG BOL HAS BEEN A STAPLE QUICK MEAL FOR GENERATIONS OF UNDERGRADUATES.
ITALIANS SERVE THIS TRADITIONAL MINCE-AND-TOMATO SAUCE WITH TAGLIATELLE,
BUT ANY SHAPE WILL DO.

THIS ISN'T A QUICK SAUCE TO PREPARE, SO MAKE A LARGE BATCH AND FREEZE HALF
OR KEEP IT COVERED IN THE FRIDGE FOR UP TO THREE DAYS, READY TO REHEAT WHEN YOU
WANT A QUICK MEAL – THE SAUCE WILL BE PIPING HOT IN LESS TIME THAN IT TAKES TO
BOIL THE PASTA.

200 g/7 oz dried pasta, such as tagliatelle or spaghetti
Grated Parmesan cheese, to serve
Salt and pepper

FOR THE BOLOGNESE SAUCE:
$1/2$ carrot
$1/2$ celery stick
$1/2$ onion
1 garlic clove
2 rashers smoked bacon
1 tablespoon olive oil
250 g/8 oz lean minced beef
1 tablespoon plain white flour
1 can (400 g/14 oz) chopped tomatoes
4 tablespoons dry red wine
1 tablespoon tomato puree
1 teaspoon dried mixed herbs

1. To make the sauce, peel or scrub and finely dice the carrot. Finely chop
the celery. Peel and chop the onion. Peel and finely chop the garlic. Put the
bacon on a chopping board and cut off the rinds, if necessary, then chop.

2. Heat the oil in a frying pan or saucepan with a tight-fitting lid over
a medium-high heat. Add the carrot, celery, onion and bacon and fry,
stirring occasionally, for about 8 minutes until the carrot is tender.

3. Add the garlic and minced beef, stirring to break up the mince.
Continue frying and stirring until the meat is no longer red. Sprinkle
over the flour and stir it in.

4. Add the tomatoes with the juice from the can, the wine, the tomato puree, the herbs and salt and pepper to taste and bring to the boil. Turn the heat to its lowest setting, partially cover the pan and leave the sauce to simmer for 20–25 minutes, stirring occasionally, until thick with very little liquid remaining.

5. Bring another large saucepan of salted water to the boil over a high heat. Stir in the pasta, return the water to the boil and continue boiling for 10–12 minutes, or according to the packet instructions, until the pasta is tender to the bite.

6. Set a colander or sieve in the sink and drain the pasta. Return the pasta to the un-rinsed pan and add the sauce. Use 2 forks to lift and toss the pasta with the sauce until it is coated. Serve with cheese for sprinkling over the top.

Leftovers
► Reheat any leftovers and spoon over Crispy Baked Potatoes (page 42).

VARIATIONS
► Add wiped and sliced chestnut or button mushrooms, or seeded and chopped red or green peppers, with the other vegetables in Step 2 of the master recipe.
► To bulk this out to make 3–4 servings, add a drained can (400 g/14 oz) of chickpeas or cannelloni beans about 5 minutes before the sauce finishes cooking.

Pasta with Tomatoes, Ricotta & Basil

MAKES **2 SERVINGS**
PREP TIME: **ABOUT 10 MINUTES, PLUS MARINATING**
COOKING TIME: **10–12 MINUTES**

SAVE THIS PASTA DISH FOR DURING THE HOT SUMMER MONTHS, WHEN TOMATOES HAVE
THEIR BEST FLAVOUR. PLAN AHEAD, HOWEVER, BECAUSE THE LONGER YOU CAN LEAVE THE
TOMATOES TO MARINATE IN STEP 1, THE BETTER: TWO HOURS IS IDEAL, BUT FIFTEEN
MINUTES IS BETTER THAN NOTHING IF THAT IS ALL THE TIME YOU HAVE.

2 or 3 tomatoes, depending on how large they are
1 large garlic clove
$^{1}/_{2}$ small bunch fresh basil
4 tablespoons olive oil
200 g/7 oz pasta shapes, such as short tubes or corkscrews,
    or spaghetti
125 g/4 oz ricotta cheese
Salt and pepper

1. Seed (see below) and coarsely chop the tomatoes, then put them in
a large bowl. Peel and crush the garlic clove and add to the tomato. Tear
the basil leaves into thin strips and add to the bowl along with the olive
oil. Gently stir together and leave to stand at room temperature for up
to 2 hours.

2. Bring a large saucepan of salted water to the boil over a high heat. Stir in
the pasta, return the water to the boil and continue boiling for 10–12 minutes,
or according to the packet instructions, until the pasta is tender to the bite.

3. Set a colander or sieve in the sink and drain the pasta. Return the
pasta to the un-rinsed pan. Add the tomato sauce and ricotta cheese
and gently toss together until the cheese starts to melt and the pasta
and other ingredients are mixed together.

VARIATIONS
▶ Add chopped, stoned olives with the sauce and ricotta cheese in
Step 3 of the master recipe above.
▶ Replace the basil with another fresh herb, such as parsley or thyme leaves.
▶ For a real gutsy flavour, mash 1 canned anchovy fillet and add it to the
sauce with 1 teaspoon of red-wine vinegar in Step 1.

SEEDING TOMATOES
Use a small knife to remove and discard the stem end of the tomato.
Cut it in half and use a small spoon to scoop out and discard the seeds.
Chop or slice the tomato flesh as the recipe specifies.

Pasta with Sausage Sauce

MAKES **2 SERVINGS**
PREP TIME: **ABOUT 10 MINUTES**
COOKING TIME: **ABOUT 20 MINUTES**

1 onion
1 garlic clove
2 pork sausages, such as Cumberland or Italian sweet sausages
2 tablespoons olive oil
$^1/_2$ tablespoon tomato puree
1 can (400 g/14 oz) chopped tomatoes
Pinch of sugar
200 g/7 oz dried pasta, such as macaroni or tubes
Salt and pepper
Grated Parmesan cheese, to serve

1. Peel and chop the onion. Peel and crush the garlic. Cut the sausages into bite-size pieces.

2. Heat the oil in a large frying pan over a medium heat. Add the onion and garlic and fry, stirring occasionally, for about 5 minutes until the onion is soft, but not brown. Stir in the tomato puree.

3. Add the tomatoes with the juice from the can, then the sugar and season with salt and pepper to taste. Bring to the boil, then lower the heat and simmer for about 15 minutes, stirring occasionally.

4. Meanwhile, bring a large saucepan of salted water to the boil over a high heat. Stir in the pasta, return the water to the boil and continue boiling for 10–12 minutes, or according to the packet instructions, until the pasta is tender to the bite.

5. Set a colander or sieve in the sink. Drain the pasta well. Add the pasta to the sausage sauce and stir together. Taste and adjust the seasoning, if necessary. Serve with grated cheese for sprinkling over the top.

VARIATIONS
► Bulk this out with 90 g/3 oz of fresh or frozen shelled peas. Add frozen peas straight from the freezer to the pasta cooking water after 5 minutes; add fresh peas after 8 minutes.
► If you have any red wine left in the bottom of a bottle, add it to the sauce in Step 2 when the onions are tender. Leave it to bubble before stirring in the tomato puree.

Spaghetti with Meatballs

 MAKES **4 SERVINGS, 12 MEATBALLS** PREP TIME: **ABOUT 20 MINUTES, PLUS MAKING THE SAUCE IF YOU ARE MAKING YOUR OWN** COOKING TIME: **30–40 MINUTES, DEPENDING ON HOW MANY BATCHES IT TAKES TO FRY THE MEATBALLS**

THIS IS ANOTHER PASTA DISH FOR WHEN YOU'RE IN THE MOOD TO SPEND A BIT OF TIME IN THE KITCHEN, SO IT'S WORTH MAKING DOUBLE QUANTITIES OF THE SAUCE AND MEATBALLS AND STORING THEM IN THE FRIDGE OR FREEZER. THAT WAY YOU'LL HAVE A SECOND, SPEEDY MEAL.

About 2 tablespoons olive oil
700 ml/23 fl oz tomato sauce, either home-made (page 48) or bottled
400 g/14 oz dried noodles, such as spaghetti or tagliatelle
Grated Parmesan cheese, to serve

FOR THE MEATBALLS:
2 onions
1 large garlic clove
600 g/20 oz lean minced beef
60 g/2 oz fresh white breadcrumbs (page 102)
1 large egg
4 tablespoons chopped fresh parsley, or 1 tablespoon dried thyme
Salt and pepper

1. If you are using home-made sauce, begin by making it with double the quantity of ingredients on page 48.

2. Meanwhile, make the meatballs. Peel and finely chop the onions. Peel and very finely chop the garlic clove.

3. Put the onions, garlic, minced beef, breadcrumbs, egg, parsley or thyme, and salt and pepper to taste in a bowl and use your hands to squeeze all the ingredients together until they are blended.

4. Slightly wet your hands and shape the meat mixture into 12 equal-size balls.

5. Heat 2 tablespoons of the oil in a large frying pan or saucepan with a tight-fitting lid over a medium-high heat. Add as many meatballs that fit in a loose single layer and fry, uncovered, until they are brown and crispy all over. (It is important not to overcrowd the pan, so work in batches, if necessary. As each batch is fried, transfer it to a plate lined with paper towels to drain. Add a little extra oil to the pan between batches, if necessary. Continue until all the meatballs are fried.)

6. When the meatballs are fried, pour off any excess oil in the pan. Return all the meatballs to the pan and stir in the sauce. Slowly bring to the boil, then lower the heat, cover the pan and leave the meatballs and sauce to simmer for 20 minutes. Remove one of the meatballs from the pan and cut in half to check that it is cooked through.

7. Meanwhile, bring another large saucepan of salted water to the boil over a high heat. Stir in the spaghetti, return the water to the boil and continue boiling for 10–12 minutes, or according to the packet instructions, until the pasta is tender to the bite.

8. Set a colander or sieve in the sink and drain the spaghetti. Divide the pasta between individual plates and top with the meatballs and sauce. Serve with grated cheese for sprinkling over the tops.

VARIATIONS
► Spice up the meatballs by adding dried chilli flakes or a pinch of cayenne pepper.
► To reduce the fat content of the dish, make the meatballs with half minced beef and half minced pork or chicken.

Meat Matters
► To determine how much seasoning the meatball mixture needs in Step 3 of the master recipe, fry a small piece and taste. This prevents you from eating raw meat.
► Wetting your hands in Step 4 stops the meatball mixture sticking to them.
► If you only have one pan and want to use a home-made sauce, put the raw meatballs in the fridge at the end of Step 4 until the sauce finishes simmering. Transfer the sauce to a bowl, then wash and dry the pan and proceed with the recipe. Keep the sauce and meatballs warm in a low oven while you boil the pasta.

Pasta with Broccoli and Anchovies

☐ ☐ ☐ ☐

MAKES **2 SERVINGS**
PREP TIME: **ABOUT 5 MINUTES**
COOKING TIME: **ABOUT 20 MINUTES**

THE ROBUST FLAVOURS IN THIS DISH, PACK QUITE A PUNCH! THE SMALL, ROUND
PASTA DISCS, CALLED ORECCHIETTES, OR 'LITTLE EARS', ARE SOLD AT SUPERMARKETS,
BUT IF YOU DON'T HAVE ANY USE MACARONI OR BOWS.

250 g/8 oz broccoli
2 large garlic cloves
$^1/_2$ can (50 g/$1^1/_2$ oz) anchovy fillets in oil
200 g/7 oz orecchiette or macaroni
2 tablespoons olive oil
60 g/2 oz Parmesan cheese
Salt and pepper

1. Bring a saucepan of salted water to the boil. Cut the broccoli florets
and stems into small, bite-size pieces. Peel and crush the garlic cloves.
Chop the anchovy fillets.

2. Add the broccoli pieces to the boiling water and return the water to
the boil. Continue boiling the broccoli for about 8 minutes until it is very
tender, but the florets aren't falling apart. Put a colander or sieve in the
sink and use a slotted spoon to transfer the broccoli to the sink to drain.

3. Return the broccoli-cooking water to the boil over a high heat. Stir
in the pasta, return the water to the boil and continue boiling for 10–12
minutes, or according to the packet instructions, until the pasta is
tender to the bite.

4. Meanwhile, heat the oil in a large frying pan or saucepan over a
medium heat. Add the garlic and stir it around for 2–3 minutes until
it is golden, but not brown.

5. Stir the anchovies into the pan with the garlic and mash them with
a wooden spoon or a fork until they break up into the oil.

6. Drain the pasta in the colander or sieve with the broccoli, shaking
to remove as much water as possible. Add the pasta and broccoli to the
pan with the anchovy-flavoured oil. Gently stir everything together.
Grate the cheese directly into the pan and stir again.

7. Season with pepper to taste – the anchovies and cheese are salty
so you won't need salt.

Pasta with Chickpeas & Pesto

MAKES **4 SERVINGS**
NO PREP TIME
COOKING TIME: **10–12 MINUTES**

HERE'S A SUPER-QUICK TASTE OF THE MEDITERRANEAN THAT MOSTLY COMES FROM
YOUR CUPBOARD – OR THE CORNER SHOP WHEN THE CUPBOARD IS BARE. IF YOU HAVE
ANY PARMESAN CHEESE IN THE FRIDGE, GRATE IT OVER THE DISH JUST BEFORE EATING,
BUT THIS IS FLAVOURSOME ENOUGH NOT TO NEED ANY.

200 g/7 oz pasta shapes, such as bows, corkscrews or radiators
1 can (400 g/14 oz) chickpeas
6 tablespoons bottled pesto sauce
Salt and pepper

1. Bring a large saucepan of salted water to the boil over a high heat.
Stir in the pasta, return the water to the boil and continue boiling for
10–12 minutes, or according to the packet instructions, until the pasta
is tender to the bite.

2. Meanwhile, place a colander or sieve in the sink, tip the can of
chickpeas into it and rinse them in cold water. Add the chickpeas
to the pasta after 8 minutes cooking to warm them through.

3. Drain the pasta and chickpeas, reserving about 2 tablespoons of
the water in the pan. Stir the pesto sauce into the pasta cooking water.

4. Return the pasta and chickpeas to the pan and quickly toss in the
sauce. Season with salt and pepper to taste.

Pasta with Puttanesca Sauce

☐ ☐ ☐ ☐   **SERVES 2** PREP TIME: **ABOUT 10 MINUTES**
COOKING TIME: **ABOUT 25 MINUTES, MOST OF WHICH
CAN BE DONE AHEAD**

WHEN YOU'RE FEELING DECADENT, OR IN THE MOOD FOR SEDUCTION, TRY THIS DISH
FROM NAPLES. LOCAL LEGENDS MAINTAIN THAT THE WOMEN OF THE NIGHT, LA PUTTANE,
SEDUCED THEIR CLIENTS WITH THIS SPICY DISH.

10 black olives
2 tinned anchovy fillets in oil, drained
   (see page 136 for storing leftover anchovy fillets)
1 small garlic clove
2 tablespoons olive oil
Small pinch of dried chilli flakes
$^1/_2$ tablespoon tomato puree
1 can (400 g / 14 oz) chopped tomatoes
Pinch of dried oregano, thyme or mixed herbs
2 teaspoons capers in brine, drained (optional)
200 g / 7 oz dried spaghetti or tagliatelle
Salt and pepper

1. Use a small knife to slice the olive flesh off the stones. Finely chop
the anchovies. Peel and chop the garlic clove.

2. Heat the oil in a large frying pan or saucepan over a medium heat.
Add the chilli flakes and garlic and stir around for 2–3 minutes until the
garlic is golden, but not brown. Add the anchovies and mash them with
a wooden spoon or fork.

3. Stir in the tomato puree, then add the tomatoes with the juice, the
olives, herbs and capers, if you are using. Bring to the boil, stirring.
Lower the heat and simmer, covered, for 20 minutes, stirring occasionally.

4. Meanwhile, bring a large saucepan of salted water to the boil over
a high heat. Stir in the pasta, return the water to the boil and continue
boiling for 10–12 minutes, or according to the packet instructions, until
the pasta is tender to the bite.

5. Place a colander or sieve in the sink and drain the pasta well. Add
the pasta to the pan with the sauce and toss together. Taste and adjust
the seasoning, if necessary.

Plan Ahead
You can make the sauce through to Step 3 in the master recipe in
advance. Store it in a tightly covered jar in the fridge for up to 2 days.
Reheat while the pasta boils.

Spaghetti with Fried Breadcrumbs

MAKES **2 SERVINGS**
PREPARATION TIME: **ABOUT 10 MINUTES**
COOKING TIME: **10–12 MINUTES**

WHEN YOU ARE FEELING REALLY BROKE, TAKE A TIP FROM FRUGAL SICILIAN COOKS
AND CONJURE UP THIS TASTY, FILLING MEAL FROM THE MOST MEAGRE INGREDIENTS.
YOU MIGHT BE SURPRISED HOW DELICIOUS THIS IS!

1 garlic clove
2 tablespoons olive oil
100 g/3½ oz breadcrumbs, ideally made from day-old bread
   (see page 102)
200 g/7 oz dried pasta, such as spaghetti, fettucine or tagliatelle
Salt and pepper

1. Bring a large saucepan of salted water to the boil over a high heat.
Stir in the pasta, return the water to the boil and continue boiling for
10–12 minutes, or according to the packet instructions, until the
pasta is tender to the bite.

2. Meanwhile, peel and very finely chop the garlic clove.

3. Heat the oil in a large frying pan or saucepan over a medium-high
heat. Add the garlic and stir around for 1 minute. Stir in the breadcrumbs
and stir them around for 8–10 minutes until they are toasted and crisp;
do not let them become too brown. Immediately tip the breadcrumbs
out of the pan onto a plate.

4. Place a colander or sieve in the sink and drain the pasta well. Divide
the pasta between serving plates and top with the breadcrumb mixture.
Season with salt and pepper to taste.

VARIATIONS
▸ Add chopped canned anchovy fillets with the garlic, and stir it around
until it starts to dissolve.
▸ Stir in chopped fresh herbs when the breadcrumbs are crisp.
▸ Grate fresh Parmesan or pecorino cheese over the breadcrumbs
just before serving.

Three-Cheese Macaroni

SERVES 2
PREP TIME: **ABOUT 8 MINUTES**
COOKING TIME: **10–12 MINUTES**

NOTHING LIGHT AND FROTHY ABOUT THIS. THIS IS COMFORT FOOD THAT FILLS YOU UP! AND THE ONE-STEP CHEESE SAUCE SAVES TIME. IF YOU ARE NOT IN A RUSH, TAKE A LOOK AT THE VARIATION RIGHT FOR A BAKED DISH WITH A GOLDEN BROWN TOP.

200 g/7 oz dried macaroni or other pasta shapes,
   such as bows, corkscrews or twists
60 g/2 oz mozzarella cheese, drained
60 g/ 2 oz Cheddar cheese
60 g/2 oz Emmental cheese
2 spring onions
125 ml/4 fl oz milk
3 tablespoons plain white flour
$^1/_2$ teaspoon English mustard powder
$^1/_2$ teaspoon dried thyme
Salt and pepper
Tomato ketchup, to serve

1. Bring a large saucepan of salted water to the boil over a high heat. Stir in the pasta, return the water to the boil and continue boiling for 10–12 minutes, or according to the packet instructions.

2. Meanwhile, chop the mozzarella cheese. Grate the Cheddar and Emmental cheeses on the coarse side of a grater. Finely chop the white and green parts of the spring onions.

3. Put all the cheeses, the spring onions, milk, flour, mustard powder, thyme and salt and pepper to taste in a saucepan over a medium-high heat and stir constantly until the cheeses melt and the sauce is blended. Do not boil the sauce.

4. Set a colander or sieve in the sink and drain the pasta. Add the hot pasta to the cheese sauce and stir around to mix together. Serve at once, while it is hot – you'll get lots of long strings from the mozzarella when you scoop up the pasta. (See the following variation if you would like a baked dish, which will take about 35 minutes longer.) Serve with ketchup.

VARIATIONS

▸ *Three-Cheese Macaroni Bake:* Heat the oven to 180°C/350°F/Gas 4. After the cheese sauce and pasta are combined in Step 4 of the master recipe, spoon it into an ovenproof dish and cover with a piece of kitchen foil, shiny side down. Bake for 20 minutes. Remove the foil and return the dish to the oven for 15 minutes longer, or until the top is golden brown and bubbling. Leave to stand for a few minutes before eating.

▸ For a non-vegetarian version of the master recipe or the baked variation above, add 100 g/3$\frac{1}{2}$ oz diced cooked ham with the other ingredients in Step 3.

▸ Other ingredients to add to the master recipe or baked variation above include 150 g/5 oz frozen peas straight from the freezer, 1 finely chopped red onion, chopped fresh parsley and/or chives, or sliced drained sun-dried tomatoes in oil.

Vegetable Lasagne

MAKES **4–6 SERVINGS** PREP TIME: **15–20 MINUTES,
PLUS MAKING THE SAUCE IF YOU ARE MAKING
YOUR OWN** COOKING TIME: **10–15 MINUTES**

ANOTHER CROWD-PLEASER THAT FILLS YOU UP FOR NOT A LOT OF CASH.

A TRADITIONAL ITALIAN LASAGNE CAN TAKE HOURS TO ASSEMBLE, BUT THIS SCALED-DOWN VERSION IS JUST AS SATISFYING.

THIS IS, HOWEVER, THE MOST TIME-CONSUMING RECIPE IN THE BOOK TO PREPARE, SO IT'S NOT A GOOD IDEA TO TACKLE THIS AFTER A LATE NIGHT AT THE PUB, OR WHEN YOU WANT TO HAVE A MEAL ON THE TABLE IN TWENTY MINUTES. (TRY SOME OF THE OTHER PASTA RECIPES IN THIS CHAPTER INSTEAD.) BUT, ONCE YOU'VE GOT THE LASAGNE ASSEMBLED, IT WILL BE PIPING HOT, BUBBLY AND GOLDEN WITHIN FIFTEEN MINUTES. SO PLAN AHEAD AND ASSEMBLE THE LASAGNE UP TO A DAY IN ADVANCE AND KEEP IT COVERED IN THE FRIDGE UNTIL YOU'RE READY TO POP IT IN THE OVEN. JUST REMEMBER TO HEAT THE OVEN IN ADVANCE, AND TAKE THE LASAGNE OUT OF THE FRIDGE ABOUT TWENTY MINUTES BEFORE YOU PUT IT IN THE OVEN TO BRING IT TO ROOM TEMPERATURE.

BE SURE TO READ THROUGH ALL THE STEPS BEFORE YOU BEGIN. AND DON'T LET THE LENGTH OF THIS RECIPE PUT YOU OFF GIVING IT A GO. IT LOOKS MUCH MORE COMPLICATED THAN IT IS – AND YOU CAN SAVE TIME BY USING BOTTLED TOMATO SAUCE.

Olive oil for the dish
700 ml/23 fl oz tomato sauce, either home-made (page 48) or bottled
1/2–1 tablespoon tomato puree (optional)
250 g/8 oz button or chestnut mushrooms, wiped
125 g/4 oz broccoli florets
2 courgettes, scrubbed
2 large garlic cloves (optional)
1 tablespoon dried basil (optional)
250 g/8 oz ricotta cheese
125 g/4 oz mozzarella cheese, drained
125 g/4 oz Parmesan cheese
Pinch of grated nutmeg
7 no-cook spinach or plain lasagne noodles
Salt and pepper

1. Heat the oven to 230°C/450°F/Gas 8. Lightly grease a 23 cm/9-inch square ovenproof dish that is about 5 cm/2 inches deep.

2. If you are using home-made sauce, begin by making it with double the quantity of ingredients on page 49. If the flavour isn't as gusty or robust as you like, stir in the tomato puree. If you are using bottled sauce, have a taste, because it might be flavourful enough that you don't need to add the extra garlic or the basil in Step 4.

3. Trim the mushroom stalks, if necessary, then thinly slice the caps. Cut the broccoli florets into small, bite-size pieces, then cut each in half lengthways. Cut the courgettes in half lengthways, then put each half, cut side down, on a chopping board and cut into 0.5 cm/$^1/_4$-inch slices. Peel and crush the garlic cloves, if you are using.

4. Add the mushrooms and courgettes, along with the garlic and basil, if using, to the tomato sauce in a saucepan over a medium heat. Bring to the boil, then lower the heat and simmer, stirring occasionally, for about 8 minutes until the courgettes and broccoli are tender, but still holding their shape with a little bite left.

5. Meanwhile, put the ricotta cheese in a bowl and beat until smooth. Cut the mozzarella into 0.5 cm/$^1/_4$-inch slices and then cut into 0.5 cm/$^1/_4$-inch dice. Add the mozzarella to the bowl with the ricotta. Grate the Parmesan into the bowl, setting aside about 2 tablespoons of the Parmesan that will be used for the topping. Stir the cheeses in the bowl together and season with nutmeg and salt and pepper to taste, but remember, the Parmesan is salty so add salt sparingly.

6. Spread 2 tablespoons of the tomato sauce over the base of the ovenproof dish, and set aside another 2 tablespoons that will be used for the topping. Top the sauce with 2 lasagne noodles, placed next to each other in the same direction, overlapping if necessary, so that they cover the base of the dish. Break one of the noodles into pieces to fill any gaps, if necessary.

7. Add half the cheese mixture, dropping it in small blobs and spreading it around with the back of the spoon. Top with half the tomato-and-vegetable sauce, spreading it around.

8. Top with 2 more lasagne noodles and fill any gaps, as in Step 6. Add the remaining cheese mixture, as in Step 7. Add the remaining half of the tomato-and-vegetable sauce, spreading it around.

9. Top with the final 2 lasagne noodles and fill any gaps, if necessary. Spread the reserved 2 tablespoons tomato-and-vegetable sauce over the top and sprinkle with the reserved 2 tablespoons grated Parmesan cheese.

10. Bake the lasagne for 15–20 minutes until hot, bubbling and golden brown. Leave to stand for 5 minutes, then cut into squares to serve.

Tuna-Noodle Bake

☐ ☐ ☐ ☐   MAKES **4–6 SERVINGS**
PREP TIME: **ABOUT 20 MINUTES, INCLUDING BOILING
THE PASTA** COOKING TIME: **20–25 MINUTES**

200 g/7 oz fettucini, spaghetti or tagliatelle
  – wholemeal is good for this
2 celery sticks
1 red pepper
1 green pepper
125 g/4 oz mature Cheddar cheese
1 can (400 g/14 oz) cream of mushroom soup
125 ml/4 fl oz milk
1 can (200 g/7 oz) tuna in brine, drained

1. Heat the oven to 220°C/425°F/Gas 7. Bring a large saucepan of salted water to the boil over a high heat. Stir in the pasta, return the water to the boil and continue boiling for 10–12 minutes, or according to the packet instructions, until the pasta is tender to the bite.

2. Meanwhile, finely slice the celery sticks. Core, seed and chop the peppers. Coarsely grate the cheese.

3. Put a colander or sieve in the sink and drain the pasta well. To save on washing-up use the same pan to make the sauce in. Tip the tin of soup into the pan over a medium heat. Stir in the milk, flake in the tuna and stir in the celery, peppers and half the cheese. Do not boil the sauce.

4. Return the pasta to the saucepan and stir until it and the vegetables are evenly distributed. Spoon this mixture into an ovenproof dish.

5. Sprinkle the remaining cheese over the top. Bake for 20–25 minutes until golden brown on top. Serve straight from the dish.

VARIATIONS
▸ Add whatever vegetables you have. Try finely chopped onion, drained sweet corn kernels or sliced sun-dried tomatoes. Or add 150 g/5 oz frozen peas straight from the freezer.

Rice-stuffed Peppers

MAKES **2 SERVINGS**
PREP TIME: **ABOUT 15 MINUTES, INCLUDING COOKING
THE RICE** COOKING TIME: **ABOUT 25 MINUTES**

100 g/3^1/$_2$ oz short-grain Italian rice, such as arborio or carnaroli
2 large green, orange, red or yellow peppers
1 onion
1 garlic clove
1 tablespoon olive oil, plus a little extra for drizzling
2 teaspoons tomato puree, dissolved in 2 tablespoons water
45 g/1^1/$_2$ oz raisins
2 tablespoons chopped fresh herbs, such as parsley,
    or 1 teaspoon dried mixed herbs or thyme
4 tablespoons fresh breadcrumbs (page 102)
2 tablespoons grated fresh Parmesan cheese
Salt and pepper

1. Heat the oven to 180°C/350°F/Gas 4 and grease a small ovenproof dish. Bring a small saucepan of salted water to the boil over a high heat. Stir in the rice and continue boiling for 10 minutes, or until the rice is tender.

2. Meanwhile, break the stalks off the peppers. Cut each pepper in half from top to bottom so you have 4 boat-shaped cups. Use a small, sharp knife to scrape out the cores and seeds; set aside. Peel and finely chop the onion. Peel and crush the garlic clove.

3. Place a sieve in the sink and drain the rice well, shaking off any excess water; set aside.

4. Heat the oil in the washed and dried saucepan over a medium heat. Add the onion and garlic and fry for about 5 minutes until the onion is soft, but not brown.

5. Stir in the tomato puree, cooked rice, raisins, herbs and salt and pepper to taste.

6. Spoon the stuffing into the pepper halves. Mix the breadcrumbs and Parmesan together, then sprinkle the crumb mixture over the top of the rice stuffing. Drizzle very lightly with a little olive oil.

7. Place the peppers in the dish and bake for 25 minutes, or until the peppers are tender and the topping is crisp. Eat hot or at room temperature.

Courgette & Sun-dried Tomato Risotto

MAKES **2 SERVINGS**
PREP TIME: **ABOUT 10 MINUTES**
COOKING TIME: **ABOUT 25 MINUTES**

RISOTTOS ARE CREAMY ITALIAN RICE DISHES THAT REALLY COME INTO THEIR OWN WHEN YOU WANT A CHEAP, FILLING MEAL. IN ITS MOST BASIC FORM, YOU CAN MAKE A PLAIN RISOTTO WITH JUST GRATED PARMESAN CHEESE ADDED (SEE RISOTTO IN BIANCO, RIGHT). ON THE OTHER HAND, RISOTTOS ARE GREAT VEHICLES FOR MAKING A MEAL OUT OF SMALL AMOUNTS OF VEGETABLES OR LEFTOVER COOKED CHICKEN, BEEF AND PORK.

TREAT THIS AS A MASTER RECIPE FOR THE PROPORTION OF RICE AND LIQUID, AND EXPERIMENT WITH THE FLAVOURS. IF YOU GET IN THE HABIT OF MAKING RISOTTO REGULARLY, THINK SERIOUSLY ABOUT KEEPING A SUPPLY OF HOME-MADE CHICKEN OR VEGETABLE STOCK (PAGES 51 AND 54) IN THE FREEZER. IT ADDS SUCH A BETTER FLAVOUR THAN USING STOCK CUBES. THESE QUANTITIES CAN BE DOUBLED OR TRIPLED. YOU NEED TWO SAUCEPANS TO MAKE A RISOTTO.

$^1/_2$ onion
1 courgette, rinsed
4–6 sun-dried tomatoes in oil, drained
750 ml/1$^1/_2$ pints vegetable stock, either home-made (page 54)
    or from a cube
2 tablespoons olive oil, or 2 tablespoons oil from the tomatoes
200 g/7 oz short-grain Italian rice, such as arborio or carnaroli
30 g/1 oz butter
30 g/1 oz Parmesan cheese, freshly grated
Salt and pepper

1. Peel and finely chop the onion. Cut off the courgette ends, then coarsely grate it without peeling. Thinly slice the sun-dried tomatoes.

2. Pour the stock into a small saucepan and heat until small bubbles appear around the edge. Leave it to simmer at the back of the hob.

3. Heat the oil in another saucepan over a medium heat. Add the onion and stir it around for 5 minutes until it is soft, but not brown. Add the rice and stir until all the grains are coated.

4. Add one ladleful of the simmering stock to rice and stir constantly until all the liquid is absorbed. Continue adding ladlefuls of stock after the previous one has been absorbed, stirring constantly, for about 20 minutes until all the stock is used, or the rice is creamy and tender when you bite a grain. (There aren't any shortcuts for this stage – if you want a good risotto, you have to stand at the hob and stir.)

5. Add the courgettes and sun-dried tomatoes with the last addition of stock and continue stirring until all the liquid is absorbed.

6. Stir in the butter and cheese, stirring until the butter melts. Add salt and pepper to taste, but remember the cheese is salty so you might not need much. Serve at once.

VARIATIONS
▸ *Lemon Risotto:* Replace 100 ml/3½ fl oz of the stock in the master recipe with freshly squeezed lemon juice and add it at the end of the cooking process. Add the finely grated rind of 2 lemons and 2 tablespoons chopped parsley with the butter in Step 6. Serve with grated Parmesan cheese for sprinkling over the top.
▸ *Risotto in Bianco:* The most basic, classic Italian risotto. Follow the master recipe left and above, but omit the courgette and sun-dried tomato. You can add butter in Step 6, as in the master recipe, or replace it with 2 tablespoons double cream. Serve at once, as risotto becomes stodgy if it is left to stand.

Cheese-stuffed Potatoes

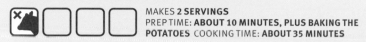

MAKES **2 SERVINGS**
PREP TIME: **ABOUT 10 MINUTES, PLUS BAKING THE
POTATOES** COOKING TIME: **ABOUT 35 MINUTES**

THIS IS NOT QUICK COOKING, BUT THE STUFFED POTATOES MAKE A VERY FILLING, CHEAP MEAL. TO SPEED THINGS UP, HOWEVER, THE POTATOES CAN BE BAKED AND STUFFED AND LEFT IN THE FRIDGE FOR UP TO A DAY, READY FOR REHEATING FOR A QUICK MEAL. SERVE THESE WITH A GREEN SALAD AND SLICED BAGUETTE FOR A VEGETARIAN MEAL.

THIS VERSION HAS A GREEK-FLAVOURED STUFFING WITH FETA CHEESE, BUT YOU CAN USE ANY FLAVOUR CHEESE YOU HAVE.

2 large floury potatoes,
  about 500 g/1 lb each, scrubbed
  (see Potato Primer 1, page 41)
Olive oil
Salt and pepper

FOR THE COURGETTE-FETA STUFFING:
$^1/_2$ courgette, rinsed
1 garlic clove
1 tablespoon olive oil
$^1/_3$ teaspoon dried oregano
125 g/4 oz feta cheese

1. Heat the oven to 230°C/450°F/Gas 8. Rub the potatoes with olive oil and salt, and bake as on page 43.

2. Meanwhile, prepare the vegetables for the stuffing. Cut the courgette into 0.5 cm/$^1/_4$-inch dice. Peel and crush the garlic clove.

3. When the potatoes are tender, remove them from the oven and reduce the temperature to 190°C/375°F/Gas 5.

4. As soon as the potatoes are cool enough to handle, slice each one in half lengthways. Use a spoon to scoop out the flesh, leaving a shell of about 0.5 cm/$^1/_4$ inch thick; set aside.

5. Heat the oil in a frying pan or saucepan over a high heat. Add the courgette and garlic and fry, stirring frequently, for about 4 minutes until the courgette is tender-crisp. Stir in the potato flesh and oregano and stir around until the potato is broken down. Crumble in the feta cheese. Season to taste with pepper, but remember the feta is salty so you might not need any extra salt.

6. Loosely spoon the stuffing into the potato shells, mounding it up. Put the stuffed potato halves on a baking sheet and bake for about 35 minutes until the filling is piping hot.

VARIATIONS

▶ For an all-British stuffing, replace the courgette, feta and oregano in the master recipe with 6 tablespoons each of grated Cheddar cheese and chopped cooked ham, and some chopped fresh parsley.
▶ Crumbled cooked bacon also makes a good stuffing with Cheddar cheese.

Fruity-Veg Couscous

MAKES **4 SERVINGS**
PREP TIME: **ABOUT 10 MINUTES**
COOKING TIME: **ABOUT 30 MINUTES**

THERE IS A TASTE OF THE MIDDLE EAST IN THIS SPICY, STEAMING FRUIT AND VEGETABLE STEW.

1 large onion
1 large garlic clove
1 large red pepper
1 large carrot
1 large courgette, rinsed
1 can (400 g/14 oz) chickpeas
2 tablespoons olive oil
1 teaspoon ground coriander
1 teaspoon ground cumin
1 teaspoon turmeric

Pinch of dried chilli flakes
1 can (400 g/14 oz) chopped tomatoes
60 g/2 oz dried apricots
60 g/2 oz dried figs
Handful of raisins
125 g/4 oz instant couscous
30 g/1 oz butter
Salt and pepper
Chopped fresh coriander, to serve (optional)

1. Peel and chop the onion. Peel and crush the garlic. Core, seed and slice the pepper. Scrub or peel and cut the carrot into thick slices. Cut the courgette in half lengthways, then put each half, cut side down, on a chopping board and cut into 0.5 cm/¼-inch slices.

2. Place a sieve in the sink, tip in the can of chickpeas and rinse under cold water; set aside.

3. Heat the oil in a large frying pan or saucepan over a medium heat. Add the onion, garlic, coriander, cumin, turmeric and chilli flakes, and fry, stirring often, for about 5 minutes until the onion is soft.

4. Stir in the tomatoes with the juice from the can, the chickpeas and the dried fruit. Bring to the boil, stirring, then lower the heat and leave to simmer, partially covered, for 20–25 minutes until the carrots are tender. Add salt and pepper to taste.

5. Meanwhile, bring a kettle or small saucepan of water to the boil. Put the couscous in a heatproof bowl and stir in ½ teaspoon of salt. Pour just enough boiling water over to cover the couscous. Cover the bowl with a folded tea towel and leave to stand for about 10 minutes until all the liquid is absorbed and the grains are tender.

6. Stir the butter into the couscous and fluff up the grains with a fork. Serve the couscous in bowls with the fruit and vegetables and lots of the broth. Sprinkle with coriander, if you have any.

Spaghetti with Rocket

MAKES **2 SERVINGS**
PREP TIME: **LESS THAN 5 MINUTES**
COOKING TIME: **10–12 MINUTES**

FOR ITALIAN STUDENTS, SIMPLE, QUICK PASTA DISHES LIKE THIS ARE SECOND-NATURE. YOU'LL FIND BUNCHES OF PEPPERY-TASTING ROCKET IN THE SUPERMARKET, BUT BABY SPINACH LEAVES MAKE A GOOD SUBSTITUTE. OR TRY WATERCRESS, BUT BE PREPARED TO SPEND TIME PICKING THE LEAVES OFF THE STALKS. YOU CAN SPRINKLE GRATED PARMESAN CHEESE OVER JUST BEFORE COOKING, BUT IT'S NOT TRADITIONAL.

200 g/7 oz dried spaghetti
250 g/9 oz fresh rocket, about 2 bunches
2 large garlic cloves
2–3 tablespoons olive oil
Pinch dried chilli flakes
Salt and pepper

1. Bring a large saucepan of salted water to the boil over a high heat. Stir in the pasta, return the water to the boil and continue boiling for 10–12 minutes, or according to the packet instructions, until the pasta is tender to the bite.

2. In the meanwhile, remove the rocket leaves from the stalks; set aside. Peel and very finely chop the garlic.

3. Heat 2 tablespoons oil in a large frying pan or saucepan over a high heat. Add the chopped garlic and stir around for about 1 minute, but watch carefully so it doesn't burn. Remove the pan from the heat. Stir in the chilli flakes.

4. Just before the pasta finishes cooking, add the rocket leaves to the boiling water and stir around until they are wilted.

5. Set a colander or sieve in the sink and drain the pasta and rocket, shaking the colander well to remove the excess water. Tip the pasta into a bowl and immediately add the hot oil. Use 2 forks to toss all the ingredients together, adding a little extra oil if the pasta seems dry. Add salt and pepper to taste and toss again.

Pasta with Gorgonzola

MAKES **2 SERVINGS, OR 3–4 FIRST-COURSE SERVINGS**
PREP TIME: **LESS THAN 5 MINUTES**
COOKING TIME: **10–12 MINUTES**

THIS IS TOO CALORIFIC TO EAT EVERY DAY BUT IS UNBEATABLE WHEN YOU NEED COMFORT
FOOD. IT IS ALSO GOOD TO SERVE AS A FIRST COURSE BEFORE A PLAIN DISH, SUCH AS
ROAST CHICKEN.
THIS RECIPE ONLY USES A SMALL ABOUT OF FRESH SAGE OR PARSLEY LEAVES, BUT IT IS
WORTH BUYING SOME – LOOK FOR THEM IN THE SUPERMARKET AT THE END OF THE DAY
WHEN PERISHABLE FOOD IS BEING REDUCED.

250 g/9 oz pasta shells or twists
250 g/9 oz Gorgonzola cheese
100 g/3¹/₂ oz shelled walnuts
Several sprigs fresh sage or parsley (optional)
25 g/1 oz butter
200 g/7 oz ricotta cheese
3–4 tablespoons milk
Salt and pepper

1. Bring a large saucepan of salted water to the boil over a high heat. Stir
in the pasta, return the water to the boil and continue boiling for 10–12
minutes, or according to the packet instructions, until the pasta is tender
to the bite.

2. Meanwhile, cut the rind off the Gorgonzola cheese. Cut the cheese
into small pieces, put in a bowl and use a fork to mash; set aside. Finely
chop the walnuts with a knife – don't do this in a blender or food
processor because they will be too fine. If you are using the fresh herb
leaves, finely shred them.

3. Melt the butter in a large saucepan over a medium heat. Remove the
pan from the heat and stir in the ricotta cheese. Return the pan to a low
heat, add the mashed Gorgonzola cheese and stir. Add just enough milk
to make a smooth, creamy sauce. Add pepper and taste – the cheese is
salty, so it probably won't need much.

4. Set a colander or sieve in the sink and drain the pasta, shaking well to
remove any water trapped inside the shells. Add the hot pasta to the
sauce and stir, then stir in the walnuts and herbs, if using. Serve at once.

POSITIVE PROTEINS

Your body can't thrive on a steady diet of fast food and lager. You won't feel good and you won't look good unless you get a daily dose of protein.

Protein is a vital nutrient because it contains essential amino acids that are necessary for every bodily function. They are what keep your skin, hair, teeth and nails looking great. And, if you want to get noticed, it's protein that will help you look healthy.

There are two kinds of proteins: complete and incomplete. The best complete protein comes from animal products. Good sources include lean meat, chicken, milk, eggs and dairy products, such as cheese and yogurt. In this chapter you'll find favourite student standbys of Chilli con Carne, Curried Mince and Shepherd's Pie – inexpensive and high in protein.

Incomplete proteins come from vegetable sources, such as pulses (dried beans and peas), nuts and seeds, and other vegetables. None of these, however, contain all the essential amino acids you need. But when you eat a combination of these foods they make a complete protein. Examples of this include Red Beans & Rice and Dahl with Chapatis, both of which combine a pulse with grain.

The amount of protein your body needs to keep functioning in top form, however, is a modest amount of your overall diet. So team the recipes in this chapter with plenty of vegetables and carbohydrates, such as rice and whole grains.

Other protein-rich dishes to try:
- ► Beef in Beer (page 201)
- ► Belly of Pork with Cider (page 169)
- ► Chicken & Veg Parcels (page 192)
- ► Curried Lentil Soup (page 116) with bread
- ► Garlic Chicken with Roast Veg (page 197)
- ► Hummus (page 88)
- ► Lamb Shanks with Dried Fruit (page 171)
- ► Mary's Beef & Mushroom Casserole (page 175)
- ► Spaghetti with Meatballs (page 130)
- ► Poached Fish in Green Broth (page 199)
- ► Stir-fried Beef with Broccoli & Mangetouts (page 184)
- ► Stir-fried Chicken & Bean Sprouts (page 180)
- ► Stir-fried Ginger Pork (page 183)

Chicken with Rice & Peppers

MAKES **2–4 SERVINGS**
PREP TIME: **ABOUT 10 MINUTES**
COOKING TIME: **ABOUT 30 MINUTES**

WHEN IT'S YOUR TURN TO COOK FOR ALL THE FLAT- OR HOUSEMATES, THIS IS A DISH
YOU CAN'T BEAT. IT'S QUICK, IT'S EASY AND, BEST OF ALL, IT'S A WHOLE MEAL MADE IN
ONE PAN, SO THERE IS HARDLY ANY WASHING-UP. IF YOU WANT ANYTHING EXTRA, TOSS
UP A MIXED GREEN SALAD.

IT'S EASY TO DOUBLE OR TRIPLE THIS RECIPE. JUST MAKE SURE THERE IS ENOUGH
LIQUID TO COVER THE RICE IN STEP 5.

60 g/2 oz button or chestnut mushrooms, wiped
1 garlic clove
$^1/_2$ onion
$^1/_2$ red pepper
$^1/_2$ green pepper
4 chicken thighs on the bone
2 tablespoons olive or sunflower oil
1 bay leaf (optional)
4 tablespoons dry white wine
125 g/4 oz long-grain rice
250 ml/8 fl oz chicken stock, home-made (page 51)
    or from a cube
Salt and pepper

1. Cut off the mushroom stalks, if necessary, then slice the caps. Peel
and chop the garlic. Peel and chop the onion. Remove the cores and
seeds from the pepper halves, then finely chop each one. Sprinkle the
chicken thighs with salt and pepper to taste.

2. Heat the oil in a flameproof casserole or large frying pan with a tight-
fitting lid over a medium-high heat. Add the chicken thighs, skin sides
down, and leave to fry for 5 minutes, or until the skins are crisp. Remove
all but 1 tablespoon of the fat from the pan.

3. Turn the chicken thighs skin side up. Scatter the mushrooms, garlic,
onion and pepper pieces between the chicken thighs. Add the bay leaf,
if you are using one, and continue frying for 5 minutes longer.

4. Pour in the wine and let it bubble until it almost evaporates. Add
the rice and stir it around so it doesn't rest on top of the chicken pieces.
Add the chicken stock and bring to the boil. Turn the heat to its lowest
setting, cover the pan tightly and leave to simmer for 20 minutes,
without lifting the lid, or until the rice is tender and the chicken is cooked
through, and the juices run clear when you pierce with the tip of a knife.
Add salt and pepper to taste and serve straight from the pan.

▸ The white wine is a good way to use up any leftover wine. If you don't have any, however, just add an extra 4 tablespoons stock or water.
▸ Boneless chicken breasts also work well in this dish, but are more expensive than thighs.

Cut the Fat
Remove the skin from the chicken thighs before you fry them to reduce the overall fat content of the dish.

One-pot Creamy Chicken

MAKES **2 SERVINGS**
PREP TIME: **LESS THAN 5 MINUTES**
COOKING TIME: **ABOUT 25 MINUTES**

THERE IS NO SUCH THING AS 'CAN'T COOK, WON'T COOK'. THIS IS LITERALLY AS EASY AS OPENING A CAN, BUT NO ONE WILL SUSPECT YOU'VE GONE TO SO LITTLE TROUBLE. IN FACT, BE PREPARED TO ACCEPT COMPLIMENTS FOR MASTERING WHAT IS ASSUMED TO BE A COMPLICATED SAUCE RECIPE. OVEN-BAKED CHIPS (PAGE 44) OR SPINACH & CHICKPEAS (PAGE 210) GO WELL WITH THIS.

4 chicken thighs on the bone
1 tablespoon sunflower or olive oil
1 can (400 g/14 oz) cream of mushroom soup
125 ml/4 fl oz water
Salt and pepper
Chopped fresh parsley, to serve (optional)

1. Season the chicken thighs with salt and pepper.

2. Heat the oil in a flameproof casserole or large frying pan with a tight-fitting lid over a medium-high heat. Add the chicken thighs, skin sides down, and fry for about 5 minutes until golden and crisp.

3. Turn the chicken thighs skin side up. Stir the soup and water into the pan and bring to the boil. Turn the heat to its lowest setting, cover the pan and simmer for 20 minutes, or until the chicken juices run clear when a piece is pierced with the tip of a knife. Sprinkle with the chopped parsley, if you have any.

VARIATION
▸ Ring the changes by using other soups, such as cream of asparagus or cream of chicken.

Chicken & Cauliflower Curry

MAKES **2 SERVINGS**
PREP TIME: **ABOUT 10 MINUTES**
COOKING TIME: **ABOUT 20 MINUTES**

THIS IS PROBABLY AS QUICK AS WALKING DOWN TO THE LOCAL CURRY HOUSE – AND CERTAINLY A WHOLE LOT CHEAPER! BUY NAANS OR CHAPATIS FROM THE SUPERMARKET AND MAKE RICE (PAGES 47 AND 48) AND YOU'LL HAVE AN INDIAN MEAL AS GOOD AS A TAKE-AWAY. WASH THIS DOWN WITH A CHILLED LAGER OR COOLING LASSI (PAGE 83).

1 small onion
About 300 g/10 oz cauliflower
2 chicken thighs
1^1/$_2$ tablespoons sunflower oil
2 teaspoons cumin seeds
1 teaspoon mild to hot curry
   powder, to taste

1 can (400 g/14 oz) chopped tomatoes
Lemon juice
Salt and pepper
Chopped fresh coriander, to serve
   (optional)

1. Finely chop the onion and cut the cauliflower into small, bite-size florets. Remove the skin and any bones from the chicken thighs, then cut the flesh into 1 cm/^{1}/$_2$-inch pieces.

2. Heat the oil in a large frying pan or saucepan with a tight-fitting lid over a medium-high heat. Add the onion and fry, stirring occasionally, for 5–7 minutes until it starts to brown. Stir in the cumin seeds and curry powder and continue frying until the seeds brown and give off their aroma.

3. Add the cauliflower florets and stir them around for about a minute. Stir in the tomatoes with the juice from the can and season with salt and pepper to taste. Turn the heat to its lowest setting, cover the pan and simmer for about 10 minutes, stirring occasionally.

4. Stir in the chicken pieces, re-cover the pan and continue simmering for about 8 minutes longer until the chicken is cooked through and the juices run clear when you pierce them with the tip of a knife. (If the sauce seems too runny, remove the chicken pieces and keep them warm, then boil the juices until they are reduced. Return the chicken to the pan.)

5. Add lemon juice and salt and pepper to taste. Sprinkle with coriander to serve, if you have any.

VARIATIONS

► For a vegetarian version, replace the chicken with 300 g/10 oz scrubbed new potatoes, cut into 1 cm/^{1}/$_4$-inch cubes.
► To bulk this out, add 1 cubed aubergine with the tomatoes.
► Replace the cauliflower with sliced green beans or broccoli florets.
► You can also add a drained and rinsed can (400 g/14 oz) of chickpeas.

Shepherd's Pie

☐ ☐ ☐ ☐ MAKES **4–6 SERVINGS**
PREP TIME: **ABOUT 15 MINUTES, PLUS MAKING THE MASH** COOKING TIME: **ABOUT 45 MINUTES**

WHEN A BUNCH OF CARNIVORES IS COMING FOR A MEAL, THIS IS THE ULTIMATE. IT IS A TRADITIONAL WAY FOR USING UP LEFTOVER ROAST BEEF, BUT AS YOU ARE UNLIKELY TO HAVE A LEFTOVER ROAST JOINT, HERE'S A RECIPE FOR MAKING A MEAL-IN-A-DISH WITH MINCE. WHAT'S MORE, IT'S NOT EXPENSIVE TO MAKE A LARGE AMOUNT, SO THERE IS PLENTY FOR SECONDS ALL AROUND.

IF YOU WANT TO CUT DOWN ON THE PREPARATION TIME, MAKE THE MASH TOPPING UP TO TWO DAYS IN ADVANCE AND KEEP IT COVERED IN THE FRIDGE.

Double quantity Creamy Mash (page 40)
1 large onion
250 g/8 oz button, chestnut or large flat mushrooms, wiped
2 tablespoons sunflower oil
750 g/1^{1}/$_{2}$ lb lean minced beef
250 ml/8fl oz fresh, bought beef stock, or from a cube
Large pinch dried thyme (optional)
Large knob of butter
Salt and pepper

1. Begin by preparing the Creamy Mash, using double the quantity of ingredients on page 40. Set aside until required.

2. When you are ready to cook, heat the oven to 180°C/350°F/Gas 4. Lightly grease a large ovenproof dish. Peel and chop the onion. Remove the stalks from the mushrooms and thickly slice the caps.

3. Heat the oil in a large flameproof casserole or saucepan over a medium heat. Add the onion and fry for about 5 minutes until it is soft, but not brown. Add the mushrooms and fry for 1 minute longer.

4. Stir in the mince and continue frying until it turns brown, breaking up the meat as it fries.

5. Stir in the beef stock, the thyme, if using, and salt and pepper to taste, and bring to the boil.

6. Transfer the mince mixture to the ovenproof dish. Top with the mashed potatoes and spread them out to cover the surface. (Use the round tip of an upturned spoon to make a 'scalloped' pattern over the top, if you want an attractive appearance.)

7. Dot dabs of butter over the surface of the mash. Bake for 45 minutes, or until the filling is piping hot and the topping is lightly golden.

Curried Mince

ANOTHER TAKE-AWAY CHALLENGE – YOU'LL WIN HANDS DOWN WITH THIS RECIPE. THIS IS SPICY, SO MAKE A COOLING RAITA (OPPOSITE) TO CUT THROUGH THE HEAT. SERVE WITH BOILED RICE (PAGE 46) AND, IF YOU'RE TEMPTED TO TRY A LAGER-FREE INDIAN MEAL, DRINK LASSI (PAGE 83). INDIANS OFTEN SERVE LASSI, A SIMPLE YOGURT DRINK, WITH SPICY MEALS – IT HAS THE SAME COOLING AFFECT AS RAITA.

THIS RECIPE MAKES TWO SERVINGS, BUT THE QUANTITIES CAN EASILY BE DOUBLED OR TRIPLED TO FEED A CROWD.

1 tomato
$^1/_2$ onion
1 garlic clove
0.5 cm/$^1/_4$-inch piece fresh root ginger
2 tablespoons sunflower oil
1 teaspoon cumin seeds
1 bay leaf
$^1/_2$ teaspoon garam masala
$^1/_2$ tablespoon ground coriander
Large pinch of cayenne pepper, or to taste
Large pinch of ground turmeric (optional)
350 g/12 oz lean minced beef
Salt and pepper
Chopped fresh coriander or parsley, to serve (optional)

1. Finely chop the tomato, removing the seeds, if you want (see Seeding Tomatoes, page 131). Peel and grate the onion on the coarse side of a grater. Peel and crush the garlic clove. Peel and finely chop the ginger.

2. Heat a wok or large frying pan over a high heat. Add the oil and swirl it around. Add the cumin seeds and stir-fry for about 30 seconds until they start to jump.

3. Stir in the onion, garlic, ginger, bay leaf and garam masala, and continue stir-frying until the fat separates.

4. Add the tomato and stir-fry for 1 minute. Stir in the ground coriander, cayenne, turmeric, if you are using, and $^1/_2$ teaspoon each of salt and pepper to taste.

5. Stir in the mince and continue stir-frying until it becomes brown, breaking up the meat as you stir. Lower the heat and simmer, stirring occasionally, for 20 minutes. Serve sprinkled with fresh coriander or parsley, if you have any.

VARIATION
▸ Bulk this out by adding 150 g/5 oz of frozen peas straight from the freezer with the tomato in Step 4.

Leftovers
▸ *Chapati Wrap:* Buy chapatis at the supermarket or an Indian food shop. Heat the grill to high. Sprinkle a chapati with a little water and grill for 2–3 minutes on each side until softened. Spoon the leftover curried mince on half a chapati, add a dollop of Greek-style or natural yogurt and wrap up.
▸ Serve spooned over Crispy Baked Potatoes (page 42).

Cooling Raita
Grate $^1/_2$ a cucumber into a bowl, then use you hands to squeeze out all the excess water; set the cucumber aside. Tip 250–300 g/8–10 oz of Greek-style or natural yogurt into a bowl and beat in $^1/_3$ teaspoon of ground cumin, a pinch of sugar, a pinch of cayenne pepper and salt to taste. Stir in the cucumber, cover and chill until required. To serve, dust with a little extra ground cumin and sprinkle with chopped coriander, if you have any.

Chilli con Carne

MAKES **4 SERVINGS**
PREP TIME: **ABOUT 10 MINUTES**
COOKING TIME: **20–25 MINUTES**

WHEN THE PRESSURE IS ON WITH COURSEWORK OR APPROACHING EXAMS, A LARGE POT OF CHILLI IN THE FRIDGE CAN KEEP YOU GOING FOR A COUPLE OF DAYS. IT REHEATS IN A FLASH, AND CAN BE WRAPPED IN A FLOUR TORTILLA FOR A QUICK MEAL ON THE GO, USED TO TOP A CRISPY BAKED POTATO (PAGE 42), OR SERVED PIPING HOT WITH GRATED CHEESE OR A DOLLOP OF SOURED CREAM. (LEAVE ANY LEFTOVERS TO COOL COMPLETELY BEFORE YOU PUT THEM IN THE FRIDGE.) IN FACT, CHILLI IS ONE OF THE DISHES THAT TASTE BEST WHEN IT IS MADE A DAY IN ADVANCE AND REHEATED.

OR MAKE A REALLY BIG POT OF THIS FOR AN ECONOMICAL MEAL WHEN A GANG OF FRIENDS COME ROUND. A VEGETARIAN VERSION IS GIVEN ON PAGE 159.

2 large garlic cloves	1 teaspoon ground cumin
1 large onion	1 teaspoon dried oregano or thyme
1 red pepper	750 g/1$^1/_2$ lb lean ground beef
1 green pepper	1 can (400g /14 oz) red kidney beans
1 fresh red chilli	1 can (400 g/14 oz) chopped tomatoes
2 tablespoons sunflower oil	Salt and pepper

1. Peel and finely chop the garlic cloves. Peel and chop the onion. Core, seed and chop the red and green peppers. Seed and finely chop the chilli (page 189).

2. Heat the oil in a large frying pan or flameproof casserole over a medium-high heat. Add the garlic, onion, peppers and chilli, and fry, stirring frequently, for about 5 minutes until the vegetables are soft, but not brown.

3. Stir in the cumin and oregano or thyme. Add the beef and continue frying, using the spoon to break up the meat, until it changes colour and loses its redness.

4. Meanwhile, place a colander or sieve in the sink. Tip in the kidney beans and rinse with cold water. Add the kidney beans to the meat, along with the tomatoes and the juice in the can, and bring to the boil, stirring. Lower the heat, cover the pan and leave to simmer for 15–20 minutes until the beef is cooked through and the flavours blend. Add salt and pepper to taste.

Leftovers
▶ *Chilli Tacos:* You'll find crisp corn taco shells in supermarkets with other Tex-Mex or Mexican ingredients or health food shops. Reheat the taco shells according to the packet instructions, then fill with shredded Iceberg lettuce and leftover chilli con carne. Top with soured cream.

VARIATIONS
▶ *Vegetarian Chilli:* Replace the meat in the master recipe above with an extra can of red kidney beans and 1 can (400 g/14 oz) of cannelloni beans or chickpeas. (Rinse the extra beans under cold water before you add them to the other ingredients.) Serve with Boiled Rice (page 46) for a complete vegetarian protein.
▶ Chilli is traditionally served with boiled rice, but it also tastes good spooned over hot, freshly boiled spaghetti, or other pasta.
▶ If you don't have a fresh red chilli, use 2 teaspoons of cayenne pepper, or to taste.
▶ Untraditional ingredients to add in Step 4 include drained canned sweet corn kernels, grated carrots and fresh or frozen peas.

Cola-Glazed Pork

MAKES **2 SERVINGS** PREP TIME: **LESS THAN 5 MINUTES**
COOKING TIME: **10–12 MINUTES, DEPENDING ON THE
THICKNESS OF THE CHOPS**

NO DOUBT YOU CAN REMEMBER THE CHILDHOOD EXPERIMENTS OF LEAVING A NAIL
TO CORRODE IN A JAR OF CARBONATED COLA DRINK. SO, EVEN IF YOU KNOW DRINKING
CARBONATED COLAS ON A REGULAR BASIS ISN'T RECOMMENDED AS PART OF A HEALTHY
DIET, YOU MIGHT BE SURPRISED HOW USEFUL COLAS CAN BE IN COOKING. THESE CHOPS
TASTE LIKE THEY'VE BEEN BARBECUED, WITHOUT THE HASSLE OF LIGHTING COALS.

THE COLA SAUCE IS RICH AND FILLING, SO KEEP ANY VEGETABLES PLAIN – BOILED
NEW POTATOES OR STEAMED BROCCOLI OR CARROTS. IF YOU WANT REAL COMFORT FOOD,
TRY THIS WITH CREAMY MASH (PAGE 40).

2 tablespoons dark-brown sugar
2 tablespoons tomato ketchup
1 tablespoon English, Dijon or wholegrain mustard
6 tablespoons carbonated cola drink – go ahead, drink the rest!
Sunflower oil
2 large boneless pork loin chops or leg steaks,
 each about 1 cm/¹/₂ inch thick
Salt and pepper

1. Stir the sugar, ketchup and mustard together in a small bowl. Add the
cola, stirring to dissolve the sugar. (The mixture will fizz up and splash
when you add the cola.)

2. Heat a large frying pan with a lid over a medium-high heat until you
can feel the heat rising from the surface. Very lightly brush one side of
each piece of pork with oil. Put the pork, oiled sides down, into the pan
and fry for about 2 minutes.

3. Lightly oil the top of each piece of pork and season with salt and
pepper to taste. Turn the pork over and fry for 2 minutes longer until
golden brown.

4. Carefully pour the sauce into the pan – it will bubble up and sputter.
Turn the heat to its lowest setting, cover the pan and leave the pork to
cook for 6–8 minutes until both pieces are cooked through and the
juices run clear if you pierce one with the tip of a knife.

5. If the sauce is still very liquid, remove the pork from the pan and keep
warm. Increase the heat to high and bring the sauce to the boil, stirring,
until it reduces and thickens. Add salt and pepper to taste, then spoon
the cola sauce over the pork.

Sausages with Lentils

☐☐☐☐ MAKES **2 SERVINGS**
PREP TIME: **ABOUT 5 MINUTES**
COOKING TIME: **30–35 MINUTES**

BUY GREEN-GREY LENTILS FOR THIS, BECAUSE THEY HOLD THEIR SHAPE DURING COOKING.
IF YOU ONLY HAVE RED OR YELLOW LENTILS IN THE CUPBOARD, TRY DHAL WITH CHAPATIS
(PAGE 163) INSTEAD.

1–2 large garlic cloves
1 onion
Sunflower oil
4 sausages, such as Cumberland
150 g/5 oz green lentils

500 ml/16 fl oz vegetable stock,
   home-made (page 54) or from a cube
Salt and pepper
Chopped fresh parsley, to serve (optional)
Balsamic vinegar, to serve (optional)

1. Peel and crush the garlic cloves. Peel and chop the onion.

2. Coat the base of your frying pan with a small amount of oil and put
over a medium heat. Prick each sausage in a couple places with a fork.
Add the sausages to the pan and fry, shaking the pan occasionally, for
6–10 minutes until the skins are brown all over and the juices run clear
when you pierce one with a knife: the exact cooking time will depend on
the thickness of the sausages. Remove the sausages from the pan and
set aside; leave the sausage fat in the pan.

3. Add the garlic and onion to the pan and fry, stirring occasionally, for
5 minutes, or until the onion is soft, but not brown. Stir in the lentils and
stock. Return the sausages to the pan and bring the stock to the boil.
Lower the heat, cover the pan and leave the lentils to simmer for
20–25 minutes until they are tender.

4. Season to taste with salt and pepper. Stir in the parsley, if you have
any. Add a splash of balsamic vinegar over each portion, if you have any.
It tastes great with this.

Leftovers
▸ *Lentil & Sausage Salad:* Leave any leftover lentils and sausages to
cool completely. Cut the sausages into bite-size pieces and stir them
through the lentils. Add 2 drained and chopped canned anchovy fillets
and 1 or 2 finely chopped Hard-boiled Eggs (page 35). Splash with
home-made Vinaigrette (page 55) or bottled salad dressing and gently
stir together.

COOK'S TIP
WHENEVER YOU COOK PULSES, SUCH AS LENTILS, DO NOT ADD SALT UNTIL THEY HAVE
BECOME TENDER. IF YOU SEASON THEM WHILE THEY COOK, THE SALT WILL DRAW OUT
MOISTURE, MAKING THE TEXTURE TOUGH.

Red Beans & Rice

MAKES **2 SERVINGS**
PREP TIME: **ABOUT 10 MINUTES**
COOKING TIME: **ABOUT 20 MINUTES**

IN THE SOUTHERN AMERICAN STATES, RED BEANS & RICE, FLAVOURED WITH HAM HOCKS, IS TRADITIONALLY SERVED ON NEW YEAR'S DAY IN THE BELIEF IT WILL BRING GOOD LUCK FOR THE FOLLOWING YEAR – PERHAPS YOU SHOULD GIVE THIS RECIPE A GO BEFORE EXAMS.

THIS IS AN INEXPENSIVE VEGETARIAN VERSION OF THE AMERICAN DISH, IN WHICH THE BEANS AND RICE COMBINE TO MAKE A COMPLETE PROTEIN. IF YOU'RE A MEAT-EATER, HOWEVER, TAKE A LOOK AT THE VARIATION BELOW.

1 can (400 g/14 oz) red kidney beans
2 celery sticks
1–2 garlic cloves, to taste
1 green pepper
1 onion
6 sun-dried tomatoes in oil, drained
$1^{1}/_{2}$ tablespoons sunflower oil
125 g/4 oz long-grain rice
250 ml/8 fl oz vegetable stock, home-made (page 54) or from a cube
Pinch of cayenne pepper
Salt and pepper

1. Place a colander or sieve in the sink. Tip in the can of beans and rinse with cold water; set aside to drain.

2. Thinly chop the celery sticks. Peel and crush the garlic cloves. Core, seed and finely chop the pepper. Peel and chop the onion. Thinly slice the sun-dried tomatoes.

3. Heat the oil in a large frying pan or saucepan with a tight-fitting lid over a medium-high heat. Add the celery, garlic, pepper and onion and fry for about 5 minutes until the vegetables are soft, but not brown. Stir in the sun-dried tomatoes.

4. Add the rice and stir until the grains are coated. Pour in the stock, stir in cayenne and salt to taste and bring to the boil, without stirring.

5. Turn the heat to the lowest setting, cover the pan tightly and leave the rice and beans to simmer, without lifting the lid, for 20 minutes. Remove the pan from the heat and set it aside to stand for 5 minutes, still covered. Uncover the pan and use a fork to fluff up the rice.

VARIATIONS

▶ For a meat-based version, fry 2–4 rashers of streaky smoked bacon in the pan at the beginning of Step 3 in the master recipe above, without any extra oil. When the bacon is cooked through, but not crisp, remove it from the pan and cut it into bite-size pieces. Fry the vegetables in the bacon fat, adding an extra tablespoon of oil, if necessary. Continue with the master recipe as above.

▶ Replace the kidney beans with other canned pulses, such as adzuki beans, black beans, butter beans, cannelloni beans or chickpeas.

Dhal with Chapatis

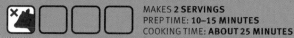

MAKES **2 SERVINGS**
PREP TIME: **10–15 MINUTES**
COOKING TIME: **ABOUT 25 MINUTES**

THIS IS THE ANSWER WHEN YOU'RE IN THE MOOD FOR A CURRY, BUT ARE HARD UP
OR CAN'T BE BOTHERED TO GO OUT. IT IS A CROSS BETWEEN A VEGETABLE CURRY AND
A LENTIL STEW THAT MAKES A VERY RICH, INEXPENSIVE MEAL. WHEN YOU TEAM IT WITH
SHOP-BOUGHT CHAPATIS OR BOILED RICE (PAGE 46), THE RESULT IS A COMPLETE PROTEIN.
　　RED OR YELLOW LENTILS ARE THE ONES TO USE FOR THIS DISH, BECAUSE THEY WILL
LITERALLY FALL APART WHILE THEY COOK, SO DON'T TRY IT WITH GREEN LENTILS. THIS ISN'T
LIGHTNING-QUICK TO PREPARE (ALTHOUGH MOST OF THE TIME IT SIMMERS UNATTENDED),
SO IT MAKES SENSE TO COOK DOUBLE OR TRIPLE QUANTITIES AND KEEP THE LEFTOVERS IN
THE FRIDGE, TIGHTLY COVERED WITH CLINGFILM, FOR UP TO THREE DAYS, OR FROZEN FOR
UP TO A MONTH.

180 g/6 oz red lentils
1^1/$_2$ teaspoons ground coriander
Large pinch of ground turmeric
1 fresh green chilli
2 tomatoes, seeded (page 131) and chopped
1 onion
30 g/1 oz butter
1 tablespoon vegetable oil
2–4 shop-bought chapatis
Salt and pepper
Chopped fresh coriander, to serve (optional)

1. Put the lentils, coriander and turmeric in a saucepan over a medium-
high heat with enough water to cover the lentils by about 1 cm/½ inch
and bring to the boil. Lower the heat and simmer for about 15 minutes,
stirring occasionally, until the lentils are very tender.

2. For a thin, smooth dhal, put the lentils in a blender and whiz until
smooth. Alternatively, you can serve the lentils the texture they are
or mash them with a potato masher or a large fork in the pan.

3. Return the lentils to the pan, if necessary. Stir in the chilli, tomatoes
and salt and pepper to taste. Stir a little extra water if the mixture seems
too thick. Cover the pan, turn the heat to its lowest setting and simmer
for 10 minutes.

4. Meanwhile, slice the onion very thinly . Melt the butter with the oil
in a small frying pan or another saucepan over a medium-high heat.
Add the onion and fry, stirring frequently, for 8–10 minutes until light
golden brown. Do not leave the hob at this point and watch carefully
because the onions can burn quickly.

5. Heat the grill to its highest setting. Sprinkle the chapatis with a little water and grill them for 20–30 seconds on each side.

6. Top the dhal with the onions and coriander, if you have any. Serve with the warm chapatis.

Leftovers
▶ Spoon any leftovers over Crispy Baked Potatoes (page 42).
▶ Use the leftover as a filling for Quesadillas (page 104).

VARIATIONS
▶ Add chopped green beans, small broccoli or cauliflower florets, or peas in Step 3 of the master recipe left.
▶ Drained tinned corn kernels are an unconventional, but suitable, addition.

Bean & Pasta Stew

MAKES **4 SERVINGS**
PREP TIME: **ABOUT 15 MINUTES**
COOKING TIME: **ABOUT 25 MINUTES**

THIS COUNTRY-STYLE ITALIAN VEGETARIAN STEW IS A HEARTY MEAL IN A POT. FRENCH BREAD OR ITALIAN FOCACCIA IS THE ONLY ACCOMPANIMENT IT NEEDS.
STORE ANY LEFTOVERS IN A BOWL IN THE FRIDGE, COVERED WITH CLINGFILM, AND REHEAT THE NEXT DAY, OTHERWISE THE PASTA WILL BECOME SOGGY.

2 celery sticks
2 garlic cloves
1 carrot
1 onion
1 waxy potato (see Potato Primer 2, page 73), scrubbed
1 leek
1 can (400 g/14 oz) borlotti beans
2 tablespoons olive oil
1 teaspoon dried thyme
250 ml/8 fl oz tomato passata (see Variations, overleaf)
450 ml/16 fl oz vegetable stock, home-made (page 54) or from a cube
100 g/3$^{1}/_{2}$ oz wholemeal or plain pasta shapes, such as bows, corkscrews or twists
60 g/2 oz French beans
Chopped fresh basil or parsley (optional)
Salt and pepper
Freshly grated Parmesan cheese (optional), to serve
Olive oil, to serve

1. Finely chop the celery. Peel and crush the garlic. Scrub or peel the carrot, then cut it into thick slices. Peel and chop the onion. Scrub the potato and cut it into bite-size chunks.

2. Cut the leek in half lengthways, then place, cut sides down, on a chopping board and slice thinly. (If the leek has grit between the layers, put the slices in a sieve and run cold water over them.)

3. Place a colander or sieve in the sink. Tip in the beans and rinse with cold water, then set aside to drain.

4. Heat the oil in a large saucepan or flameproof casserole over a medium-high heat. Add the celery, garlic, carrot, leek, onion, potato and thyme and fry, stirring occasionally, for about 5 minutes until the vegetables are soft, but not brown.

5. Stir in the passata and stock and bring to the boil. Lower the heat, cover the pan tightly and leave to simmer for 15 minutes.

6. Meanwhile, bring a large saucepan of salted water to the boil over a high heat. Stir in the pasta, return the water to the boil and continue boiling for 12–15 minutes, or according to the packet instructions, until the pasta is tender to the bite. Drain well and set aside.

7. Top and tail the French beans, then cut them into 2.5 cm/1-inch pieces. Add the French beans to the stew, re-cover the pan and continue simmering for about 10 minutes longer, or until the carrots and potatoes are tender when you pierce them with the tip of a knife.

8. Add the borlotti beans to the stew and stir in the basil or parsley, if you have any. Simmer for another couple of minutes to warm the beans, then add salt and pepper to taste. Serve in bowls with a sprinkling of Parmesan, if you have any, and olive oil drizzled over the tops.

VARIATIONS
▸ If you don't have borlotti beans, use butter beans, chickpeas or cooked lentils.
▸ Tomato passata, a thin tomato puree that has been strained to remove the seeds, is sold in supermarkets and health food shops. If you can't find any, increase the amount of stock by 200 ml/7 fl oz and stir in 1 tablespoon tomato puree.

LEAVE - ALONE COOKING

These are the recipes to make when you have an essay to write or a book to read and don't want to spend time fussing in the kitchen, but still want something comforting to eat. Once you put these in the oven to cook, you can almost forget about them for an hour or so while you concentrate on other things. The most attention these recipes require is a stir or two, except the roast chicken, which needs basting for the final half hour, and the belly of pork that needs a quick baste every thirty minutes.

Most of these recipes also make four servings, so you have a second, hassle-free meal waiting that just needs reheating.

Other recipes that don't require much attention:
- Beef in Beer (page 201)
- Chicken or Vegetable Stock (pages 51 and 54)
- Provençale-style Leg of Lamb (page 200)
- Sesame-Lemon Chicken Wings (page 113)

Roast Chicken with Pan Gravy

MAKES **4 SERVINGS** PREP TIME: **ABOUT 5 MINUTES, PLUS 10 MINUTES STANDING AFTER ROASTING** COOKING TIME: **ABOUT 1¼ HOURS**

EVEN IF YOU ONLY COOK FOR YOURSELF AND ARE ON A REALLY TIGHT BUDGET, IT MAKES SENSE TO ROAST A CHICKEN ONCE A WEEK. YOU'LL HAVE A DELICIOUS MEAL TO EAT ON THE DAY, WITH PLENTY OF LEFTOVERS FOR SANDWICHES, SALADS AND STIR-FRIES.

1 oven-ready chicken, 1.35–1.5 kg/2½–3 lb
1 lemon, cut in half
2 garlic cloves, peeled

Butter, at room temperature
About ½ mug water
Salt and pepper

1. Heat the oven to 190°C/375°F/Gas 5. Rinse the chicken inside and out and pat dry with paper towels.

2. Squeeze the lemon halves over the chicken's breasts, then put the squeezed halves in the chicken's cavity. Peel and crush the garlic cloves and add them to the cavity. If you have kitchen string, tie the legs together for a neater shape when the bird roasts, but this isn't necessary.

3. Spread the butter over the breasts. Place the chicken in a roasting tin and roast until it is cooked through, which will take about 1¼ hours. (See Is It Cooked?, below.) Baste the bird with the juices accumulated in the pan at least twice after it has roasted for 30 minutes. (To do this, use a large metal spoon to gather up the cooking juices and spoon them over the breasts. This helps produce a crisp skin and keeps the breast meat tender and juicy.)

4. Remove the chicken from the pan and set it on a large plate with a rim that will catch any juices. Cover the chicken with a piece of kitchen foil, shiny side in, and leave it to rest for 10 minutes.

5. Use a metal spoon to skim any fat off the surface of the cooking juices left in the pan. Pour in the water, put the pan over a medium-high heat and slowly bring to a boil, stirring to scrape up any cooked bits on the bottom of the pan. Tip in any juices that have accumulated on the plate with the chicken, and boil hard for at least 2 minutes. Add salt and pepper to taste.

6. Thinly slice the chicken and serve with the juices spooned over.

Is it Cooked?
To avoid food poisoning, it is important that all chicken meat is thoroughly cooked. To test, use a fork or sharp knife to pierce the flesh at the thickest part of the thigh. If the juices that come out are clear, the bird is ready to come out of the oven; if they are pink, put the chicken back in the oven for another 5 minutes and test again. If in doubt, roast for 5 minutes longer.

Belly of Pork with Cider

MAKES **4 SERVINGS, WITH LEFTOVERS**
PREP TIME: **ABOUT 15 MINUTES, PLUS OPTIONAL MARINATING** COOKING TIME: **ABOUT 2½ HOURS**

EAST MEETS WEST WITH THIS BLEND OF CHINESE FLAVOURS AND DRY CIDER.

BELLY OF PORK IS A VERY INEXPENSIVE CUT OF MEAT THAT YOU CAN BUY IN A SLAB OF CONNECTED SPARERIBS WITH FAT LAYERED THROUGH THE MEAT. ITS TENDER, RICH MEAT CAN BE A REAL TREAT WHEN YOU ARE COOKING ON BUDGET. THE TRICK IS TO COOK THE MEAT VERY SLOWLY AT A HIGH TEMPERATURE SO THE LARGE AMOUNT OF FAT MELTS AWAY.

THIS IS FANTASTIC SERVED WITH CREAMY MASH (PAGE 40), AND THE RICHNESS IS BEST OFFSET WITH SOME SIMPLE BOILED CARROTS OR BROCCOLI.

IF YOU BUY YOUR MEAT FROM THE SUPERMARKET MEAT COUNTER OR A BUTCHER, ASK TO HAVE THE SKIN AND TOP LAYER OF FAT SCORED. OTHERWISE, TO DO THIS YOURSELF, USE A SMALL SHARP KNIFE AND MAKE DEEP SLICES ALONG THE LENGTH OF THE FAT, WITHOUT CUTTING DOWN INTO THE MEAT. THIS SCORING HELPS TO RENDER SOME OF THE FAT JUST UNDER THE SKIN AND PRODUCES CRISP CRACKLING.

2 garlic cloves
1 tablespoon Chinese five-spice powder
1 orange
1 tablespoon olive oil
900 g/1¾ lb belly of pork in one slab, about 4 long spareribs, scored (see introduction, above)
400 ml/14 fl oz dry cider
Salt and pepper

1. Heat the oven to 230°C/450°F/Gas 8 (if you are cooking straight away, otherwise do not heat the oven until the start of Step 4).

2. Peel and crush the garlic cloves. Put the garlic in a pestle and mortar or small bowl and add the Chinese five-spice powder. Grate in the orange rind. Add the olive oil and mash together. Add salt and pepper to taste.

3. Spread the garlic paste over the belly of pork, rubbing it into the slits. If you have time, leave the meat to marinate for at least 1 hour in the fridge, although longer or overnight is better. (In which case, remove the meat and leave it to come to room temperature while you heat the oven.)

4. Put a rack in a roasting tin and place the belly of pork on top. Put the tin in the oven and roast for 30 minutes

5. Lower the oven temperature to 190°C/375°F/Gas 5 and continue roasting for 2 hours, basting the meat every 30 minutes or so with the juices that accumulate in the base of the roasting tin until the crackling is crisp and the meat feels very tender when you pierce it with the tip of a knife, and the juices that run out are clear.

6. Transfer the belly of pork to a plate, cover with foil, shiny side in, and leave it to rest for 10 minutes while you make the gravy.

7. Pour out the excess fat from the roasting tin. Put the tin over a medium-high heat and stir in the cider, using a wooden spoon to scrape up any of the crispy bits on the bottom of the pan. Turn the heat to high and bring the cider to the boil, stirring. Add salt and pepper to taste.

8. Use a sharp knife to cut the crackling off the meat, and then cut this into thin strips. Cut the belly of pork into individual ribs, then remove the meat from the ribs and serve with the crackling. Strain the gravy through a fine sieve and serve with the pork.

COOK'S TIP
THE CRACKLING SHOULD BE CRISPY. IF IT NEEDS ADDITIONAL COOKING, ONCE THE PORK IS COOKED, SLICE IT OFF THE MEAT IN A SINGLE LAYER AND PUT IT UNDER A HOT GRILL UNTIL IT CRISPS AND BROWNS.

Lamb Shanks with Dried Fruit

☐ ☐ ☐ ☐ MAKES 4 **SERVINGS**
PREP TIME: **ABOUT 10 MINUTES**
COOKING TIME: **2 HOURS**

THIS EXOTIC TASTE OF THE MIDDLE EAST REQUIRES NO COOKING SKILLS AT ALL.
PRACTICALLY ANYONE CAN MAKE THIS DELICIOUS, HEARTY DISH.

LAMB SHANK IS ANOTHER VERY INEXPENSIVE CUT OF MEAT THAT BECOMES MELTINGLY
TENDER AFTER SLOW COOKING. YOU JUST HAVE TO BE PREPARED TO SKIM THE EXCESS FAT
FROM THE SURFACE BEFORE YOU SERVE THIS.

QUICK-COOKING COUSCOUS IS AN IDEAL ACCOMPANIMENT THAT DOESN'T INVOLVE
EFFORT OR SKILL TO PREPARE, EITHER. OR SERVE THIS WITH EITHER OF THE RICE RECIPES
ON PAGES 47 AND 48, CREAMY MASH (PAGE 40) OR SPINACH & CHICKPEAS (PAGE 210).

2 onions
2 large garlic cloves
4 lamb shanks
400 ml/14 fl oz water
100 g/3^1/$_2$ oz prunes
60 g/2 oz ready-to-eat apricot halves
3 tablespoons ready-to-eat dried cranberries or raisins
3 cinnamon sticks
4 whole cloves
1 bay leaf
Salt and pepper
Chopped fresh coriander or parsley, to serve (optional)

1. Heat the oven to 180°C/350°F/Gas 4. Peel and cut the onion into
quarters. Peel and crush the garlic clove.

2. Put the lamb shanks in an ovenproof casserole or ovenproof dish and
season to taste with salt and pepper. Add the onion and garlic, scattering
the pieces around, and spoon 4 tablespoons of the water over. Cover the
casserole and put in the oven for 1 hour. (If you are using an ovenproof
dish, cover it tightly with kitchen foil, shiny side in.)

3. Meanwhile, put the dried fruit, spices, bay leaf and the remaining
water in a saucepan over a high heat. Bring to the boil, then remove from
the heat, cover the pan and set aside while the lamb shanks cook.

4. After 1 hour's cooking, using oven gloves, remove the casserole from
the oven and stir in the fruit mixture. Re-cover the casserole and return it
to the oven for another hour, or until the meat is falling off the bone and
the fruit is very soft and plump.

5. Use a metal spoon to skim any excess fat from the surface of the
cooking juices.

6. Add salt and pepper to taste. Transfer the lamb shanks to a soup plate and spoon the fruit and cooking juices over. Sprinkle with fresh herbs, if you have any.

Leftovers
▸ *Middle Eastern Pittas:* Spread a small amount of Hummus (page 88) inside a split pitta bread. Cut the leftover lamb into small pieces and toss with a chopped tomato, some sliced cucumber and grated carrot. Stuff into the pitta.
▸ *Oriental Wraps:* Spread hoisin sauce on to a soft flour tortilla. Add thin strips of cucumber, shredded lettuce and thin slices of leftover lamb. (Sliced red plums also taste fantastic with the lamb.) Wrap up for a quick sandwich on the go.

VARIATIONS
▸ Use whatever dried fruit you have handy, or all apricots.
▸ You can also make the Oriental Wraps using rice paper wrappers, sold at Chinese food shops. Soak the wrappers as instructed on the packet and line with crisp lettuce leaves.

Ratatouille

MAKES **4–6 SERVINGS**
PREP TIME: **ABOUT 10 MINUTES**
COOKING TIME: **ABOUT 1½ HOURS**

THIS MEDITERRANEAN DISH IS THE ULTIMATE VEGETARIAN CASSEROLE. RATATOUILLE IS INEXPENSIVE AND VERY VERSATILE – SERVE IT HOT OR COLD, ON ITS OWN OR AS A TOPPING FOR CRISPY BAKED POTATOES (PAGE 42) OR WITH A BOWL OF BOILED PASTA. FOR MEAT-EATERS, THIS PERKS UP SIMPLY GRILLED CHOPS OR CHICKEN BREASTS, OR MAKES A MEAL OUT OF ROAST CHICKEN WITH PAN GRAVY (PAGE 168). TO SERVE A CROWD, JUST DOUBLE THE QUANTITIES AND TAKE A LOOK AT THE VARIATIONS RIGHT.

PURISTS SAY EACH VEGETABLE SHOULD BE COOKED SEPARATELY AND THEN COMBINED AT THE END, BUT THAT IS FAR TOO LABOUR-INTENSIVE, AND NOT AT ALL NECESSARY. ONCE YOU'VE DONE THE INITIAL COOKING, JUST LET THIS SIMMER OVER A LOW HEAT WHILE YOU GET ON WITH STUDYING, OR PARTYING. IT'S WORTH MAKING A LARGE POT OF THIS, BECAUSE LEFTOVERS WILL KEEP IN THE FRIDGE FOR UP TO FOUR DAYS. THE FLAVOURS ARE BEST IF YOU TAKE THE LEFTOVERS OUT OF THE FRIDGE ABOUT 15 MINUTES BEFORE SERVING AT ROOM TEMPERATURE. TO REHEAT, TRANSFER THE VEGETABLES TO A SAUCEPAN OVER A MEDIUM-HIGH HEAT AND STIR UNTIL THEY ARE HEATED THROUGH. IF THE STEW SEEMS TOO DRY, STIR IN A LITTLE WATER, VEGETABLE STOCK OR TOMATO PUREE DISSOLVED IN WATER.

2 large onions
4–6 garlic cloves
4 courgettes, scrubbed
1 large aubergine, wiped
2 red peppers
4 tablespoons olive oil
1 can (400 g/14 oz) chopped tomatoes
1 tablespoons tomato puree
2 sprigs fresh thyme, or 1 teaspoon dried thyme
½ teaspoon sugar
1 bay leaf, fresh or dry, broken in half
Salt and pepper
Chopped fresh parsley or coriander, to serve (optional)

1. Peel and chop the onions. Peel and finely chop the garlic cloves. Cut the courgettes into 1 cm/½-inch slices. Cut the aubergine into 1 cm/½-inch slices crossways, then cut each slice into quarters. Core, seed and slice the red peppers.

2. Heat the olive oil in a flameproof casserole or a large saucepan with a tight-fitting lid over a medium heat. Add the onion and garlic and fry, stirring occasionally, for 3–5 minutes until the onion soft, but not brown.

3. Add the remaining ingredients, stirring to dissolve the tomato puree. Reduce the heat to its lowest setting, cover the pot tightly and leave the vegetables to simmer for about an hour. (If you don't have a tight-fitting lid, check after 20 minutes and add water if the liquid is evaporating.)

4. After an hour, check the amount of liquid in the pot – it is up to you to decide how soupy or dry you like it. If it is too liquid, turn up the heat and let the stew slowly bubble, uncovered, until the excess evaporates, stirring occasionally to make sure the vegetables don't catch on the bottom.

5. Serve straight away, while it's still hot, or leave to cool to room temperature. Add salt and pepper to taste and sprinkle with chopped herbs, if you have any.

VARIATIONS
▸ Thin, French-style green beans also go well with this. Add them with the other vegetables in Step 3 of the master recipe.
▸ To bulk this out, stir in a drained and rinsed can (400 g/14 oz) of chickpeas after 40 minutes. Or add drained and rinsed tins of borlotti, cannelloni or red kidney beans.
▸ If you have any fresh basil, finely slice it and stir it in just before serving.
▸ Stir in a handful of raisins when you take the stew off the heat.

Mary's Beef & Mushroom Casserole

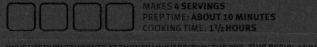

MAKES **4 SERVINGS**
PREP TIME: **ABOUT 10 MINUTES**
COOKING TIME: 1½ **HOURS**

'INVENTED' BY STUDENTS AT SYDNEY UNIVERSITY IN THE 70S, THIS RECIPE CERTAINLY ISN'T GOURMET COOKING, BUT IT HAS STOOD THE TEST OF TIME. IT CAN'T BE BEATEN FOR A WARMING, HASSLE-FREE WINTER CASSEROLE. SERVE WITH CREAMY MASH (PAGE 40), CRISPY BAKED POTATOES (PAGE 42) OR CHUNKS OF FRENCH BREAD TO MOP UP THE RICH, HEARTY SAUCE.

THE QUANTITIES CAN EASILY BE DOUBLED OR TRIPLED AS LONG AS THE LIQUID COVERS THE INGREDIENTS BY 1 CM/½ INCH. TOP UP WITH VEGETABLE STOCK OR WATER, IF NECESSARY.

600 g/1½ lb button or chestnut mushrooms, wiped
2 tablespoons plain white flour
Vegetable oil
600 g/1½ lb stewing beef, cubed
40 g/1½ oz dry French onion soup mix
1 beer mug red wine (600 ml/1 pint)
1 beer mug tomato juice (600 ml/1 pint)
Chopped fresh parsley, to serve (optional)

1. Lightly grease the inside of a flameproof casserole or large saucepan with a tight-fitting lid. Remove the mushroom stalks, if necessary, and thickly slice the caps.

2. Put the flour in a plastic bag and add the beef. Hold the bag closed and shake until the beef cubes are lightly coated with flour. Tip the beef and any excess flour into the casserole. Add the mushrooms and onion soup mix. Pour over the red wine and tomato juice.

3. Place the casserole over a high heat and bring to the boil. Stir once, reduce the heat to its lowest setting, cover the casserole tightly and leave to simmer for 1½ hours, or until the meat is tender when you pierce it with a fork.

4. Sprinkle with parsley, if you like, and serve straight from the casserole.

Leftovers
► Slowly simmer any leftover stew for an extra hour, or until the meat literally starts to fall apart. Shred the meat with two forks and serve as a thick ragú sauce for freshly boiled pasta or use to spoon over Crispy Baked Potatoes (page 42). Add a little extra water if the sauce appears too thick before the meat is ready. If the flavour becomes too strong and concentrated, stir in a little sugar.

IN THE FLASH OF A WOK

Whatever you do, don't leave home without a wok. You can live on stir-fried dishes practically all year, and the wok can do double duty as a frying pan if your kitchen equipment is really minimal.

Stir-frying is the Chinese version of quick, one-pot cooking – and that means there are fewer pots and pans for you to wash up. The shape of the wok, with its rounded base and deep sloping side, conducts heat evenly over the whole surface, so ingredients cook quickly over a high heat. As you move the ingredients around constantly while they are cooking – hence the name stir-frying – there is less chance of them sticking, so you can use less fat.

Stir-frying is also budget cooking. You will soon appreciate that, when you get your wok hot, small amounts of leftover cooked chicken and meat or a few fresh vegetables can be transformed into a filling meal with rice or Asian noodles, for pennies.

You'll always have time for these recipes, no matter how hectic your social life is. Stir-fries are the ultimate in one-pot meals. They are easy to make and more satisfying than most quickies.

If you're new to stir-frying, start by reading Golden Rules of Stir-frying (below).

Golden Rules of Stir-frying
▸ Prepare all the ingredients before you begin stir-frying. This is quick cooking, so there won't be time to chop once the wok heats up.
▸ Cut the ingredients into small, uniform-size pieces.
▸ Heat the wok before you add the oil. This prevents the ingredients from sticking.
▸ Add the thickest ingredients that will take the longest to cook before you add the quicker-cooking ingredients.
▸ Use chopsticks or a wooden spatula to keep the ingredients constantly moving around the wok.

Other recipes suitable for wok cooking:
▸ Chicken & Cauliflower Curry (page 155)
▸ Curried Mince (page 157)
▸ Dhal with Chapatis (page 163)
▸ Scrambled Eggs (page 38)

Stir-fried Vegetables with Oyster Sauce

MAKES **2 SERVINGS**
PREP TIME: **ABOUT 10 MINUTES**
COOKING TIME: **ABOUT 5 MINUTES**

SERVE THIS WITH EGG-FRIED RICE (PAGE 185) FOR AN ORIENTAL VEGETARIAN FEAST. OR
ADD SOME QUICKLY SOAKED RICE NOODLES WITH THE VEGETABLES FOR A ONE-POT MEAL.

1 garlic clove
$^1/_2$ onion
125 g/4 oz broccoli florets
1 red or green pepper
1 head bok choy
1 tablespoon groundnut or sunflower oil
1 teaspoon salt
1 tablespoon bottled oyster sauce
1 tablespoon water

1. Peel and thinly slice the garlic. Peel and finely chop the onion. Cut
the broccoli into small florets. Core, seed and thinly slice the pepper.
Cut the bok choy lengthways into quarters.

2. Heat a wok or large frying pan over a high heat. Add the oil, swirl
it around and heat until it shimmers.

3. Add the garlic and salt and stir-fry for about 30 seconds.

4. Add the onion, broccoli, pepper and bok choy and stir-fry for 3 minutes
until the vegetables are starting to become tender. Stir in the oyster
sauce and water and continue stir-frying for 1–2 minutes longer until
the vegetables are tender.

VARIATION
► For a vegetarian version, replace the oyster sauce with bottled
hoisin sauce.

Hoisin Chicken with Soba Noodles

MAKES **2 SERVINGS**
PREP TIME: **10–15 MINUTES**
COOKING TIME: **ABOUT 5 MINUTES**

150 g/5 oz dried soba noodles
2 chicken thighs
2 garlic cloves
1 green pepper
1 onion
2.5 cm/1-inch piece fresh root ginger
1¹/₂ tablespoons groundnut or sunflower oil
2 tablespoons bottled hoisin sauce
¹/₂ tablespoon light soy sauce
Salted roasted peanuts, to serve (optional)

1. Bring a large saucepan of water to the boil over a high heat. Add the soba noodles, bring the water back to the boil and continue boiling for 6–7 minutes, or according to the packet instructions, until tender. Place a colander or sieve in the sink and drain the noodles. Shake the noodles to remove the excess moisture and set them aside.

2. Remove the skin and any bones from the chicken thighs. Cut the flesh into thin strips and set aside.

3. Peel and crush the garlic cloves. Core, seed and finely chop the green pepper. Peel and thinly slice the onion. Peel the and very finely chop the ginger.

4. Heat a wok or large frying pan over a high heat. Add the oil, swirl it around and heat until it shimmers.

5. Add the garlic, onion and ginger and stir-fry for about 30 seconds. Add the chicken and pepper and continue stir-frying for 3–5 minutes until the pepper is soft, but not brown, and the chicken is cooked through so the juices are clear if you pierce a piece with the tip of a knife.

6. Stir in the hoisin sauce and soy sauce. Add the noodles and continue stir-frying until they are warmed through and all the ingredients are mixed together. Sprinkle with the nuts, if you are using, and serve.

VARIATIONS

▶ Replace the chicken in the master recipe with thinly sliced pork fillet, or cubed firm tofu for a vegetarian and vegan dish.
▶ If you're using leftover chicken or pork, remove any skin or bones and cut it into thin strips. Add it in Step 5 of the master recipe, after the pepper has been stir-fried for about 2 minutes.

Stir-fried Chicken & Bean Sprouts

MAKES **2 SERVINGS**
PREP TIME: **ABOUT 10 MINUTES**
COOKING TIME: **8–10 MINUTES**

2 chicken thighs
1 large red pepper
$^{1}/_{2}$ can (220 g/7$^{1}/_{2}$ oz) water chestnuts
1 large garlic clove
1 cm/$^{1}/_{2}$-inch piece fresh root ginger
$^{1}/_{2}$ onion
1$^{1}/_{2}$ tablespoons groundnut or sunflower oil
1 tablespoon soy sauce
1 tablespoon bottled black bean sauce
100 g/3$^{1}/_{2}$ oz fresh bean sprouts

1. Remove the skin and any bones from the chicken thighs. Cut the flesh into thin strips, then set aside.

2. Core, seed and very thinly slice the red pepper. Drain and thinly slice the water chestnuts. Peel and finely chop the garlic. Peel and finely chop the ginger. Peel and finely chop the onion.

3. Heat a wok or large frying pan over a high heat. Add the oil, swirl it around and heat until it shimmers.

4. Add the garlic, ginger and onion to the wok and stir-fry for about 30 seconds. Add the chicken and red pepper to the wok and continue stir-frying for about 5 minutes until the pepper is soft, but not brown, and the chicken is cooked through so the juices are clear if you pierce a piece with the tip of a knife.

5. Stir the soy sauce and black bean sauce into the wok. Add the bean sprouts and water chestnuts and stir-fry until all the ingredients are mixed together and hot.

VARIATION
▶ This is a mild-flavoured stir-fry. For extra heat, add $^{1}/_{2}$ seeded and finely chopped fresh red chilli, or a pinch of dried chilli flakes with the garlic, ginger and onion in Step 4 of the master recipe.

COOK'S TIP
WATER CHESTNUTS ARE USED IN CHINESE COOKING TO ADD AN EXTRA CRUNCH TO DISHES. THIS RECIPE ONLY USES HALF A CAN, BUT THE REMAINDER WILL STAY CRUNCHY IN THE FRIDGE FOR UP TO FIVE DAYS. TIP THE CHESTNUTS AND WATER IN THE CAN INTO A BOWL AND COVER TIGHTLY WITH CLINGFILM.

Chow Mein

MAKES **2 SERVINGS** PREP TIME: **12–15 MINUTES**
COOKING TIME: **ABOUT 20 MINUTES, INCLUDING
FRYING THE NOODLES**

CHICKEN OR PORK (SEE VARIATION) AND VEGETABLES GO WELL WITH BOILED RICE
(PAGE 46) OR EGG-FRIED RICE (PAGE 185).

2 chicken thighs
1 cm/$^1/_2$-inch piece fresh root ginger
1 large garlic clove
1 celery stick
60 g/2 oz button or chestnut mushrooms, wiped
$^1/_2$ head Chinese cabbage
$^1/_2$ tablespoon cornflour
4 tablespoons water
1$^1/_2$ tablespoons soy sauce
3 tablespoons groundnut or sunflower oil
60 g/2 oz fresh bean sprouts

1. Remove the skin and any bones from the chicken thighs. Cut the flesh into thin strips and set aside.

2. Peel and finely chop the ginger. Peel and crush the garlic clove. Thinly slice the celery. Trim the stalks from the mushrooms, if necessary, and thinly slice the caps. Remove the core from the Chinese cabbage and thinly slice the leaves.

3. Put the cornflour in a small bowl and stir in the water and soy sauce, then set aside.

4. Heat a wok or large frying pan over a high heat. Add 2 tablespoons oil and heat it until it shimmers.

5. Add the ginger, garlic and celery and stir-fry for 2 minutes. Add the mushroom slices to the pan and continue stir-frying for 2 minutes longer. Spoon the vegetables on to a plate and set aside.

6. Add another tablespoon of oil to the wok or pan, if necessary, and heat until it shimmers. Add the chicken and stir-fry for 2–3 minutes until it is cooked through and the juices are clear if you pierce a piece with the tip of a knife.

7. Spoon the chicken pieces on to the plate with the stir-fried vegetables. Stir the sauce and add it to the wok or pan and bring it to the boil, stirring, until it thickens.

8. Return the vegetables and chicken to the pan along with the cabbage and bean sprouts and stir-fry for about 2 minutes longer until all the ingredients are blended and hot.

VARIATIONS
▸ Replace the chicken with 200 g/7 oz of pork fillet, cut across the grain into thin slices.
▸ This recipe is also a wonderful dish for using up small amounts of leftover cooked chicken and pork. Skip Step 6 and add the finely sliced meat with the other ingredients in Step 7.

COOK'S TIP
CHINESE EGG NOODLES ARE THE NATURAL ACCOMPANIMENT TO SERVE WITH THIS. BRING A KETTLE OR SAUCEPAN OF WATER TO THE BOIL. PUT 60 G / 2 OZ DRIED CHINESE EGG NOODLES IN A LARGE HEATPROOF BOWL AND POUR OVER ENOUGH BOILING WATER TO COVER. SET ASIDE TO SOAK FOR 3 MINUTES, OR ACCORDING TO THE INSTRUCTIONS ON THE PACKET, UNTIL TENDER. DRAIN WELL.
YOU CAN SOAK THE NOODLES UP TO SEVERAL HOURS IN ADVANCE IF YOU LIGHTLY TOSS THEM WITH A LITTLE GROUNDNUT, SUNFLOWER OR SESAME OIL AS SOON AS THEY ARE DRAINED, TO PREVENT THEM FROM STICKING TOGETHER.

Stir-fried Ginger Pork

MAKES **2 SERVINGS**
PREP TIME: **ABOUT 10 MINUTES, INCLUDING SOAKING THE NOODLES** COOKING TIME: **ABOUT 8 MINUTES**

IN AUTHENTIC CHINESE COOKING, THIS DISH WOULD PROBABLY BE MADE WITH THIN SLICES OF BONELESS, LEAN PORK, SUCH AS FILLET, BUT PORK MINCE IS MUCH CHEAPER.

200 g/7 oz dried Chinese egg noodles
2 cm/³/₄-inch piece fresh root ginger
1 garlic clove
¹/₂ carrot
1 leek
1 tablespoon groundnut or sunflower oil
200 g/7 oz lean pork mince
1 tablespoon soy sauce
Salt and pepper

1. Bring a saucepan of water to the boil. Add the noodles, turn off the heat and leave to soak for 4 minutes, or according to the packet instructions, until tender. Drain well and set aside.

2. Meanwhile, peel and finely grate the ginger. Peel and crush the garlic. Scrub or peel the carrot and coarsely grate it. Cut the leek in half lengthways, then place, cut sides down, on a chopping board and slice thinly. (If the leek has grit between the layers, put the slices in a sieve and run cold water over them.)

3. Heat a wok or large frying pan over a high heat. Add the oil, swirl it around and heat until it shimmers.

4. Add the ginger and garlic and stir-fry for about 30 seconds. Stir in the minced pork and continue stir-frying, using wooden chopsticks or a wooden spoon to break up any large pieces, for 5 minutes, or until the pork is cooked through and no longer pink.

5. Stir the soy sauce, leek, carrot and drained noodles into the wok and continue stir-frying for 2 minutes until the ingredients are blended and the noodles are hot. Add salt and pepper to taste.

VARIATIONS
► Stir the soy sauce, leek, carrot and drained noodles into the wok and omit the noodles. Serve the pork mixture with Egg-fried Rice (page 185).
► To stretch this dish to feed an extra person, add 100 g/3 ¹/₂ oz of fresh bean sprouts with the other ingredients in Step 5 of the master recipe.
► If you like hot, spicy food, add a large pinch of dried chilli flakes with the garlic and ginger in Step 5.

Stir-fried Beef with Broccoli & Mangetouts

MAKES **2 SERVINGS**
PREP TIME: **ABOUT 10 MINUTES**
COOKING TIME: **ABOUT 10 MINUTES**

STIR-FRYING IS A GOOD TECHNIQUE FOR STRETCHING A SMALL AMOUNT OF LEAN BEEF.
SERVE THIS WITH EGG NOODLES, BOILED RICE (PAGE 46) OR EGG-FRIED RICE (PAGE 185).

250 g/8 oz lean beef, such as frying steak or rump
100 g/3^{1}/$_{2}$ oz broccoli florets
2 spring onions
60 g/2 oz mangetouts
1 tablespoon cornflour
5 tablespoons vegetable stock, home-made (page 54) or from a cube
2 tablespoons bottled oyster sauce
2 tablespoons soy sauce
2 tablespoons rice wine or dry sherry
2 tablespoons groundnut or sunflower oil
Salt and pepper

1. Cut the beef across the grain into thin strips. Cut the broccoli florets into small, bite-size pieces. Cut the spring onions into 2.5 cm/1-inch pieces. Break the stem end off the mangetouts and pull away the thin 'string' that runs along the side of each one.

2. Put the cornflour in a bowl and stir in the vegetable stock, oyster sauce, soy sauce and rice wine or sherry. Set the sauce aside.

3. Heat a wok or large frying pan over a high heat. Add 1 tablespoon of the oil, swirl it around and heat until it shimmers.

4. Add the beef and stir-fry for about 2 minutes until it is cooked through and brown on both sides. Remove the beef from the pan and set aside.

5. Heat the remaining tablespoon of oil in the wok and swirl it around. Add the broccoli and stir-fry for 2 minutes. Add the sliced spring onions and mangetouts and continue stir-frying for a minute longer.

6. Stir the sauce mixture, add it to the wok and bring to the boil, stirring. Return the beef to the wok and stir-fry until the sauce thickens and the broccoli florets and mangetouts are tender. Add salt and pepper to taste.

Egg-fried Rice

MAKES **2 SERVINGS**
PREP TIME: **ABOUT 5 MINUTES**
COOKING TIME: **ABOUT 5 MINUTES**

THERE IS A HIGH PROFIT MARGIN ON FRIED RICE AT YOUR LOCAL CHINESE TAKE-AWAY, SO IF YOU WANT TO KEEP THE MONEY IN YOUR POCKET, RATHER THAN THE PROPRIETOR'S, GET IN THE HABIT OF MAKING EXTRA RICE WHENEVER YOU COOK ANY.

EGG-FRIED RICE IS A SUPER-SPEEDY RECIPE, THAT CAN EITHER BE A SIDE DISH OR A MEAL IN ITSELF, BUT YOU HAVE TO START WITH COOKED RICE THAT HAS HAD TIME TO COOL, SO IT IS HANDY TO HAVE SOME ON HAND. IF YOU DON'T HAVE ANY COOKED RICE IN THE FRIDGE OR FREEZER, HOWEVER, COOK SOME FRESH AND LEAVE IT TO BECOME COMPLETELY COOL BEFORE YOU START COOKING THIS. (YOU MIGHT AS WELL ALWAYS COOK DOUBLE QUANTITIES OF RICE SO YOU HAVE SOME AT THE READY THE NEXT TIME YOU PREPARE THIS DISH.)

THIS IS A SIMPLE DISH TO SERVE WITH OTHER ORIENTAL DISHES, BUT TAKE A LOOK AT THE IDEAS THAT FOLLOW FOR TURNING IT INTO A FILLING MEAL.

$1/2$ onion
1 small garlic clove
1 cm/$1/2$-inch piece fresh root ginger
1 tablespoon groundnut or sunflower oil
200 g/7 oz cooked, cool rice
1 large egg
1 tablespoon soy sauce
Salt and pepper

1. Peel and finely chop the onion. Peel and crush the garlic clove. Peel and finely chop the ginger. Combine the 3 ingredients in a bowl and set aside.

2. Break the egg into a small bowl and beat with a fork.

3. Heat a wok or frying pan over a high heat until you can feel the heat rising from the surface. Add the oil, swirl it around and heat until it shimmers.

4. Add the onion, garlic and ginger to the wok and stir-fry for about 15 seconds.

5. Pour the egg into the pan and immediately begin stir-frying until it is scrambled and set.

6. Add the rice to the pan and continue stir-frying for about 2 minutes until the rice is heated through and the egg is mixed with the rice.

7. Add the soy sauce and stir it into the rice and egg. Add salt and pepper to taste, but remember the soy sauce is salty so you might not need to add any salt.

VARIATIONS

▸ **Broccoli Fried Rice:** Add leftover cooked broccoli with the rice in Step 6 of the master recipe left, then continue with the recipe.

▸ **Cantonese Fried Rice:** This could just as easily be called 'Store Cupboard Rice' because it makes a meal out of small amounts of ingredients from your cupboard or fridge. Stir-fry finely chopped cooked ham, thinly sliced spring onions, drained canned sweet corn kernels and finely diced red pepper in the wok with the onion, garlic and ginger in Step 4 of the master recipe left.

▸ **Chicken Fried Rice:** This is an economical way of making a meal out of just a little leftover cooked chicken. Remove any skin and bones from the cooked chicken and shred the flesh into fine strips, or cut it into small pieces. Add the chicken at the beginning of Step 6 in the master recipe left and stir-fry for about 30 seconds before adding the rice and continuing with the recipe.

This variation is also good made with leftover cooked pork, beef or lamb.

▸ **Omelette Fried Rice:** For a more filling dish, begin by making a thin omelette to slice and add to the rice. Lightly beat 2 eggs in a bowl with $1/2$ teaspoon sesame oil, then set aside. Heat a wok or large frying pan over a high heat until you can feel the heat rising from the surface. Add 1 tablespoon groundnut or sunflower oil, swirl it around and heat until it shimmers. Add the eggs and swirl the pan, so they set in a thin, crepe-like layer. Leave to cook for 35–45 seconds, or until the underside is set. Slide the omelette onto a plate and flip it over. Slide the omelette back into the pan and continue cooking until the second side sets.

Slide the omelette out of the pan and leave it to cool. Roll up the omelette, place it on a chopping board and cut into 0.5 cm/$1/4$-inch slices. Unroll the slices and set them aside. Follow Steps 1, 2, 3, 4 and 5 in the master recipe. Add the omelette strips with the rice in Step 6 and finish frying as in the recipe.

▸ **Sesame-Egg Fried Rice:** Add 1 tablespoon sesame seeds with the onion, garlic and ginger in Step 4 of the master recipe left. Omit the soy sauce and instead stir $1/2$ a tablespoon of sesame oil into the rice-and-egg mixture just before serving.

▸ **Prawn-Corn Fried Rice:** You need 60–90 g/2–3 oz of small peeled prawns, which you can buy inexpensively, fresh or frozen, at the supermarket. (Put frozen ones in a strainer over the sink and run cold water over them until they thaw.) Pat fresh or thawed prawns dry with paper towels. Add the prawns to the wok at the start of Step 6. Add 4 tablespoons drained canned sweet corn kernels and stir-fry for about 30 seconds before adding the rice. Continue as in the master recipe.

▸ Add finely chopped fresh parsley or snipped chives with the rice.

Pad Thai

☐ ☐ ☐ ☐ MAKES **2 SERVINGS**
PREP TIME: **ABOUT 15 MINUTES, PLUS SOAKING THE
NOODLES** COOKING TIME: **ABOUT 10 MINUTES**

THIS IS A MEAL-IN-A-BOWL THAT THAIS EAT AT ANYTIME OF THE DAY OR NIGHT. IT IS VERY
RICH AND FILLING.

CLEAR RICE NOODLES, ALSO CALLED CELLOPHANE NOODLES, ARE TRADITIONAL FOR
THIS DISH, BUT YOU HAVE TO PLAN AHEAD BECAUSE THEY NEED TO SOAK FOR 90 MINUTES
–2 HOURS BEFORE THEY BECOME SOFT. (MANY PACKETS HAVE INSTRUCTIONS FOR BOILING
THE NOODLES FOR 6–8 MINUTES, BUT YOU CAN END UP WITH A SOGGY MESS.) IF YOU
DON'T HAVE TIME, USE THE QUICK-SOAKING EGG NOODLES INSTEAD.

100 g/3$^{1}/_{2}$ oz rice noodles
1 shallot or small onion
30 g/1 oz fresh tofu
1 spring onion
1 tablespoon soft brown sugar
$^{1}/_{2}$ tablespoon tamarind paste (page 24)
$^{1}/_{2}$ tablespoon hot water
2 tablespoons salted peanuts
1 teaspoon sunflower oil
150 g/5 oz small peeled prawns, thawed if frozen
1 egg
1 tablespoon Thai fish sauce
Pinch of white sugar
30 g/1 oz fresh bean sprouts
Pinch of dried chilli flakes

1. Put the rice noodles in a large bowl and pour over enough water
to cover them. Use your hand to swirl the noodles around, then leave
to stand until they are tender, which can take up to 2 hours.

2. Meanwhile, peel and finely chop the shallot or onion. Crumble the
tofu, rubbing it between your fingers. Finely chop the white and green
parts of the spring onion and set aside.

3. Put the sugar, tamarind paste and hot water in a small bowl and stir
until the tamarind paste dissolves, then set aside.

4. Heat a wok or large frying pan over a high heat until you can feel the
heat rising off the surface. Add the peanuts without any oil and quickly
stir them around until they turn golden – watch carefully because this
takes only seconds and they can easily burn. Immediately tip the
peanuts out of the pan. Coarsely chop the peanuts and set them aside.

5. Add the oil to the wok or frying pan, swirl it around and continue
heating until it shimmers.

6. Add the shallot or onion and stir-fry for about 2 minutes, or until it just starts to colour. Add the prawns and continue stir-frying for 30 seconds longer. Turn the heat to medium, crack in the egg and stir-fry until it is scrambled.

7. Add the noodles, the tamarind mixture, the Thai fish sauce, white sugar and bean sprouts and stir-fry for about 2 minutes longer until the noodles are heated through and all the ingredients are mixed together.

8. Stir in the dried chilli flakes and sprinkle with the spring onion.

VARIATIONS
► Fresh tofu is sold at Chinese supermarkets and some health food shops. If you can't find any, however, use firm tofu, cut into fine cubes. It is sold in supermarkets with other Oriental ingredients.
► If you don't have tamarind paste (page 24), use 1 tablespoon lemon juice.
► Thais often add rehydrated dried shrimps, which are sold at Oriental food shops. They are not expensive and add a slightly crunchy texture.

COOK'S TIP
IF YOU DON'T HAVE TIME TO THAW FROZEN PRAWNS IN THE FRIDGE, EMPTY THEM INTO A SIEVE AND RUN COLD WATER OVER THEM UNTIL THEY THAW. DRY WELL BEFORE ADDING TO THE OTHER INGREDIENTS IN STEP 6 OF THE MASTER RECIPE.

Singapore Noodles

MAKES **2 SERVINGS**
PREP TIME: **ABOUT 10 MINUTES, PLUS SOAKING THE NOODLES** COOKING TIME: **ABOUT 5 MINUTES**

PLAN AHEAD SO THE NOODLES HAVE PLENTY OF TIME TO SOAK.

100 g/3½oz thin rice noodles
60 g/2 oz button or chestnut
  mushrooms, wiped
90 g/3 oz broccoli florets
1 spring onion
1 garlic clove
1 fresh red chilli

1½ tablespoons soy sauce
1½ tablespoons sugar
1½ tablespoons sunflower oil
4 tablespoons salted peanuts
About 100 g/3½ oz leftover cooked, skinless and boneless chicken or pork

1. Put the rice noodles in a large bowl and pour over enough water to cover them. Use your hand to swirl the noodles around, then leave them to stand until they are tender, which can take up to 2 hours. (Or soak in boiling water for 6–8 minutes, or according to packet instructions, until tender, but be warned – they can turn into a soggy mess!)

2. Meanwhile, trim the stalks from the mushroom, if necessary, and thinly slice the caps. Cut the broccoli florets into small pieces. Finely chop the white and green parts of the spring onion. Peel and crush the garlic. Set aside each vegetable separately.

3. Hold the chilli at the stem end and cut in half lengthways. Use the tip of the knife to scrape out the seeds, then thinly slice the chilli.

4. Mix the soy sauce and sugar together in a small bowl, then set aside.

5. Heat a wok or large frying pan over a high heat until you can feel the heat rising off the surface. Add the peanuts without any oil and quickly stir them around until they turn golden – watch carefully because this take only seconds and they can easily burn. Immediately tip the peanuts out of the pan and coarsely chop, then set aside.

6. Add the oil to the wok or frying pan, swirl it around and continue heating until it shimmers. Add the chilli and garlic to the pan and swirl around. Add the broccoli and stir-fry for about 1 minute.

7. Add the mushrooms and chicken to the pan and stir-fry until the chicken is warmed through. Stir in the sauce and noodles and continue stir-frying, tossing all the ingredients together, until the noodles are hot. Sprinkle with the chopped spring onions.

VARIATIONS
▶ Make this recipe a couple of times and you'll appreciate how fantastic it is for giving a new lease of life to small amounts of leftover chicken, pork, beef, or just about anything you have in the fridge. Experiment!
▶ Make a vegetarian version with an even greater selection of vegetables, such as bean sprouts, mangetout and peppers.
▶ The broccoli can be replaced by one finely sliced cored and seeded red or green pepper.

Hot Stuff: Seeding Chillies
▶ Use the tip of the knife to remove the seeds from a chilli – it is the seeds that contains the substance known as capsaicin, which makes them hot.
▶ Always wash your hands after handling fresh chillies. You'll know instantly that you've forgotten to do this if you touch your eyes or lips!

Chicken Ramen Noodles

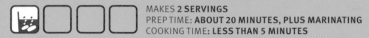

MAKES **2 SERVINGS**
PREP TIME: **ABOUT 20 MINUTES, PLUS MARINATING**
COOKING TIME: **LESS THAN 5 MINUTES**

THE SECRET TO THIS DISH IS IN THE PREP WORK – EVERYTHING HAS TO BE CUT THINLY SO IT
COOKS QUICKLY. THIS MIGHT SEEM MORE TIME CONSUMING THAN YOU ARE USED TO, BUT
YOUR REWARD WILL BE WHEN YOU COME TO COOK. IF YOU HAVE YOUR ACT TOGETHER, DO
ALL THE PREP WORK BEFORE YOU GO TO LECTURES, YOU'LL BE READY TO EAT WITHIN 15
MINUTES OF COMING HOME.

$1^1/_2$ tablespoons sunflower or
   groundnut oil
2 teaspoons Chinese rice wine
1 teaspoon light soy sauce,
   plus extra to serve
$1^1/_2$ teaspoons sesame oil
pepper
2 chicken thighs

75 g/3 oz mangetouts
3 spring onions
1 small red pepper
1 carrot
150 g/5 oz fresh udon or ramen noodles
75 g/3 oz fresh beansprouts
fresh coriander (optional)
toasted sesame seeds (optional)

1. Put 1 tablespoon of the sunflower oil, the rice wine, soy sauce and 1
teaspoon of the sesame oil in a large mixing bowl with pepper to taste.

2. Remove the skin and bones from the chicken thighs and cut the flesh
into very thin strips; add to the bowl. Cut the mangetout into long, thin
strips. Finely chop the spring onions. Cut the pepper in half, remove the
core and seeds, then cut into thin strips – a vegetable peeler is ideal for
this, otherwise use a knife. Coarsely grate the carrot.

3. Put all the vegetables, noodles and beansprouts in the bowl with the
marinade and chicken strips, and use your hands to mix together. Add
pepper to taste. If not cooking at once, cover with cling film and put in
the fridge.

4. When you're ready to cook, heat a wok or frying pan over a high heat
until you can feel the heat rising. Add the remaining $1/_2$ tablespoon oil
and swirl around.

5. Tip in the chicken and vegetables and stir-fry for 3–5 minutes until the
chicken pieces are cooked through, the vegetables are tender and the
noodles are hot. Sprinkle with fresh coriander leaves and toasted
sesame seeds if you have any, and add the remaining sesame oil. If it
needs more salt, sprinkle with a little soy sauce.

COME TO DINNER

What can be nicer than having friends around for a meal?

It's a great idea and can be great fun, but what a minefield – there's bound to be someone who doesn't eat meat, someone who doesn't eat fish, someone with a religious diet that doesn't let them mix dairy and meat, and maybe even a vegan, who doesn't even eat what the vegetarians will.

Here's a mix of recipes that should get you through most social occasions, including some posh nosh for when someone you want to seduce through their stomach is on the guest list – or when your parents come to visit.

If you're new to cooking for dinner parties, the best tips are to keep the menu simple, and prepare as much as you can in advance. Or take a tip from the French and buy the dessert.

Other easy recipes to try when company comes:
- ► Belly of Pork with Cider (page 169)
- ► Chicken with Rice & Peppers (page 153)
- ► Chilli con Carne (page 158)
- ► Courgette & Sun-dried Tomato Risotto (page 145)
- ► Curried Lentil Soup (page 116)
- ► Curried Mince (page 157)
- ► Fruidités with Yogurt-Vanilla Dip (page 121)
- ► Lamb Shanks with Dried Fruit (page 171)
- ► One-pot Creamy Chicken (page 154)
- ► Pasta Bolognese (page 129)
- ► Potato & Leek Soup (page 117)
- ► Roast Chicken with Pan Gravy (page 168)
- ► Shepherd's Pie (page 156)
- ► Smoked Fish Spread (page 93)
- ► Spinach, Orange & Avocado Salad (page 110)
- ► Take-away Pizzas at Home (page 57)
- ► Vegetarian Lasagne (page 141)

And, don't forget The Cocktail Hour chapter, beginning on page 228.

Stuffed Mushrooms

MAKES **4 SERVINGS**
PREP TIME: **ABOUT 10 MINUTES**
COOKING TIME: **ABOUT 20 MINUTES**

THIS IS A GOOD FIRST COURSE WHEN YOU'VE GOT A MIX OF VEGETARIAN OR VEGAN
AND MEAT-EATING GUESTS. THE PORTOBELLO MUSHROOMS HAVE A CHUNKY AND
THICK MEAT-LIKE TEXTURE.

1 large garlic clove
1 red or green pepper
$1/2$ onion
4 large Portobello mushrooms, wiped
Olive oil
Salt and pepper
Chopped fresh parsley, to serve (optional)
Grated Parmesan cheese, to serve (optional)

1. Heat the oven to 180°C/350°F/Gas 4. Peel and very finely chop the
garlic clove. Core, seed and cut the pepper into 0.5 cm/$1/4$-inch pieces.
Peel and cut the onion into very fine pieces, about the same size as the
pepper. Finely chop the mushroom stalks setting aside the caps.

2. Heat 2 tablespoons of olive oil in a large frying pan over a medium-
high heat. Add the garlic, pepper, onion and mushroom stalks and
fry, stirring frequently, for 3–5 minutes until the onion and pepper are
soft, but not brown. Remove the vegetable mixture from the pan and
set aside.

3. Heat another 1 or 2 tablespoons of oil in the pan. Add the mushroom
caps, gill sides down, and fry for about 5 minutes, or until they begin to
soften. Transfer the mushrooms, gill sides up, to a baking sheet.

4. Equally divide the vegetable stuffing between the mushroom caps.
Put the mushrooms in the oven and bake for about 10 minutes until the
filling is hot and the flesh is tender when you poke one with the tip of
a knife. Sprinkle with chopped parsley for vegans or grated cheese
for everyone else.

Plan Ahead
The mushrooms can be stuffed, ready for cooking, up to a day in
advance. Keep them covered with clingfilm in the fridge, and remove
them about 15 minutes before you put them in the oven.

Miso Broth

MAKES **4 SERVINGS**
PREP TIME: **ABOUT 15 MINUTES, INCLUDING SOAKING
THE NOODLES** COOKING TIME: **ABOUT 5 MINUTES**

LOOK FOR THE INSTANT MISO SOUP AT THE SUPERMARKET OR ORIENTAL FOOD SHOP.

60 g/2 oz thin rice noodles
3 button or chestnut mushrooms
2 Chinese cabbage leaves
$\frac{1}{2}$ carrot
2 sachets (8 g/$\frac{1}{2}$ oz) instant miso soup
Chopped fresh parsley (optional)

1. Bring a saucepan of water to the boil over a high heat. Stir in the rice noodles, then turn off the heat, cover the pan and leave the noodles to soak and soften for 4 minutes, or according to the instructions on the packet. Place a colander or strainer in the sink and drain the noodles. Set them aside until required.

2. Meanwhile, trim the mushroom stalks and very thinly slice the caps. Remove any hard cores from the cabbage leaves. Roll the leaves up like a cigar, then cut them crossways into very thin slices. Scrub or peel the carrot, then cut it into very thin slices.

3. Empty the instant miso soup into a saucepan with 900 ml/1$\frac{1}{2}$ pints water and bring to the boil over a high heat. Drop in the mushrooms, cabbage and carrot and turn the heat to its lowest setting. Cover the pan and leave the soup to simmer for about 5 minutes until the vegetables are tender.

4. Stir in the noodles and let them just heat through. Spoon into bowls and sprinkle with parsley, if you have any.

VARIATION
▶ For a burst of heat, add one thinly sliced seeded green chilli (page 189) with the vegetables in Step 3.

Tofu Stroganoff

THIS DINNER PARTY POSH NOSH IS USUALLY MADE WITH BEEF FILLET, BUT THIS IS
A PENNY-SAVING VEGETARIAN VERSION. YOU CAN SERVE WITH BOILED RICE (PAGE 46),
OR BUTTERED TAGLIATELLE. IT'S RICH AND FILLING.

500 g/ 1 lb firm tofu
250 g/8 oz button or chestnut mushrooms, wiped
2 large garlic cloves
1 large onion
2 tablespoons sunflower oil
30 g/1 oz butter
$\frac{1}{2}$ tablespoon plain flour
1 teaspoon mustard powder
$\frac{1}{2}$ teaspoon salt
300 ml/10 fl oz soured cream or crème fraîche
Pepper
Chopped fresh parsley, to serve

1. Cut the tofu into 1 cm/$\frac{1}{2}$-inch cubes. Remove the stalks from the
mushrooms, then slice the caps. Peel and very finely chop the garlic.
Peel and thinly slice the onion.

2. Heat 2 tablespoons of oil in a large frying pan over a medium-high
heat. Add the tofu cubes and fry, turning them over frequently, for about
10 minutes until golden on all sides. Remove the tofu cubes from the
pan and set aside.

3. Reduce the heat to medium, add the butter to the pan and swirl
it around until it melts. Add the mushroom, garlic and onion and fry,
stirring frequently, for 5 minutes. Stir in the flour, mustard powder
and salt and continue frying for at least 2 minutes.

4. Return the tofu cubes to the pan. Stir in the soured cream or crème
fraîche and slowly bring to the boil to reheat the tofu, stirring. Adjust
the seasoning, if necessary. Sprinkle with chopped parsley.

Plan Ahead
The tofu can be fried up to 4 hours in advance and then kept covered
with clingfilm in the fridge. Remove it from the fridge about 15 minutes
before you continue with the master recipe from Step 3.

Tofu Skewers with Peanut Dip

MAKES **2 SERVINGS** PREP TIME: **ABOUT 20 MINUTES,
PLUS MARINATING** COOKING TIME: **ABOUT 20 MINUTES,
INCLUDING MAKING THE SAUCE**

THIS VEGETARIAN VERSION OF INDONESIAN CHICKEN SATAY.

500 g/1 lb firm tofu
1 garlic clove
2 spring onions
2 tablespoons soy sauce
2 tablespoons orange juice
1 teaspoon sugar

FOR THE SPICY PEANUT SAUCE:
60 g/2 oz cream of coconut
125 g/4 oz crunchy peanut butter
3 tablespoons lemon juice
2 tablespoons soy sauce
¹/₂ teaspoon dried red chilli flakes

1. Cut the tofu into 2.5 cm/1-inch chunks. Peel and thinly slice the garlic clove. Finely chop the white and green part of the spring onions and set aside until you are ready to serve.

2. Put the soy sauce, orange juice and sugar in a bowl large enough to hold the tofu and stir until the sugar dissolves. Add the tofu and garlic and stir to coat, then set aside for at least 30 minutes, or up to 2 hours, to marinate. Put 8 bamboo skewers in a glass of water to soak for at least 30 minutes. (This prevents them burning under the grill.)

3. Meanwhile, make the Spicy Peanut Sauce. Put the cream of coconut in a bowl and pour over 300 ml/10 fl oz boiling water. Stir and set aside to dissolve.

4. Put the peanut butter, lemon juice, soy sauce and chilli flakes in a saucepan over a low heat. Add the dissolved coconut, stirring until all the ingredients are blended, then set aside until you are ready to grill the tofu skewers.

5. When you are ready to cook, heat the grill to high. Thread the tofu onto the bamboo sticks, alternating with the thin slices of garlic. Line a baking sheet with foil and place the skewers on top. Grill, turning the skewers frequently, for 6–10 minutes until they are golden brown.

6. Meanwhile, reheat the peanut sauce. Serve the skewers with the peanut sauce for dipping and sprinkle with the chopped spring onions.

Plan Ahead

Make the sauce up to two days in advance and leave it to cool complètely at the end of Step 4 in the master recipe. Store tightly covered with clingfilm in the fridge until it is time to reheat.

If the sauce seems too thick when reheated, stir in water, tablespoon by tablespoon.

Garlic Chicken with Roast Veg

MAKES **4 SERVINGS**
PREP TIME: **ABOUT 10 MINUTES**
COOKING TIME: **ABOUT 45 MINUTES**

IT CAN BE VERY DAUNTING TO FACE A MOUND OF WASHING-UP AFTER A DINNER PARTY, SO GIVE THIS RECIPE A TRY – THE MAIN COURSE AND VEGETABLES ARE COOKED IN ONE PAN.

1 head garlic
2 red peppers
600 g/20 oz new potatoes, scrubbed
2 large courgettes
8 chicken thighs on the bone, or 4 chicken breasts
Olive oil
Salt, ideally coarse sea salt
Pepper
Chopped fresh parsley, to serve (optional)

1. Heat the oven to 220°C/425°F/Gas 7.

2. Separate the garlic into cloves, but don't bother to peel them. Core, seed and chop the peppers. Finely chop the potatoes. Remove both ends of the courgettes, then cut them into 1 cm/^{1}/$_2$-inch slices.

3. Put the chicken pieces into a roasting tin and add the garlic cloves, pepper pieces and potatoes. Lightly drizzle with olive oil and use your hands to toss all the ingredients so they are coated. (You do not want the chicken swimming in oil, just a light coating will do.)

4. Sprinkle with salt and pepper. Put in the oven and roast for 20 minutes. Stir the vegetables around, add the courgettes and continue roasting for 20–25 minutes longer until the potatoes and courgettes are tender and the chicken is cooked through (page 168).

5. Serve the chicken and a selection of vegetables straight from the pan, sprinkled with lots of chopped fresh parsley.

VARIATION
▸ In the winter, include root vegetables, such as peeled and chopped parsnips or quartered fennel bulbs. Orange-fleshed sweet potatoes, scrubbed and cut into 1 cm/^{1}/$_2$-inch cubes, are also good.

Plan Ahead
The chicken and vegetables can be prepared ahead, through to Step 3 of the master recipe. Cover the roasting tin with clingfilm and put in the fridge until 15 minutes before you are ready to cook.

Chicken & Veg Parcels

□ □ □ □ MAKES **4 SERVINGS**
PREP TIME: **15–20 MINUTES**
COOKING TIME: **25 MINUTES**

TV CHEF JAMIE OLIVER WOULD PROBABLY CALL THIS 'PUKKA'. HE MADE COOKING FOOD IN FOIL PARCELS POPULAR, AND THIS IS A WAY TO GET THE SAME AROMATIC RESULTS USING GREASEPROOF PAPER – THE POSH-SOUNDING FRENCH NAME FOR THIS STYLE OF COOKING IS *EN PAPILLOTE* IF YOU WANT TO IMPRESS YOUR GUESTS. THIS IS A REAL DINNER PARTY WINNER. YOU CAN ASSEMBLE THE PAPER PARCELS SEVERAL HOURS IN ADVANCE AND, EVEN BETTER, THERE ISN'T MUCH WASHING-UP TO FACE WHEN THE PARTY'S OVER.

Olive oil

2 carrots

2 courgettes

150 g/5 oz button or chestnut
  mushrooms, wiped

4 boneless chicken breasts

4 teaspoons Dijon or wholegrain mustard

Dried thyme

Paprika

Salt and pepper

1. Heat the oven to 230°C/450°F/Gas 8. Cut out 8 circles of greaseproof paper, each 35 cm/14 inches across. Put 2 circles together, one on top of the other, and lightly brush the top piece with olive oil. Repeat to make 3 more double circles, then set them aside.

2. Scrub or peel the carrots and cut them into thin slices. Remove both ends of the courgettes, then thinly slice them. Remove the mushroom stalks, then thinly slice the caps.

3. Put a chicken breast on half of the first set of greaseproof circles. Spread it with 1 teaspoon of mustard, then top with one-quarter of the carrots, one-quarter of the courgettes and one-quarter of the mushrooms. Sprinkle with thyme, paprika and seasoning to taste.

4. Very lightly drizzle with olive oil. Fold the paper over to make a half-moon shape, enclosing the chicken breast and vegetables. Very tightly twist and fold the edge together to seal the parcel, and place it on a baking sheet. Repeat to make 3 more sealed parcels.

5. Bake the paper parcels for 25 minutes. To test if the chicken breasts are cooked through, carefully open one of the parcels (stand back because there will be lots of hot steam) and cut into the chicken breast. The juices should be clear; if the are pink, return all the parcels to the oven for 5 minutes longer, then test again.

6. Serve the sealed parcels to your guests. As they open them, the most wonderful aromas will be released. Remove the paper and throw away.

Plan Ahead
The parcels can be assembled up to 5 hours in advance and refrigerated until 15 minutes before you want to cook.

Poached Fish in Green Broth

MAKES 2 SERVINGS
PREP TIME: ABOUT 8 MINUTES
COOKING TIME: ABOUT 10 MINUTES

WHEN YOUR GRANT IS BURNING A HOLE IN YOUR POCKET AND YOU FEEL LIKE LASHING OUT ON SOMETHING EXTRAVAGANT, TRY THIS DISH WITH COD. HOWEVER, FOR LATER IN TERM WHEN YOU'RE WATCHING THE PENNIES, HADDOCK, ROCKFISH AND FARMED SALMON, OR ANY OTHER FIRM, MEATY FISH, WORK JUST AS WELL. THIS ISN'T A DISH TO TRY WITH PLAICE FILLETS.

FRESH SEAFOOD IS EXPENSIVE, SO STICK TO SIMPLE COOKING TECHNIQUES AND DON'T ADD TOO MANY STRONG FLAVOURS THAT WILL MASK THE SEAFOOD'S DELICATE TASTE. LESS IS DEFINITELY MORE WHEN YOU COOK SEAFOOD.

2 large garlic cloves
6 spring onions
4–6 sprigs fresh parsley
2 tablespoons plain white flour
4 thick fish fillets (see introduction), about 150 g/5 oz each
4 tablespoons olive oil
125 ml/4 fl oz dry white wine
Salt and pepper

1. Heat the oven to 230C/450°F/Gas 8. Peel and very finely chop the garlic. Thinly slice the white and green parts of the spring onions. Remove the parsley leaves from the stalks and finely chop them.

2. Season the flour generously with salt and pepper on a flat plate. Dredge the skin side of the fish fillets in the seasoned flour, then shake off the excess and set aside.

3. Heat a frying pan with an ovenproof handle or a shallow flameproof casserole over a high heat until you can feel the heat rising. Add the oil to the pan and heat until it almost sizzles. Add the fish fillets, skin sides down, and cook for 3 minutes until the skin is golden brown.

4. Turn the fish over and season with salt and pepper to taste. Take the pan off the heat and pour in the wine. Add the garlic, spring onions and parsley. Transfer the pan or casserole to the oven, uncovered, and cook for 5 minutes, or until the flesh flakes easily. Add salt and pepper to taste and serve the fish fillets with the herby liquid spooned over.

COOK'S TIP
COOKING THE RECIPE FROM START TO FINISH IN AN OVENPROOF PAN OR CASSEROLE SAVES ON WASHING-UP. IF YOUR FRYING PAN HAS A PLASTIC HANDLE, HOWEVER, GENTLY TRANSFER THE FISH TO AN OVENPROOF DISH IN A SINGLE LAYER AT THE START OF STEP 3, THEN CONTINUE WITH THE RECIPE.

Provençale-style Leg of Lamb

□ □ □ □ MAKES **6–8 SERVINGS** PREP TIME: **ABOUT 5 MINUTES, AFTER THE LAMB IS THAWED, IF NECESSARY, PLUS OPTIONAL MARINATING** COOKING TIME: **ABOUT 1½ HOURS**

OK, CERTAINLY NOT FOR EVERYDAY COOKING, BUT WHEN YOU'VE GOT A GROUP OF FRIENDS COMING ROUND AND SOMETHING TO CELEBRATE, A LEG OF LAMB GIVES THE MEAL A SENSE OF OCCASION. FROZEN LEGS OF LAMB ARE USUALLY LESS EXPENSIVE THAN FRESH, SO BUY ONE SEVERAL DAYS IN ADVANCE AND LEAVE IT TO THAW ON THE BOTTOM SHELF OF THE FRIDGE. (JUST BE SURE TO WRITE DOWN THE WEIGHT BEFORE YOU THROW THE LABEL AWAY, BECAUSE YOU WILL NEED IT TO CALCULATE THE ROASTING TIME.)

RATATOUILLE (PAGE 173) IS AN IDEAL 'DO-AHEAD' ACCOMPANIMENT, WITH THE ADDED ADVANTAGE THAT IT CAN BE SERVED HOT, WARM OR AT ROOM TEMPERATURE. OR TRY THE SPICED RICE ON PAGE 208.

2 garlic cloves
1 leg of lamb, about 2.5–3 kg/5–6 lb
1 jar (125g/4 oz) black olive tapenade
Fresh rosemary sprigs (optional)

1. Heat the oven to 230°C/450°F/Gas 8 (if you are cooking straight away, otherwise do not heat the oven until the start of Step 3). If you have not kept a record of the joint's weight, weigh it. (Use the bathroom scales.) Peel and cut the garlic cloves into thin slivers.

2. Use the tip of a small knife to make slits all over the leg of lamb. Push the garlic slivers into the slits. Empty the jar of tapenade onto the leg and use your hands to rub it all over. (See Plan Ahead, below.)

3. Put the leg in a roasting pan and roast for 10 minutes. Lower the oven temperature to 180°C/350°F/Gas 4 and continue roasting for 15 minutes per 500 g/1 lb, plus 15 minutes for medium, or 20 minutes per 500 g/1 lb, plus 20 minutes for well done. Remove the leg of lamb from the oven and leave it to stand for 10–15 minutes before you carve.

VARIATIONS
▸ Instead of tapenade, use 1 jar (100 g/3½ oz) of crushed garlic.
▸ For an Indian flavour, replace the tapenade with a mixture of 125 ml/ 4 fl oz lemon juice, 4 tablespoons olive oil, 4–6 crushed garlic cloves, 2 tablespoons ground cumin and 2 tablespoons tomato puree.
▸ Or, for a different Indian flavour, make double the quantity of the tikka mixture on page 207, and use that instead of the tapenade.

Plan Ahead
Insert the garlic and rub the leg of lamb with the tapenade up to a day in advance. Leave the joint on the bottom shelf of the fridge overnight, then remove it about an hour before you plan to cook, to bring it back to room temperature.

Beef in Beer

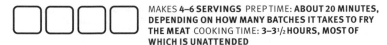

MAKES **4–6 SERVINGS** PREP TIME: **ABOUT 20 MINUTES, DEPENDING ON HOW MANY BATCHES IT TAKES TO FRY THE MEAT** COOKING TIME: **3–3¹/₂ HOURS, MOST OF WHICH IS UNATTENDED**

NO, LAGER ISN'T JUST FOR GUZZLING. THIS BELGIAN RECIPE IS AN EXAMPLE OF HOW IT CAN BE USED LIKE WINE FOR ADDING FLAVOUR TO SLOWLY COOKED CASSEROLES. THIS IS A PERFECT 'DO-AHEAD' WINTER WARMER.

WHEN YOU'RE NEW TO COOKING FOR DINNER PARTIES, THINK CASSEROLES. YOU CAN PREPARE THIS DISH UP TO TWO DAYS IN ADVANCE AND THEN LEAVE IT IN THE FRIDGE UNTIL IT IS TIME TO REHEAT. NOT ONLY DOES THIS HELP ELIMINATE LAST-MINUTE PANICS AND A SINK FULL OF DIRTY DISHES, THE FLAVOURS OF THE CASSEROLE ACTUALLY IMPROVE. JUST BE SURE TO LEAVE THE CASSEROLE TO COOL COMPLETELY BEFORE YOU PUT IT IN THE FRIDGE.

FOR AN AUTHENTIC FLAVOUR, LASH OUT ON A BELGIAN BEER, BUT YOU CAN ALSO USE LAGER OR LIGHT ALE. SERVE THIS WITH FRESHLY COOKED TAGLIATELLE OR BOILED RICE (PAGE 46) AND A TOSSED GREEN SALAD.

AND TO DRINK? PLENTY OF CHILLED LAGER, OF COURSE.

4 large onions
1 large garlic clove
About 4 tablespoons sunflower oil
750 g/1 ¹/₂ lb boneless stewing beef or chuck steak, cut into large cubes
2 bottles (330 ml) lager or Belgian beer
300 ml/10 fl oz beef stock, bought fresh or made from a cube
3 tablespoons red-wine vinegar
1¹/₂ tablespoons soft light-brown sugar
Pinch of grated nutmeg
1 bouquet garni (see overleaf)
Salt and pepper
Chopped fresh parsley, to serve (optional)

1. Heat the oven to 150°C/300°F/Gas 2. Peel and thinly slice the onions. Peel and chop the garlic clove.

2. Heat 4 tablespoons of oil in a large flameproof casserole or frying pan with an ovenproof handle and a tight-fitting lid over a medium-high heat. Add the onions and garlic and fry for 3–5 minutes until the onions are soft, but not brown. Use a slotted spoon to remove them from the pan and set aside.

3. Add as many meat cubes as will fit in a loose single layer to the fat remaining in the pan, and fry to brown on all sides. (It is important not to overcrowd the pan, so work in batches, if necessary. As each batch is fried, remove it from the pan. Add a little extra oil to the pan between batches, if necessary. Continue until all the beef cubes are fried.)

4. When all the beef has been fried, return it and the onions to the pan. Add the lager, stock, vinegar, sugar, nutmeg, bouquet garni and salt and pepper to taste. Bring to the boil, then remove the pan from the heat.

5. Put the casserole in the oven and cook for 3–3$\frac{1}{2}$ hours until the meat is tender when pierced with the tip of a fork, but not falling apart. Adjust the seasoning, if necessary, and sprinkle with chopped parsley, if you have any.

Bouquet Garnis
A bouquet garni is a small bundle of fresh or dried herbs, and sometime spices, that is added to simmering casseroles, stews and soups for extra flavour. You can buy bouquet garnis in packets at the supermarket, or make your own.

To make a fresh bouquet garni, tie together a fresh bay leaf, a couple of sprigs of fresh parsley and a sprig or two of fresh thyme with kitchen string. To make a dried bouquet garni, tie one small bay leaf, a pinch of dried mix herbs, six peppercorns and a pinch of dried parsley in a small square of muslin.

Plan Ahead
If you make this in advance and chill it overnight, any excess fat will solidify on the surface and can be lifted off with a spoon or fork. You can, however, prepare this up to two days in advance. Cook the casserole for 2$\frac{1}{2}$ hours in Step 5 of the master recipe, then leave it to cool completely and refrigerate. Leave the casserole to return to room temperature while you heat the oven, then continue cooking until the meat is tender and the casserole is hot.

Moroccan Lamb & Apricot Tagine with Couscous

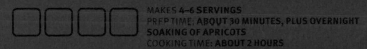

MAKES **4–6 SERVINGS**
PREP TIME: **ABOUT 30 MINUTES, PLUS OVERNIGHT SOAKING OF APRICOTS**
COOKING TIME: **ABOUT 2 HOURS**

COST-WISE, YOU HAVE TWO CHOICES WITH THIS DISH. YOU CAN MAKE IT WITH EITHER BONELESS LEG OR SHOULDER OF LAMB. SHOULDER IS THE LESS-EXPENSIVE CHOICE, BUT IT DOES COME WITH A DIFFERENT COST – THAT OF TIME. THE REASON SHOULDER IS SO MUCH CHEAPER IS BECAUSE IT IS FATTY, WHICH MEANS A TAGINE WITH SHOULDER IS BEST MADE A DAY BEFORE, SO THERE IS PLENTY OF TIME FOR IT TO CHILL AND THE FAT SOLIDIFY SO YOU CAN EASILY GET RID OF IT. (SEE PLAN AHEAD, BELOW.)

IF YOU AREN'T WORRIED ABOUT CUTTING COSTS OR ORGANIZED ENOUGH TO START COOKING A DAY AHEAD, USE BONELESS LEG. IN EITHER CASE, HOWEVER, DON'T FORGET TO SOAK THE DRIED APRICOTS IN THE ORANGE JUICE OVERNIGHT BEFORE YOU START COOKING. THEY SLOWLY FALL APART DURING COOKING TO THICKEN THE TAGINE. SERVING THIS TAGINE WITH COUSCOUS MAKES A COMPLETE MEAL, BUT IF YOU WANT ANOTHER ACCOMPANIMENT, TRY SPINACH & CHICKPEAS (SEE PAGE 210).

350 g/12 oz dried apricots
300 ml/10 fl oz orange juice
2 large onions
2 garlic cloves
5 tablespoons sunflower or
   other vegetable oil
1.3 kg/3 lb boneless leg or
   shoulder of lamb
   (see introduction, above)
2 tablespoons ground ginger
1 1/2 tablespoons ground
   cinnamon
1 1/2 tablespoons ground cumin

250–300 ml/9–10 fl oz water
Dried chilli flakes (optional)
2 tablespoons honey
Salt and pepper
Toasted flaked almonds (optional)
Chopped fresh coriander, to garnish
   (optional)

For the Couscous
125 g/4 oz quick-cooking couscous
30 g/1 oz butter

1. Use a pair of scissors or a knife to cut the dried apricots in half. (See page 77 for a tip to prevent the dried apricots sticking.) Put them in a bowl and pour over the orange juice. Cover the bowl with a piece of cling film and put it in the fridge overnight. If you are using lamb shoulder, do this two days before you start cooking.

2. Peel and finely chop the onion. Peel and crush the garlic cloves.

3. Heat 4 tablespoons of the oil in a flameproof casserole or large frying pan with a lid over a medium-high heat. Add a few pieces of lamb and cook until they are brown on all sides. Use a pair of tongs or two forks to transfer the lamb pieces to a plate when they are brown – take care not to pierce the flesh.

4. Continue frying the lamb until all pieces are brown. Add the extra tablespoon of oil to the pan and heat.

5. Add the onion to the pan and stir around for 3 minutes. Add the garlic and continue stirring for about 2 minutes, or until the onions are tender. Add the ginger, cinnamon, cumin and pepper to taste and stir around for another minute or so.

6. Return the lamb pieces with any accumulated juices to the pan and stir all the ingredients together. Pour over just enough water to cover. Increase the heat and bring the liquid to the boil. Cover the pan, reduce the heat to very low and leave to simmer for $1^1/_2$ hours.

7. Uncover the pan, add the apricots and the orange juice and stir in the honey until it dissolves. Add chilli flakes, to taste, if liked. Re-cover the pan and leave the tagine to simmer for 30 minutes longer, or until the meat is tender when you pierce it with a fork. Add salt and pepper to taste. (The tagine is now ready to serve, or it can be left to cool for reheating later.)

8. About 15 minutes before you plan to serve, bring a kettle or small saucepan of water to the boil. Put the couscous in a heatproof bowl and stir in $^1/_2$ teaspoon salt. Pour over just enough boiling water to cover the couscous. Cover the bowl with a folded tea towel and leave to stand for 10 minutes until all the liquid is absorbed and the grains are tender.

9. Stir the butter into the couscous and fluff up the grains with a fork.

10. Reheat the tagine, if necessary, and sprinkle with almonds and/or coriander, if you have any. Serve with the couscous.

VARIATION
If you don't have dried apricots, use other dried fruit, such as dates, figs or raisins.

PLAN AHEAD
If you use shoulder of lamb, turn off the heat after Step 6 and leave the tagine to cool completely. Cover the pan and put it in the fridge overnight. This will cause the fat to solidify, so it is easy to lift off and discard. Return the pan to the heat, reheat the tagine and continue with the recipe from Step 7.

Vietnamese Pork

SERVES **4–6**
PREP TIME: **ABOUT 20 MINUTES,
PLUS UP TO 24 HOURS MARINATING**
COOKING TIME: **35–40 MINUTES**

PORK FILLET ISN'T THE CHEAPEST MEAT YOU CAN BUY, BUT IT CAN BE GOOD VALUE. IT IS LEAN, THERE ISN'T ANY WASTE, AND ANY LEFTOVERS ARE IDEAL FOR STIR-FRYING FOR A SECOND, QUICK MEAL. THIS FLAVOURSOME DISH'S OTHER PLUS-POINT FOR WHEN YOU'RE ENTERTAINING IS THAT IT IS VERY EASY TO PREPARE AND DOESN'T REQUIRE MUCH ATTENTION ONCE YOU'VE MADE THE MARINADE.
THAI FISH SAUCE IS ONE OF THE INGREDIENTS THAT GIVE MANY ASIAN DISHES THEIR DISTINCTIVE FLAVOUR. LOOK FOR IT IN SUPERMARKETS AND ORIENTAL FOOD SHOPS. IF YOU HAVE TO BUY A BOTTLE ESPECIALLY FOR THIS DISH, YOU CAN ALSO USE IT IN PAD THAI (PAGE 187). GOOD ACCOMPANIMENTS FOR THIS DISH INCLUDE SPICED RICE (PAGE 208), BOILED RICE (PAGE 45) OR SIMPLY STEAMED SPINACH.

1 kg/2¹/₄ lb pork fillet

For the marinade:
4 shallots
2 garlic cloves
1 stalk lemongrass
1 tablespoon sugar
2¹/₂ tablespoons bottled Thai fish sauce
1¹/₂ tablespoon soy sauce

1. To make the marinade, peel and chop the shallots. Peel and crush the garlic cloves. Prepare the lemongrass (see below). Put the shallots, garlic and lemongrass in a blender with the sugar, Thai fish sauce and soy sauce. Whiz the ingredients together until well blended and a grainy paste forms.

2. Put the pork fillet in a glass or china bowl, pour over the marinade and use your hands to rub it all over the meat. Cover the bowl with cling film and leave it to marinate in the fridge for up to 24 hours. (It is important for hygiene reasons that the meat marinates in the fridge – do not leave it on the counter at room temperature.)

3. When you are ready to cook, remove the meat from the fridge while you preheat the oven to 200°C/400°F/Gas 6. Line a roasting pan or baking dish with foil, shiny side up. Tip the pork fillet and all the marinade into foil and loosely squeeze the foil up around the pork, but do not seal.

4. Place the pan or dish in the oven and roast the meat for 35–40 minutes until the juices are clear when you pierce the meat with a fork. Remove the pan or dish from the oven. Fold the excess foil over the top to keep the meat warm and leave it to stand for 5 minutes. Thinly slice the meat and serve it with the clear cooking juices spooned over. There will also be the thick grainy paste from the marinade, which you should leave behind.

Lemony lemongrass

To prepare lemongrass, cut off the root end and remove the other one or two layers. Press down on the wide side of the knife's blade to crush the stalk, then coarsely chop it and add to the blender. (If, however, you are using it to flavour curries or soups, add the crushed stalk whole so it can easily be removed later.)

You'll find fresh lemongrass in supermarkets and Oriental food shops. If you don't have any, however, use 3 strips of lemon peel with any white pith scraped off the back. Leftover lemongrass will keep fresh in a sealed bag in the fridge for up to a week, or it can be frozen for up to 6 weeks.

Leftovers

Cut any cooked pork into thin strips. Heat 2 tablespoons sunflower or groundnut oil in a hot wok over a high heat. Add 1 chopped onion and 1 crushed garlic clove and stir-fry for about 3 minutes until soft. Add one thinly sliced red pepper and stir-fry until it starts to soften. Stir in 400 ml/14 fl oz coconut milk, a pinch dried chilli flakes and some lime juice just to taste. Add the pork and leave to simmer until hot, then stir in a handful of fresh beansprouts.

Lamb Tikka

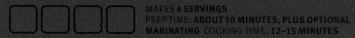

MAKES 4 **SERVINGS**
PREP TIME: **ABOUT 10 MINUTES, PLUS OPTIONAL
MARINATING** COOKING TIME: **12–15 MINUTES**

THIS IS A GOOD RECIPE TO HAVE UP YOUR SLEEVE WHEN YOU'VE INVITED FRIENDS
AROUND FOR A MEAL, BUT HAVEN'T DONE MUCH PLANNING. THE LAMB TASTES BEST
WHEN IT'S LEFT TO MARINATE FOR SIX HOURS BEFORE COOKING, BUT IT'S STILL GOOD
IF YOU MIX IT WITH THE TIKKA MIXTURE AT THE LAST MINUTE.
   SERVE THIS WITH SPICED RICE (PAGE 208) OR SPINACH & CHICKPEAS (PAGE 210),
OR MAKE THE QUICK AND SIMPLE TOMATO SALAD (PAGE 208).

750 g/1¹/₂ lb lamb neck fillets
Sunflower oil

FOR THE TIKKA MIXTURE:
1 garlic clove
150 g/5 oz Greek-style or plain yogurt
1 teaspoon ground cumin
1 teaspoon tomato puree
¹/₂ teaspoon lemon juice
¹/₂ teaspoon salt
¹/₂ teaspoon turmeric
Pinch of cayenne pepper, or to taste

1. First make the tikka mixture. Peel and crush the garlic clove. Put it in a
large bowl and stir in the yogurt, cumin, tomato puree, lemon juice, salt,
turmeric and cayenne.

2. Add the lamb neck fillets to the bowl and turn them around so they are
covered with the yogurt mixture. Ideally, cover the bowl with clingfilm
and leave the neck fillets to marinate in the fridge for up to 6 hours.

3. Heat the grill to high. Line the grill pan with foil (this saves on washing-
up later) and lightly brush the grill rack with oil.

4. Arrange the fillets on the grill rack and grill for 10–12 minutes, turning
them over once or twice, until they are brown and crispy. Remove the
fillets from the heat and set them aside to rest for about 5 minutes.
Cut the fillets across the grain into 0.5 cm/¹/₄-inch slices to serve.

Leftovers

▶ *Lamb Tikka Wraps:* Wrap any leftovers in warm shop-bought chapatis
with shredded iceberg lettuce and a dollop of Greek-style or plain yogurt
for a quick sandwich. To warm the chapatis, heat the grill to high.
Sprinkle the chapatis with a few drops of water, then grill them for 20–30
seconds on each side. Add the filling ingredients, wrap up and enjoy.

VARIATION
▸ *Chicken Tikka:* Replace the lamb neck fillets in the master recipe with 4 boneless chicken breasts. Follow the master recipe and grill the chicken breasts for 12–15 minutes, turning them over several times, until they are cooked through and the juices run clear when pierced with the tip of a knife.

Tomato Salad
This is so quick, you can put it together while the lamb fillets grill. Peel and finely slice 1 large onion, or a red onion. Thinly slice 4 tomatoes. Arrange the tomato and onion slices on lettuce leaves and sprinkle with chopped fresh coriander leaves.

Spiced Rice

MAKES **4–6 SERVINGS** PREP TIME: **ABOUT 10 MINUTES, PLUS SOAKING THE RICE, IF NECESSARY** COOKING TIME: **ABOUT 20 MINUTES, PLUS 5 MINUTES STANDING**

300 g/10 oz basmati rice
1 onion
1 cm/$\frac{1}{2}$-inch fresh root ginger
30 g/1 oz butter, or 2 tablespoons sunflower oil
6 cardamom pods, lightly crushed
1 bay leaf
1 cinnamon stick, broken in half
600 ml/20 fl oz vegetable stock, home-made (page 54)
    or from a cube
$\frac{1}{2}$ teaspoon salt
Pepper

1. Rinse and soak the basmati rice, if necessary, according to the packet instructions. (If you've bought the rice in bulk from a health food shop, see page 47.) Meanwhile, peel and finely chop the onion. Peel and grate the ginger.

2. Melt the butter or heat the oil in a flameproof casserole or a large frying pan with a tight-fitting lid over a medium-high heat. Add the cardamom pods, bay leaf and cinnamon stick and stir for about 2 minutes, or until you can smell their aromas.

3. Add the onion and ginger and continue frying, stirring occasionally, for about 5 minutes until the onion is soft, but not brown. Add the rice and stir around until all the grains are coated.

4. Pour in the stock, add the salt and stir, then bring to the boil, without stirring.

5. Reduce the heat to the lowest setting, cover the pan tightly and leave the rice to simmer, without lifting the lid, for 20 minutes. Remove the pan from the heat and leave to stand, still covered, for 5 minutes.

6. Uncover the pan and stir with a fork to fluff up the rice. Add salt and pepper to taste.

VARIATIONS

▸ *Herbed Spiced Rice:* Add about 4 tablespoons finely chopped fresh herbs, such as chives, coriander and/or parsley, with the stock in Step 4 of the master recipe.

▸ For a golden-coloured rice, fry the onion with $1/3$ of a teaspoon of ground turmeric.

▸ Using saffron is another way to add a golden colour, albeit more expensive. Lightly toast a large pinch of saffron threads in a dry frying pan over a medium-high heat for about 30 seconds until you smell the aroma. Add the toasted saffron to the rice with the liquid.

Spinach & Chickpeas

MAKES 4 **SERVINGS**
PREP TIME: **LESS THAN 5 MINUTES**
COOKING TIME: **8–10 MINUTES**

SERVE THIS WITH BREAD, SUCH AS PITTA OR FOCACCIA, FOR A VEGETARIAN MAIN COURSE, OR AS AN ACCOMPANIMENT TO ROAST CHICKEN (PAGE 168), POACHED FISH IN GREEN BROTH (PAGE 199) OR LAMB TIKKA (PAGE 207).

500 g/18 oz baby spinach leaves
1 large onion
3 garlic cloves
1 can (400 g/14 oz) chickpeas
4 tbsp olive or sunflower oil
Salt and pepper

1. Rinse the spinach in cold water and pat dry. Cut out the central stems if the leaves are large. Peel and finely chop the onion. Peel and crush the garlic cloves. Place a sieve in the sink, tip in the can of chickpeas and rinse under cold water. Shake off the excess water and set them aside.

2. Put the onion, garlic and oil in a large frying pan with a lid, over a medium heat, and fry for 3–5 minutes until the onion is soft, but not brown.

3. Lower the heat and add the spinach to the pan, cover and leave the spinach for 4–5 minutes until it is just wilted.

4. Uncover the pan, stir in the chickpeas and continue cooking until they are warmed through and all the liquid evaporates. Season to taste.

VARIATIONS
▸ Add 1 large seeded and diced tomato with the chickpeas in Step 4 of the master recipe above. Or add 250 ml/8 fl oz tomato sauce, either homemade (page 48) or bottled, with the chickpeas and boil for 2 minutes.
▸ Zip up the flavour by adding ½ teaspoon dried chilli flakes to the pan just before you add the spinach in Step 3.

Berry Fool

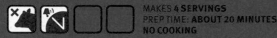

MAKES **4 SERVINGS**
PREP TIME: **ABOUT 20 MINUTES**
NO COOKING

YOU WILL FIND STRAWBERRIES ON SALE ALL YEAR ROUND, BUT SAVE THIS FOR
SUMMER WHEN THE JUICY BERRIES ARE MOST FLAVOURFUL – AND CHEAPEST.

300 g/10 oz fresh strawberries
100 g/3¹/₂ oz caster sugar, plus extra to taste
1 tablespoon orange juice
300 ml/10 fl oz heavy cream

1. Hull the strawberries to remove the green calyx. Cut the strawberries
into quarters.

2. Put half the strawberries, half the sugar and the orange juice into a
blender and whiz until smooth. Press the puree through a fine sieve to
remove the seeds. Taste and add extra sugar, if you want, then set the
puree aside.

3. Toss the remaining berries with 2 tablespoons of the remaining sugar
and mash lightly with a fork, then set aside.

4. Put the cream and remaining sugar in a bowl. Using an electric hand-
held mixer or a whisk, whip the cream until soft peaks form.

5. Beat the fruit puree into the whipped cream, then fold in the remaining
berries. Serve at once or chill for up to 2 hours.

Frozen Lemon Yogurt

MAKES **4–6 SERVINGS**
PREP TIME: **ABOUT 10 MINUTES**
NO COOKING

DON'T SAVE THIS JUST FOR WHEN COMPANY COMES. KEEP A SUPPLY OF THIS IN THE FREEZER AND YOU'LL HAVE A CREAMY, LESS-EXPENSIVE ALTERNATIVE TO THE PREMIUM BRANDS OF ICE CREAM. FOR SHEER OVER INDULGENCE, TOP SCOOPS OF THIS WITH HOT MARS BAR SAUCE (PAGE 120).

500 g/1 lb Greek-style yogurt
150 ml/5 fl oz double cream
100 g/3$^{1}/_{2}$ oz caster sugar
Freshly squeezed juice of 2 large lemons

1. Put the yogurt, cream, sugar and lemon juice in a bowl and beat until the sugar dissolves.

2. Pour into a shallow freezerproof container that will fit in the ice compartment of your fridge and smooth the surface. Cover the container with a lid or foil and freeze until solid. Remove from the freezer about 10 minutes before you want to serve.

Creamy Lemon-Rice Pudding

MAKES **4 SERVINGS**
PREP TIME: **ABOUT 5 MINUTES**
COOKING TIME: **ABOUT 25 MINUTES**

WHEN YOUR GRANT IS JUST ABOUT GONE AND FRIENDS ARE COMING ROUND, THIS IS A REALLY CHEAP DESSERT, BUT NO ONE WILL SUSPECT THAT YOU ARE PENNY PINCHING. IT IS FILLING, CREAMY AND RICH TASTING.

4 tablespoons blanched almonds (optional)
1 teaspoon cornflour
900 ml/1^{1}/$_{2}$ pints full-fat milk
125 g/4 oz short-grain pudding or risotto rice
About 2 tablespoons sugar
Finely grated rind of 1 large lemon
Lemon juice to taste

1. Heat a dry frying pan over a high heat if you are using the almonds. Add the almonds and stir them around for 1–2 minutes until they become golden brown and give off an aroma. Immediately tip the nuts out of the pan and set aside.

2. Rinse a saucepan with cold water, and do not dry it out. Put the cornflour in a small bowl and stir in 2 tablespoons of milk until the cornflour dissolves.

3. Place the remaining milk in the saucepan over a medium-high heat. Stir in the cornflour mixture and continue heating the milk, stirring occasionally, until small bubbles appear around the edge. Do not let the milk boil.

4. Stir in the rice, turn the heat to its lowest setting and stir for about 20 minutes until the mixture thickens and becomes very creamy and only about 2 tablespoons of liquid remain on the surface.

5. Remove the pan from the heat and stir in 2 tablespoons of sugar and the lemon rind. Add extra sugar and lemon juice to taste.

6. Spoon into a bowl and set aside to cool completely. Cover the top tightly with clingfilm to prevent a skin forming and chill until 10 minutes before you are ready to serve. Finely chop the nuts, if you are using them, and sprinkle them over the top of the pudding just before you serve.

VARIATION
▶ Spoon in Greek-style yogurt or add a dollop of strawberry jam just before serving.

Oranges in Spiced Wine

MAKE 4 SERVINGS
PREP TIME: **ABOUT 10 MINUTES**
COOKING TIME: **ABOUT 10 MINUTES**

ANOTHER MAKE-AHEAD, NO-HASSLE DESSERT.

2 cardamom pods
$^1/_2$ bottle dry red wine
100 g/3$^1/_2$ oz caster sugar
4 whole cloves
2 star anise
1 cinnamon stick, broken in half
1 tablespoon orange-flavour liqueur (optional)
4 oranges

1. Use the handle of a knife to lightly crush the cardamom pods. Put the wine, sugar, cloves, star anise, cardamom pods and cinnamon stick in a saucepan over a high heat and bring to the boil, stirring to dissolve the sugar. Lower the heat and simmer for 10 minutes. Do not let the wine boil.

2. Meanwhile, finely grate the rind from the oranges and set aside. Using a small serrated knife, cut off the remaining rind and any of the white pith, which is bitter tasting.

3. Cut an orange crossways into slices, cutting on a plate to collect the juices. Put the slices into a heatproof bowl and add the collected juice and reserved orange rind. Continue until all the oranges are sliced.

4. Pour the warm syrup with the spices into the bowl and stir in the liqueur, if you are using it. Set aside and leave to cool to room temperature. Cover and chill until you are ready to serve.

Chocolate Pots

MAKES 4 SERVINGS
PREP TIME: ABOUT 20 MINUTES
COOKING TIME: 30 – 35 MINUTES

ONE TIP FOR WHEN YOU START ENTERTAINING AND WANT TO IMPRESS YOUR GUESTS IS THAT CHOCOLATE DESSERTS ARE ALWAYS POPULAR – EVERYONE GOES HOME HAPPY. THIS RICH, CREAMY DESSERT IS ALSO WORTH MASTERING FOR AN OCCASIONAL TREAT, AS IT CAN BE MADE UP TO TWO DAYS IN ADVANCE.
THE FRENCH SERVE THESE IN SPECIAL WHITE POTS, BUT YOU DON'T HAVE TO SPEND MONEY ON THOSE. ANY RAMEKINS OR ANY OVENPROOF BOWLS WILL DO.

125 g/4 oz plain chocolate – look for one with 70% cocoa solids
225 ml/8 fl oz milk
50 g/2 oz sugar
2 tablespoons brandy or other liqueur you have in the house,
   or orange juice
1/2 tsp vanilla extract
4 medium egg yolks, beaten in a mixing bowl

1. Preheat the oven to 160°C/325°F/Gas 3. Use a knife to chop the chocolate into small pieces. Bring a kettle of water to the boil.

2. Put the milk in a saucepan over a medium heat, add the sugar and stir until it dissolves. Tip in the chocolate and stir until it dissolves and the mixture is smooth. Stir in the brandy, liqueur or orange juice and the vanilla extract.

3. Give the egg yolks another stir, then slowly beat in the chocolate mixture until smooth. Strain this mixture through a sieve, ideally into a large measuring jug.

4. Place 125 ml/4 fl oz ramekins or other ovenproof bowls in a roasting pan and pour an equal amount of the chocolate mixture into each. Pour just enough boiling water into the pan to come halfway up the sides of the dishes.

5. Bake for 20–35 minutes until the chocolate pots look set and the centres wobble just slightly when you shake the roasting pan.

6. Leave the pots to cool completely, then cover with cling film and chill until required.

Lemon Sorbet with Prosecco

MAKES **4–6**
PREP TIME: **LESS THAN 5 MINUTES**
NO COOKING

YOU CAN'T BEAT THE ITALIANS WHEN IT COMES TO EASY, STYLISH ENTERTAINING. PICK UP A BOTTLE OF PROSECCO AND A TUB OF LEMON SORBET AT THE SUPERMARKET AND ALL THE WORK IS DONE! IF YOU'VE GOT A FREEZER, THE INSTRUCTIONS FOR MAKING SORBET ARE BELOW, OTHERWISE YOU MIGHT AS WELL BUY IT. IT'S NOT VERY EXPENSIVE.
THIS IS A STYLISH, REFRESHING DESSERT, SO SERVE IT AFTER A FULL-FLAVOURED MAIN COURSE LIKE PROVENÇALE-STYLE LEG OF LAMB (PAGE 200) OR LAMB TIKKA WITH SPICED RICE (PAGES 207 AND 208).

1 tub ready-made lemon sorbet, or make your own
1 bottle prosecco, chilled

1. Remove the tub of sorbet from the freezer about 10 minutes before you want to serve so it is easier to scoop.

2. Put a scoop of sorbet in to 4–6 deep bowls or martini glasses and pour over the chilled prosecco.

Lemon Sorbet

1. Finely grate the rind from 3 large lemons, taking care not to include any of the bitter white pith. Roll the lemons back and forth on the work surface, pressing down, then cut them in half and squeeze until you have 175 ml/6 fl oz; set aside.

2. Put 250 ml/9 fl oz water and 200 g/7 oz caster sugar in a saucepan over a medium heat and stir until the sugar dissolves. Bring to the boil and boil, without stirring, for 3 minutes. Remove the pan from the heat and stir in the lemon rind. Leave to cool completely.

3. When the sugar mixture is cool, stir in the lemon juice. Pour the mixture into a shallow, freezer-proof container and put in the ice-cube compartment of your fridge and freeze for 2 hours. Tip the mixture into a bowl and beat. Return the mixture to the freezer and freeze for another 2 hours, then beat. Repeat this procedure once more, then chill until required.

WHEN THE CUP- BOARD IS BARE

Just been to the cash point and had your card refused? And you're hungry? Are you hung-over? And is there a week to go before term ends and you can go home and get fed? Find that emergency fiver and go straight to the corner shop.

This chapter has recipes for desperation cooking at its best – and you'll even have enough cash left over to buy a can of lager to drink in front of the TV!

The groceries at the corner shop or the petrol station certainly aren't as tempting as those from the supermarket, but they can still get you through the final week of term, when pennies count. Even if you shop on an ad hoc basis for the rest of term, this is the time to plan ahead and shop for only what you need. You can, for example, get several filling meals out of one bag of pasta. For the price of one take-away Indian or Chinese meal, you'll be able to feed yourself for several days.

When you are broke, think beans, pasta, rice, eggs, potatoes and grains. Take a good look at the back of your cupboards, as well. Pull out all the forgotten cans of beans, fish and tomatoes and the half-empty bags of pasta and grains. You might find the fixings for a meal or two. Use up all the veggies in the bottom of the fridge. Now is not the time to let anything go mouldy and have to be thrown out.

Other recipes for when you are hard up:
- Cabbage, Bacon & Tattie Fry (page 65)
- Cheese Omelette (page 74)
- Crispy Baked Potatoes (page 42)
- Curried Lentil Soup (page 116)
- Dhal with Chapatis (page 163)
- Eggs, Bacon & Beans (page 63)
- Miso Broth (page 204)
- Pasta with Almost-Instant Cheese Sauce (page 127)
- Red Beans & Rice (page 162)
- Sardines on Toast (page 109)
- Scrambled Eggs (page 38)
- Spaghetti with Fried Breadcrumbs (page 138)
- Spinach & Chickpeas (page 210)
- Tortilla (page 72)
- Tuna-Noodle Bake (page 143)
- Welsh Rarebit (page 108)

Pasta with Garlic & Chillies

MAKES **2 SERVINGS**
PREP TIME: **LESS THAN 5 MINUTES**
COOKING TIME: **10–12 MINUTES**

THIS IS A REAL WINNER WHEN YOU'RE BROKE, OR COME IN LATE FROM THE PUB AND WANT SOMETHING QUICK TO EAT. IT'S A FAVOURITE OF ROMANS AFTER A LONG NIGHT OF SOCIALISING.

200 g/7 oz dried noodles, such as spaghetti or linguini
1 or 2 large garlic cloves, or to taste
4 tablespoons olive oil
Pinch of dried chilli flakes, or to taste
Salt and pepper

1. Bring a large saucepan of salted water to the boil over a high heat. Stir in the pasta, return the water to the boil and continue boiling for 10–12 minutes, or according to the packet instructions, until the pasta is tender to the bite.

2. Meanwhile, peel and very finely chop the garlic.

3. After the pasta has cooked for about 9 minutes, heat the olive oil with the garlic in a large frying pan or another saucepan over a medium-high heat. Stir around until the garlic just starts to change colour, then add the chilli flakes and a little salt. Immediately remove the pan from the heat.

4. Set a colander or strainer in the sink and drain the pasta. Add it to the pan with the oil and garlic. Use 2 forks to lift and toss the pasta, so it is coated with the sauce.

VARIATION
► For times when you have a few pennies to spend on fresh herbs, add finely chopped parsley with the garlic in Step 2 of the master recipe.

COOK'S TIP
BE SURE TO REMOVE THE SAUCE FROM THE HEAT BEFORE THE GARLIC TURNS BROWN, OR IT WILL TASTE BITTER. THE OIL WILL STAY HOT WHILE THE PASTA FINISHES COOKING, AND THE HEAT OF THE PASTA WILL ENSURE THE DISH IS HOT.

Stuffed Pasta Broth

MAKES **2 SERVINGS**
PREP TIME: **LESS THAN 5 MINUTES**
COOKING TIME: **ABOUT 10 MINUTES**

2 vegetable stock cubes
1 package (250 g/8 oz) spinach-and-cheese stuffed tortelloni
Salt and pepper

1. Bring a large saucepan of water to the boil over a high heat. Crumble in the stock cubes and stir until they dissolve.

2. Add the pasta to the pan, return the liquid to the boil and continue boiling for about 10 minutes, or according to the packet instructions, until the pasta is just tender to the bite.

3. Add salt and pepper to taste. The stock cubes are salty so you probably won't need much salt.

Fish Finger Sandwich

MAKES **1 SANDWICH**
PREP TIME: **LESS THAN 5 MINUTES**
COOKING TIME: **ABOUT 12 MINUTES**

FAST FOOD AT HOME.

2 frozen fish fingers
2 slices processed cheese
Mayonnaise
1 hamburger bun, split in half

1. Heat the grill to high. Place the fish fingers on the grill rack and grill for 12 minutes, or according to the packet instructions, until cooked through and the flesh flakes easily.

2. Place the fish fingers on one half of the hamburger bun. Add the cheese slices and spread with a little mayonnaise. Top with the other half of the bun.

VARIATIONS
► Let your imagination loose. Add crisp lettuce leaves, pickle or mayonnaise.
► When you are really broke, hake fish fingers are cheaper than cod fish fingers.

Spiced Corn Fritters

MAKES **2 SERVINGS** PREP TIME: **ABOUT 5 MINUTES**
COOKING TIME: **10–15 MINUTES, DEPENDING ON HOW
MANY YOU MAKE**

COMBINE A CAN OF SWEET CORN KERNELS WITH A FEW STORE CUPBOARD STAPLES FOR A
QUICK, WARM MEAL.

60 g / 2 oz plain white or wholemeal flour
$^1/_2$ teaspoon garam masala
$^1/_2$ teaspoon salt
Pinch of cayenne pepper
150 ml / 5 fl oz milk
1 large egg
$^1/_2$ can (400 g / 14 oz) sweet corn kernels with red and
   green peppers, drained
Sunflower oil
Chutney or tomato ketchup, to serve

1. Heat the oven to a low setting. Put the flour in a large bowl and stir
in the garam masala, salt and cayenne and make a well in the centre.

2. Pour the milk into the well then add the egg and mix them together.
Gradually combine the liquid with the flour. Add the corn kernels to the
mixture and stir together.

3. Heat a frying pan over a medium-high heat. Add 1 teaspoon of oil and
swirl it around. Drop spoonfuls of the batter into the frying pan, spacing
them well apart: the number you can cook at once depends on the size of
your pan. (Cook all the batter in batches, if necessary.)

4. Leave the fritters to cook for 1–1$^1/_2$ minutes until golden-brown and set
on the bottoms. Use a fish slice or metal spatula to flip the fritters over
and continue cooking for about 1 minute longer until the bottoms are
golden. Remove the fritters from the pan and keep warm in the oven.

5. Continue making fritters until you have as many as you want or all the
batter is used. (Any leftover batter can be kept in a covered container in
the fridge for up to a week, to use later.) You might have to add a little
extra oil to the pan between batches. Serve with chutney or ketchup.

VARIATIONS
▶ Replace the sweet corn kernels with canned peas or carrots, cut into
small slices.
▶ Drained and rinsed canned chickpeas can also be used, to replace
the sweet corn. Or make a double quantity of the flour mixture and use
a combination of sweet corn and chickpeas.

Beans on Toast

YOU PROBABLY DON'T NEED A RECIPE FOR BEANS ON TOAST. HOW MANY TIMES HAVE YOU PREPARED IT THIS TERM? ANYHOW, WITH A BIT OF IMAGINATION, THERE ARE PLENTY OF WAYS TO GIVE IT A NEW LEASE OF LIFE – ALL CHEAP AND CHEERFUL.

▸ *Beans & Franks on Toast:* Buy a jar or can of frankfurters and cut 1 or 2 into bite-size pieces. Heat the frankfurters with the beans, then spoon over hot toast.

▸ *Cheesy Beans on Toast:* Heat the grill to high. Grill the bread for $1^1/_2$–2 minutes on each side until golden brown. Add grated Cheddar, Cheshire, Parmesan or wensleydale cheese to one side of each slice of toast, then return to the grill until the cheese melts and is golden. Top with the warmed beans.

▸ *Curried Beans on Toast:* Stir 1–2 tablespoons of curry paste, to taste, into the beans while you are reheating them.

▸ *Veggie Beans on Toast:* Coarsely grate a scrubbed or peeled carrot or a courgette into the beans while you are reheating them. Grated vegetables will become tender in the time it takes for the beans to warm up.

▸ Spoon the beans over Crispy Baked Potatoes (page 42) or a mound of Creamy Mash (page 40). Or serve them with Oven-baked Chips (page 44).

▸ Spread toast with Marmite or curry paste and top with warm beans.

Jazzing Up a Can of Kidney Beans

▸ *Bean Salad:* Combine 1 can (400 g/14 oz) of drained and rinsed red kidney beans with blanched and chopped French beans. Toss with salad dressing, either home-made (page 55) or bottled. You can top with chopped Hard-boiled Eggs (page 35) or fried crisp bacon.

▸ Heat drained and rinsed kidney beans with curry paste to taste and spoon over wholemeal or white toast.

▸ Simmer drained and rinsed kidney beans with the cola sauce on page 155 for barbecued-flavoured beans.

▸ Mix drained and rinsed kidney beans with flaked canned tuna. Add enough mayonnaise to bind them together, and season to taste with salt and pepper. (If you have any celery in the fridge, thinly slice it and stir it in, along with any chopped fresh herbs.) Eat as it is as a salad, or use as a sandwich filling or to top a Crispy Baked Potato (page 42).

Jazzing Up a Can of Tomatoes

▸ *Tortilla Soup:* Peel and finely chop 1 onion. Peel and crush 1 garlic clove. Heat ¹/₂ tablespoon sunflower oil in a large saucepan over a medium-high heat. Add the onion and garlic and fry for 3–5 minutes until soft, but not brown. Sprinkle in 1 vegetable stock cube, add ¹/₂ teaspoon ground cumin, a pinch of sugar and 1 can (400 g/14 oz) chopped tomatoes with the juice from the can. Fill the empty tomato can with water and add 2 canfuls to the saucepan, then bring to the boil. Add any finely chopped vegetables that you have – carrots, courgettes, leeks, green beans, or green, red or yellow peppers – and simmer until they are cooked through and tender. Add salt and pepper to taste and serve with crushed corn chips sprinkled over the tops.

▸ *Spanish Eggs:* Peel and slice 1 onion. Peel and crush 1 garlic clove. Core, seed and chop 2 red peppers. Heat ¹/₂ tablespoon sunflower oil in a frying pan over a medium-high heat. Add the onion, garlic and peppers and fry for 5–8 minutes until the peppers are soft, but not brown. Stir in 1 can (400 g/14 oz) chopped tomatoes with the juice from the can and a pinch of dried thyme or mixed herbs. Bring to the boil, then lower the heat and leave to simmer for about 10 minutes, stirring frequently, until the mixture thickens. Break 2 eggs into the pan, cover and leave them to cook for 10 minutes until the whites and yolks are set. (See note on Lightly Cooked Eggs, page 36.)

▸ *Store Cupboard Pasta Sauce:* Peel and finely chop 1 onion. Heat ¹/₂ tablespoon sunflower oil in a saucepan over a medium-high heat. Add the onion and fry for 3–5 minutes until it is soft, but not brown. Stir in 1 can (400 g/14 oz) chopped tomatoes with the juice from the can. What you add at this point depends on what is in the cupboard – drained and rinsed butter beans, cannillini beans, chickpeas or kidney beans, drained and flaked tuna fish, drained sardines in oil, drained sweet corn kernels or dried herbs. Add salt and pepper to taste and toss with freshly cooked pasta.

Lentil & Veg Soup

SERVES **6**
PREP TIME: **ABOUT 20 MINUTES**
COOKING TIME: **ABOUT 1 HOUR**

LENTILS ARE NUTRITIONAL AND CHEAP, SO MAKE SURE YOU ALWAYS HAVE A BAG IN THE
CUPBOARD. A BIG POT OF THIS WARMING SOUP WILL FEED YOU AND A FLATMATE FOR
SEVERAL MEALS WITHOUT COSTING VERY MUCH. IF YOU CAN AFFORD IT, BUY A FRENCH
STICK TO EAT ALONG WITH THIS, BUT IF YOU ARE TOO BROKE, THIS WILL STILL FILL YOU UP
ON ITS OWN.

2 large carrots
2 celery stalks
1 large onion
2 large garlic cloves
1 parsnip
1 tablespoon olive or sunflower oil
400 g/14 oz green or brown lentils

1.5 litres/$2^3/_4$ pints vegetables stock,
either home-made (page 54) or
from a cube, or just water
Any fresh herbs you have in the fridge,
such as parsley or thyme, or $^1/_2$
teaspoon dried thyme or mixed herbs
1 tablespoon tomato puree (optional)
salt and pepper

1. Peel and slice the carrots. Slice the celery. Peel and chop the onion.
Peel and chop the garlic. Peel the parsnip, cut it in half and remove the
core, then slice.

2. Heat the oil in a large saucepan or flameproof casserole over a
medium heat. Add the carrots, celery and onion and stir for about 5
minutes until the carrots and onion are soft.

3. Put the lentils in a sieve and rinse them under running water, then tip
them into the pan. Add the stock or water, any herbs you are using and
the tomato puree, if using. Give a good stir, increase the heat and bring
to the boil. Do not add any seasoning at this point.

4. Reduce the heat to low, partially cover the pan and leave to simmer for
about 50 minutes, or until the lentils and vegetables are very tender.
Remove any herb sprigs and add salt and pepper to taste.

VARIATIONS
▶ Take advantage of any root vegetables being sold cheaply at the end of
the day in supermarkets. Celeriac, swedes and turnips are all ideal. Or,
stir in a handful of spinach leaves 5 minutes before the soup finishes
cooking.
▶ Add diced waxy potatoes about 15 minutes before the end of cooking,
and floury ones with 10 minutes still to cook.
▶ Tip in a can of chopped tomatoes and their juices in Step 3.

Leftovers

When you think you can't face another bowl, tip everything that's left in the pan into a blender and blitz to make a pasta sauce.

Gloucestershire Mock Goose

MAKES **4 SERVINGS**
PREP TIME: **ABOUT 10 MINUTES**
COOKING TIME: **ABOUT 40 MINUTES**

BOILED CARROTS OR PEAS ARE GREAT ALONGSIDE SLICES OF THIS CHEAP-AND-CHEERFUL MEATLOAF.

1 small onion
500 g/18 oz sausagemeat
250 g/9 oz mashed potatoes – either use leftover Creamy Mash (page 40), or make up a packet of instant mash
1¹/₂ tsp dried sage
salt and pepper
1 medium egg, beaten
3 tablespoons white or brown breadcrumbs made from stale bread (page 102)

1. Preheat the oven to 190°C/375°F/Gas 5. Peel and finely chop the onion.

2. Put the onion, sausagemeat, mashed potatoes, dried sage and salt and pepper to taste in a bowl. Use your hands to squeeze the ingredients together, adding just enough of the egg to bind.

3. Pack the mixture into an ovenproof serving dish. Pat down the surface and spread any remaining egg over the top. Sprinkle with the breadcrumbs.

4. Bake, uncovered, for 40 minutes until the meat is cooked through and the top is crisp and brown. Leave to stand in the dish for about 5 minutes before serving.

COOK'S TIP
FRY A LITTLE OF THE SAUSAGE MIXTURE WHEN ALL THE INGREDIENTS ARE BLENDED AND TASTE. THAT WAY YOU'LL KNOW IF IT NEEDS MORE SALT, PEPPER OR SAGE.

Winter Goulash

MAKES **2 SERVINGS**
PREP TIME: **ABOUT 15 MINUTES**
COOKING TIME: **25–30 MINUTES**

WHEN YOU'RE HUNGRY AND BROKE, YOU CAN'T GO WRONG WITH A BIG POT OF ROOT VEGETABLES IN A SPICY TOMATO SAUCE – IT'S CHEAP AND FILLED WITH LOTS OF NUTRIENTS. STOP AT THE SUPERMARKET AT THE END OF THE DAY WHEN PERISHABLE FOOD IS BEING SOLD CHEAPLY AND PICK UP GOOD WHOLEMEAL BREAD TO GO WITH THIS. IN FACT, PICK UP ANY VEGGIES THAT ARE ON SALE, TOO, AND ADD THEM TO THE POT. JUST ABOUT ANYTHING GOES!

LOOK FOR POTATOES LABELLED AS 'WAXY' OR 'SUITABLE FOR BOILING'. YOU WANT ONES THAT WON'T TURN INTO MASH.

1 large onion
3 garlic cloves
1 large carrot
1 large turnip
1 large waxy potato, or about 450 g/1 oz new potatoes
1/2 head Savoy or green cabbage
2 tablespoons sunflower or olive oil
2 tsp paprika, or to taste
1 tsp caraway seeds (optional)
1 can (400 g/14 oz) chopped tomatoes
about 100 ml/3 1/2 fl oz water – or vegetable stock, home-made (see
     page 54) or from a cube if your finances can run to it
salt and pepper
soured cream or Greek-style yogurt (optional)

1. Peel and thinly slice the onion. Peel and crush the garlic cloves. Peel and chop the carrot. Peel and cut the turnip in half lengthwise, then cut out the core and cut into chunks. Scrub the potatoes, then cut into chunks. Cut the half head of cabbage in half again, then cut out and discard the core and finely slice the leaves.

2. Heat the oil in a large saucepan, deep-frying pan with a lid or a flameproof casserole over a medium heat. Add the onion slices and stir around for about 3 minutes. Add the garlic and continue stirring for another 2 minutes or until the onion is soft.

3. Stir in the paprika and caraway seeds, if you are using. Stir them around and watch carefully so the caraway seeds don't burn.

4. Pour in the tomatoes and their juice and the water or stock. Add the carrot, turnip and potatoes, with salt and pepper to taste. The vegetables should be covered by about 5 cm/2 in of liquid, so add more if necessary. Turn up the heat and bring the liquid to the boil.

5. Cover the pan tightly, then reduce the heat to medium-low and leave the vegetables to cook for about 15 minutes. They should all feel tender if you poke them with a knife.

6. Add the cabbage and continue cooking for about 5 minutes until it is tender. If the goulash seems too liquidy, leave the lid off so some of the liquid evaporates.

7. Taste and adjust the seasoning. Spoon into a bowl and top with a dollop of soured cream or yogurt if you're not too broke.

Leftovers
Reheat any leftovers and spoon over Crispy Baked Potatoes (page 42). Or whiz it in a blender to make a thick soup.

VARIATIONS
▸ Not quite filling enough for you? Add a drained and rinsed can (400 g/14 oz) cannellini or kidney beans with the cabbage in Step 6.
▸ If you like your food hot, add dried chilli flakes to taste with the tomatoes in Step 4.
▸ Make this with whatever vegetables you can buy cheaply. Sliced red or green peppers are good, as are chunks of butternut squash, broccoli florets and cubes of celeriac. Or, try sliced zucchini in place of the cabbage.
▸ Lots of chunky mushrooms are also good in this. Thickly slice 350 g/12 oz Portobello, chestnut or buttons. Heat 2 tablespoons sunflower oil in a large pan, add the mushrooms with salt and pepper and stir around for about 10 minutes until they are soft, but not all the liquid they give off has evaporated. Remove them and the cooking juices from the pan, then continue with Steps 2 and 3 above. Return the mushrooms to the pan with the other vegetables.
▸ Vegans can omit the soured cream or yogurt. If you like, stir silken tofu with a good pinch of paprika and chopped parsley and then spoon that on top.

THE COCKTAIL HOUR

Give yourself a break and put the books away. Get your glad rags on, hang the sparkly silver ball from the ceiling, get the music going and start shaking your cocktails. Any time, any place.

You don't need to go out and buy new glasses, and you don't need a degree in mixology to get the party started. (In fact, you don't even need a party. Most of the drinks in this chapter are for two.) All you need is a bottle or two of your favourite drink, mixers, lots of ice and a sense of style.

The sound of a cocktail shaker lifts the spirits, but a complete selection of bartenders' equipment isn't necessary. You can improvise a shaker with a glass jug – just add the spirit and ice and swirl it around. The professionals use special measures called jiggers ($1\frac{1}{2}$ oz) and ponies (1 oz), but you can use tablespoons. Each tablespoon holds $\frac{1}{2}$ oz. And there is a good reason why bartenders use measures – the drinks taste best when the ingredients are mixed in proportion. Just sloshing a whole lot of booze together won't have the same appeal.

When you've got loads of people round, it can take too long to mix individual cocktails, so try a party punch instead (page 238).

Your cocktail party can be funky. It can be retro. It can be laid back. But whatever it is, it should be fun.

Party fare to serve with cocktails:
- Aubergine Dip (page 90) with Pitta Crisps (page 100)
- Caerphilly Sausage Rolls (page 101)
- Cheesy Potato Skins with Salsa (page 97)
- Guacamole (page 91) with corn chips
- Hummus (page 88) with veggies
- Nachos (page 103)
- Potato Wedges with Blue Cheese Dip (page 95)
- Pickled Mixed Veg (page 99)
- Quesadillas (page 104)
- Sesame-Lemon Chicken Wings (page 113)
- Smoked Fish Spread (page 90) on biscuits
- Sticky Ribs (page 115)
- Tzatziki (page 89) with veggies or pitta bread

More substantial party food to act as blotting paper (without breaking the bank):
- Chicken & Cauliflower Curry (page 155)
- Chilli con Carne (page 158)
- Curried Mince (page 157)
- Three-Cheese Macaroni (page 139)
- Tuna-Noodle Bake (page 143)

VODKA

The Cosmopolitan

SIP A COUPLE OF THESE AND YOU WILL BE ABLE TO IMAGINE YOURSELF PARTYING
AROUND THE BIG APPLE WITH CARRIE AND THE GIRLS FROM *SEX AND THE CITY*.

MAKES **2 COCKTAILS**
1$^{1}/_{2}$ oz vodka
2 oz cranberry juice
1 oz triple sec
1 oz lime juice
Lemon twists

Put all the ingredients in a cocktail shaker with ice and shake. Strain into
2 cocktail glasses. Add a lemon twist.

Slow Comfortable Screw

DREAM ON . . .

MAKES **2 COCKTAILS**
2 oz vodka
1$^{1}/_{2}$ oz Southern Comfort
1$^{1}/_{2}$ oz sloe gin
150 ml/5 fl oz orange juice
Cocktail cherries

Put all the ingredients, except the cocktail cherries, in a cocktail shaker
with ice and shake. Strain into 2 cocktail glasses over crushed ice. Add
cocktail cherries.

Screwdriver

AN OLDIE, BUT A GOLDIE.

MAKES **2 COCKTAILS**
3 oz vodka
250 ml/8 fl oz orange juice
Orange slices

Put ice cubes into 2 tall glasses, add the vodka and top up with orange
juice. Stir. Add orange slices on the rims.

Harvey Wallbanger

GO ONE BETTER THAN A SCREWDRIVER AND ADD A DASH OF GALLIANO, AN ITALIAN HERB LIQUEUR. YELLOW GALLIANO IS NAMED AFTER A NINETEENTH-CENTURY ITALIAN WAR HERO. MAKE SURE YOU DON'T GET INTO ANY SKIRMISHES AFTER DRINKING THIS.

MAKES **2 COCKTAILS**
3 oz vodka
250 ml/8 fl oz orange juice
1 oz Galliano

Put ice cubes into 2 tall glasses, add the vodka and top up with orange juice. Stir. Add the Galliano on top so it floats. Do not stir.

B-52

THIS CAN WAKE YOU UP – OR KNOCK YOU OUT. YOU'LL FEEL LIKE YOU'VE BEEN HIT WITH A BOMB.

MAKES **2 DRINKS**
2 shots vodka
Hot espresso coffee

Put the vodka in 2 coffee mugs. Add a splash of hot coffee. Knock them back in one.

Sex on the Beach

YOU'LL NEVER FORGET YOUR FIRST ONE.

MAKES **2 COCKTAILS**
2 oz vodka
1$^{1}/_{2}$ oz peach schnapps
$^{1}/_{2}$ oz cranberry juice
$^{1}/_{2}$ oz orange juice
$^{1}/_{2}$ oz pineapple juice

Put all the ingredients in a cocktail shaker with ice and shake. Strain into 2 cocktail glasses.

GIN

Classic Martini

OH-SO-SOPHISTICATED. AND DEFINITELY STIRRED, NOT SHAKEN.

MAKES **2 COCKTAILS**
4 oz gin
1^1/$_2$ oz dry vermouth
Dash of orange bitters
Lemon twists or green olives

Combine the gin, vermouth and orange bitters in a mixing glass with ice cubes. Stir. Strain into 2 tumblers. Add a lemon twist to each tumbler, or olives speared on a cocktail stick.

VARIATIONS
▸ *Dry Martini:* Follow the master recipe above, but use 6 oz of gin and 2 dashes of dry vermouth.
▸ *Sweet Martini:* Follow the master recipe above, but use 4 oz of gin, 1^1/$_2$ oz sweet vermouth and a dash of orange bitters. Add a cocktail cherry to each tumbler.

G & T

THE SOUND OF THE SUBURBS.

MAKES **2 COCKTAILS**
4 oz gin
Tonic water
Lime slices (optional)

Put ice cubes into 2 tumblers, add the gin and top up with tonic water. Stir. Add a lime slice to each, if you like.

Long Island Iced Tea

THIS MIGHT LOOK LIKE ICED TEA, BUT THE SIMILARITIES END THERE.
THIS ALSO MAKES A GOOD PUNCH FOR PARTIES.

MAKES **2 COCKTAILS**

1 oz gin
1 oz vodka
1 oz light rum
1 oz tequila
Juice of 1 lemon
Carbonated cola
Lemon slices
Long straw

Put ice cubes in 2 tall glasses and add the gin, vodka, light rum, tequila
and lemon juice. Add a splash of cola to each and stir. Add a lemon slice
and straw to each glass and sip away.

Singapore Sling

A TALL TROPICAL COCKTAIL THAT CALLS OUT FOR PAPER PARASOLS. DRINK A COUPLE
OF THESE AND YOU'LL THINK YOU'RE IN THE TROPICS.

MAKES **2 COCKTAILS**

4 oz gin
2 oz cherry brandy
4 tablespoons lemon juice
A pinch of sugar
Soda water to fill
Orange slices, cocktail cherries and mint sprigs

Put the gin, cherry brandy, lemon juice and sugar in a cocktail shaker
with ice and shake. Strain into 2 tall glasses with ice cubes. Top up with
soda water. Add orange slices, cocktail cherries and mint sprigs speared
on cocktail sticks – and parasols, if you dare.

TEQUILA

Tequila Sunrise

A PRETTY, TALL DRINK THAT IS SHADED FROM ORANGE TO VIBRANT RED. DON'T EXPECT
TO SEE THE SUNRISE AFTER TOO MANY OF THESE!

MAKES **2 COCKTAILS**
3 oz white tequila
180 ml/6 fl oz orange juice
Juice of 1 lime
1^1/$_2$ oz grenadine
Lime slices

Put the tequila, orange juice and lime juice in a shaker with crushed ice
and shake. Strain into 2 tall glasses with ice cubes. Divide the grenadine
between the glasses and watch the sunrise develop. Do not stir. Add a
lime slice to each.

Tequila Slammer

MAKE SURE YOU USE HEAVY-DUTY SHOT GLASSES FOR THIS, OR IT WILL BE MORE THAN
JUST A SHATTERED HEAD YOU WILL HAVE TO DEAL WITH. A CARBONATED MIXER IS A MUST.

MAKES **2 DRINKS**
2 shots white tequila
Lemonade or other carbonated lemon drink

Put the tequila in 2 heavy-duty shot glasses. Top up with the lemonade.
Use your hand to cover the top of the shot glass tightly. Slam the shot
glass twice on a hard surface, then knock it back in one.

RUM

Cuba Libra Cooler

ACCOMPANYING SALSA MUSIC NOT OBLIGATORY. PLEASE, PLEASE DON'T EVEN THINK OF MAKING THIS WITH DIET COLA!

MAKES **2 COCKTAILS**
1 lime, cut in half
4 oz white rum
Carbonated cola drink

Squeeze ½ of the lime into each of 2 tall glasses filled with ice cubes. Divide the rum between the glasses and top up with the cola drink. Stir.

Daiquiri

BEST SIPPED FROM THE DECK OF A PRIVATE YACHT, BUT OTHERWISE THE SOFA WILL DO.

MAKES **2 COCKTAILS**
4 oz white rum
Freshly squeezed juice of 1 lime
½ oz (1 tablespoon) sugar syrup (see below)

Put all the ingredients in a cocktail shaker with ice and shake. Strain into 2 chilled cocktail glasses.

VARIATION
▶ *Frozen Daiquiri:* Put the rum, lime juice, sugar syrup and a dash of maraschino liqueur in a blender with ice, and whiz until blended and slushy. Pour into a cocktail glass and add a maraschino cherry.

Sugar Syrup
Sugar syrup, rather than just plain sugar, is used to sweeten cocktails so the bartender doesn't have to worry about dissolving the sugar. You can buy it ready made or make your own.

To make sugar syrup, put 4 tablespoons caster sugar and 4 tablespoons water in a saucepan over a medium-high heat. Stir to dissolve the sugar, then bring to the boil and boil for 1–2 minutes without stirring. Remove from the heat and leave to cool completely. Use as required in recipes. This will keep for up to two weeks in a covered container in the fridge.

AFTER-DINNER COCKTAILS

Brandy Alexander

RICH AND CREAMY, THIS IS AS MUCH A DESSERT COCKTAIL AS ONE TO SIP BEFORE DINNER.

MAKES **2 COCKTAILS**
1¹/₂ oz brandy
1 oz brown crème de cacao
1 oz double cream
Freshly grated nutmeg (optional)

Put all the ingredients in a cocktail shaker with ice and shake. Strain into 2 cocktail glasses. Add nutmeg, if you like.

Irish Coffee

YOU DON'T HAVE TO WAIT FOR ST PATRICK'S DAY TO ENJOY THIS WARM AFTER-DINNER
DRINK. THE MORE YOU MAKE THIS, THE MORE PROFICIENT YOU WILL BECOME AT FLOATING
THE CREAM ON TOP. NO INSTANT COFFEE FOR THIS – ONLY USE FRESHLY BREWED.

MAKES **2 COCKTAILS**
3 oz Irish whiskey
2 teaspoons caster sugar
Hot, freshly brewed coffee
Double cream

Divide the whiskey and sugar between 2 coffee mugs and stir together. Top up with hot coffee. Place an upturned spoon on the surface of the coffee and slowly pour cream down the back of the spoon so it floats on the coffee's surface. Do not stir – the idea is to sip the hot coffee through the layer of cream.

VARIATION
► If you can't master the cream-over-the-back-of-a-spoon technique, top the hot coffee with whipped cream.

Golden Cadillac

MAYBE AFTER YOU PASS YOUR COURSE YOU'LL BE ABLE TO AFFORD A VINTAGE GOLDEN CADILLAC. IN THE MEANTIME, TRY THIS FOR A SOPHISTICATED AFTER-DINNER DRINK.

MAKES **2 COCKTAILS**
3 oz white crème de cacao
3 oz Galliano
2 oz heavy cream

Put all the ingredients in a cocktail shaker with ice and shake. Strain into 2 chilled cocktail glasses.

Buck's Fizz

WAKE UP WITH THIS SUNNY COCKTAIL. MAKE THIS FOR YOURSELF, OR FOR A CROWD. HALF-FILL A CHAMPAGNE GLASS WITH SPARKLING WINE AND TOP UP WITH ORANGE JUICE. NOTHING COULD BE EASIER. OF COURSE, IF YOU'RE FEELING FLUSH USE FRENCH CHAMPAGNE, BUT OTHERWISE DRY SPARKLING WINE IS JUST AS ENJOYABLE, AND MUCH MORE AFFORDABLE.

IF YOU'RE MIXING DRINKS FOR A PARTY, PLAN ON USING AT LEAST 250 ML/8 FL OZ ORANGE JUICE FOR EACH BOTTLE OF SPARKLING WINE.

AND IF YOU GET BORED WITH THE SPARKLING WINE-ORANGE JUICE COMBINATION, TRY ANY OF THE POPULAR VARIATIONS BELOW.

VARIATIONS

▸ *Bellini:* Fill a champagne glass one-third full with peach juice, then top up with sparkling wine and add a dash of grenadine.

▸ *Black Velvet:* Half fill a champagne glass with Guinness, then top up with sparkling wine.

▸ *Christmas Sparkler:* Mix equal quantities of cranberry juice and orange juice together. Half fill a champagne glass with the juice mixture, then top up with sparkling wine.

▸ *Kir Royale:* Add 2 teaspoons of crème de cassis to a glass of sparkling wine.

PARTY PUNCHES

When it's party time, opening bottles of wine is the easy option. But if you want to make an impression, mix up a big bowl of punch. Use the largest bowl you have, or a clean washing-up bowl (buy a new one), and make a batch just before the party starts. If the punch has fruit in it, prepare plenty and have it waiting in the fridge. Also, make sure you have plenty of ice, which you can buy from most off-licences. (If you don't have a freezer, slow down the melting process by keeping the ice in its bags in a large bin of cold water.)

Sangria

GET THE MUSIC PUMPING AND CONJURE UP IMAGES OF IBIZA NIGHTS.
THIS IS THE ULTIMATE IN PARTY DRINKS. IT PACKS QUITE A PUNCH!

MAKES **ABOUT 8 GLASSES**
4 large oranges
3 lemons
100 g/3½ oz caster sugar
250 ml/8 fl oz brandy
1 bottle (1 litre) dry red wine, such as Rioja
Soda water
Extra fruit slices, to serve

1. Cut the oranges and lemons into slices and put them into a large pitcher or bowl. Add the sugar and brandy and use a wooden spoon to smash the fruit to release the juices.

2. Stir in the wine. If you have time, set aside for up to 2 hours to chill.

3. Add ice cubes to the pitcher or bowl. You want the punch to be very cold.

4. Pour into wine glasses and top up with soda water. Stir to blend and add the extra fruit slices.

INDEX